THE BIG BOOK OF DECKS

BY THE EDITORS OF TIME-LIFE BOOKS, ALEXANDRIA, VIRGINIA

The Consultants

Richard Day has built three homes for himself and his family, the most recent with a wraparound redwood deck. Mr. Day spent eight years with the Portland Cement Association as a writer and editor and has written numerous articles on home improvement for *Popular Science*. Based in California, he has written two books about building decks; in 1992 his most recent deck book won first prize in the National Association of Home and Workshop Writers/Stanley Tools Do-It-Yourself Writing Contest.

Jeff Palumbo is a registered journeyman carpenter who has a home-building and remodeling business in northern Virginia. His interest in carpentry was sparked by his grandfather, a master carpenter with more than 50 years experience. Mr. Palumbo teaches in the Fairfax County Adult Education program.

Mark M. Steele is a professional home inspector in the Washington, D.C., area. He has developed and conducted training programs in home-ownership skills for first-time homeowners. He appears frequently on television and radio as an expert in home repair and other consumer topics.

J. Paul Trueblood consults and teaches in the civil engineering field. He served in the U.S. Marine Corps as a civil engineer for 25 years before retiring in 1983.

Michael Tustin has formal training in architectural drafting and commercial construction and has been working in the home improvement and decking industry for 25 years. He is owner of M.R.T. Home Improvement, and in 1987 he founded Supreme Sundeck Industries, specializing in custom-built decks for the Montreal area.

CONTENTS

1 PLANS AND PRELIMINARIES 4

Evaluating the Site 6
Deciding on a Design 8
Considering the Details 13
Selecting Materials 14

2 BUILDING THE UNDERSTRUCTURE 16

Engineering a Deck 18
A Solid Foundation 21
Putting Up Beams 28
Installing Joists 34
Decks with Distinctive Shapes 40

3 DECKING, RAILINGS, AND STAIRS 46

Laying a Deck 48
Stairs and Ramps 60
Railings and Gates 69

4 RUSTIC DECKS AND ELEGANT PORCHES 82

Framing Multilevel Decks 84
Incorporating a Hot Tub 90
Decks for the Second Story 92
Custom Details for a Second-Story Deck 102
Spacious Porches
  with a Choice of Views 108
The All-Important Stairway 120
A Hip Roof for a Wraparound Porch 122
Ceilings and Railings 132

5 BENCHES, PLANTERS, SCREENS, AND SKIRTS 134

Built-In Seating 136
Planters 146
A Screen for Privacy 150
Skirting the Deck 154
Shade for a Hot Summer's Day 160
Adding Screens to Bugproof a Porch 166

6 PATIOS OF BRICK AND CONCRETE 172

Patterns to Set in Sand or Mortar 174
Bricks Without Mortar 176
Groundwork for a Concrete Slab 182
Pouring and Finishing Concrete 190
A Curved Bench Beside a
  Free-Form Patio 195
Brick or Flagstone Set in Mortar 196
The Many Possibilities of Tile 200

7 MAINTENANCE, REPAIRS, AND REFURBISHMENTS 206

Protecting the Deck with a Finish 208
Fixing Screens 210
Extending the Life of Wood Structures 213
Making Repairs in Concrete 218

Index 220
Picture Credits 223
Acknowledgements 223

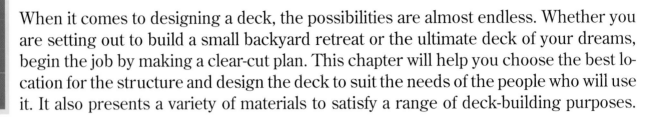

Plans and Preliminaries

When it comes to designing a deck, the possibilities are almost endless. Whether you are setting out to build a small backyard retreat or the ultimate deck of your dreams, begin the job by making a clear-cut plan. This chapter will help you choose the best location for the structure and design the deck to suit the needs of the people who will use it. It also presents a variety of materials to satisfy a range of deck-building purposes.

Evaluating the Site   6

Deciding on a Design   8

Transforming an Ordinary Deck
A Gallery of Layouts

Considering the Details   13

Selecting Materials   14

Mixing Concrete By Hand

Even the most beautiful deck may go largely unused if it is constantly baked by the sun or has an unattractive setting. These and other problems can often be avoided if you select an appropriate location before you begin planning.

Mapping Your Lot: To choose a good spot for a deck, you need to find out what factors may influence its use. The first step in this process is to draw up a site plan *(opposite)*—a sketch of your lot that includes such features as sun and shade, wind direction, and views; as well as other considerations like changes in lot level and locations of downspouts. In some cases, you may be able to obtain the original architect's site plan or deed maps from your municipal government, the mortgage company, or the property's previous owner. Otherwise, you'll have to take measurements and draw up the plan yourself.

Legal Restrictions: A number of regulations affect the placement of a deck. Zoning ordinances stipulate what percentage of your lot can be covered by structures. They also specify how far the deck must be set back from the property lines. Architectural review boards in certain neighborhoods or requirements in the house deed itself may put additional restrictions on the location.

Sketching in the Deck: Once you've completed the site plan, choose a spot, taking into consideration the factors listed in the box below. Then, roughly sketch in the shape and size of the deck on the site plan. Once you are satisfied with the location, you are ready to begin designing the deck itself.

Choosing a Deck Location

✔ Will the deck violate zoning restrictions, setback laws, or lot-coverage requirements?

✔ Will the deck be accessible from the desired room of the house, or can you add a door there if necessary?

✔ Will you need to move trees or large shrubs to make room for the proposed deck?

✔ Will water from gutters and downspouts drain onto the deck or undermine posts, or can you divert it to another area?

✔ Will the deck block light to rooms underneath it?

✔ How much sun does the spot receive, and during what parts of the day? Will an overhead provide enough shade for a too-sunny deck?

✔ Is the location private, or can you shield the deck with screens?

✔ Is the site excessively windy, or can screens or plantings serve as windbreaks?

✔ Will the location offer attractive views from the deck?

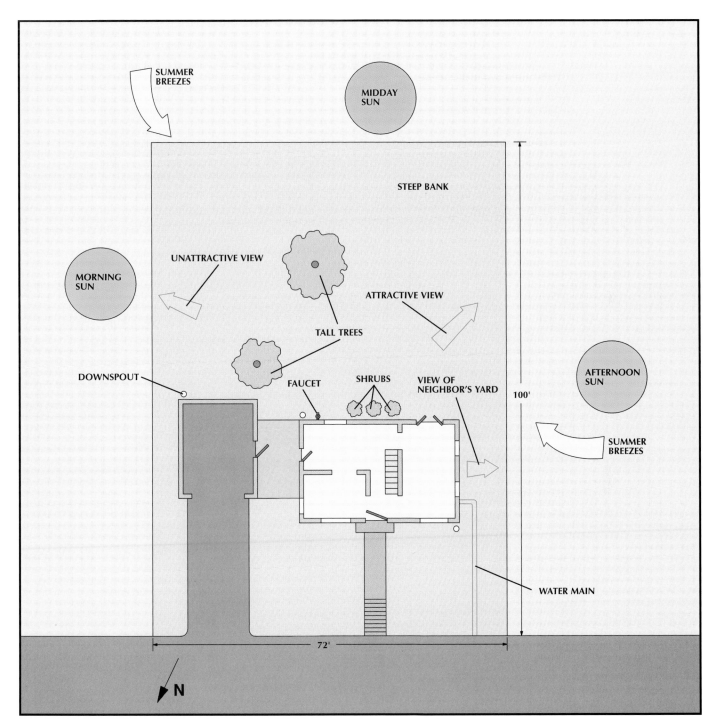

SUMMER BREEZES

MIDDAY SUN

STEEP BANK

UNATTRACTIVE VIEW

ATTRACTIVE VIEW

MORNING SUN

TALL TREES

AFTERNOON SUN

DOWNSPOUT

FAUCET

SHRUBS

VIEW OF NEIGHBOR'S YARD

100'

SUMMER BREEZES

WATER MAIN

72'

N

Developing a site plan.

◆ On a sheet of graph paper, draw a map of your lot to scale and mark the dimensions. Then add a floor plan of the house's ground floor.

◆ Draw in downspouts, outdoor faucets, and underground utilities.

◆ Indicate attractive and unattractive views, as well as views into neighboring yards.

◆ Note level changes and steep banks.

◆ Indicate existing trees, shrubs, and plantings.

◆ Show the sun's morning, midday, and afternoon positions, as well as the direction of summer breezes.

Once you've settled on a location for the deck, you can experiment with designs. On the next pages are illustrations that suggest some of the possibilities. From the starting point of a simple rectangle *(pages 18-39),* you can make minor modifications to add interest or solve a certain construction problem. Some of these changes include cutting off a corner or building around an obstacle *(pages 40-45).* You can also vary the height of the deck, adding one or more levels to define areas of activity or highlight special features *(pages 84-91).*

Planning the Deck: When you have decided on a design for the deck, review the framing methods presented in Chapter 2 to find the ones that are appropriate for your design. Choose among these examples and combine those that will best create the shape and style you want. You can also begin thinking about the details that influence its final appearance, such as the decking pattern and the stair and railing styles *(Chapter 3)*; as well as the accessories such as benches, planters, screens, and overheads *(Chapter 5).*

TRANSFORMING AN ORDINARY DECK

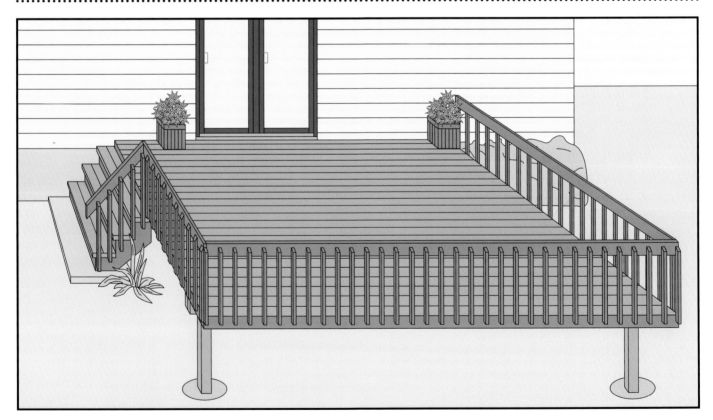

A simple deck.
The design shown above is one of the easiest designs to build: It is a simple rectangle attached to the house, with a set of stairs added at a right angle. While this deck is perfectly functional, it has few interesting features to give it charm and character.

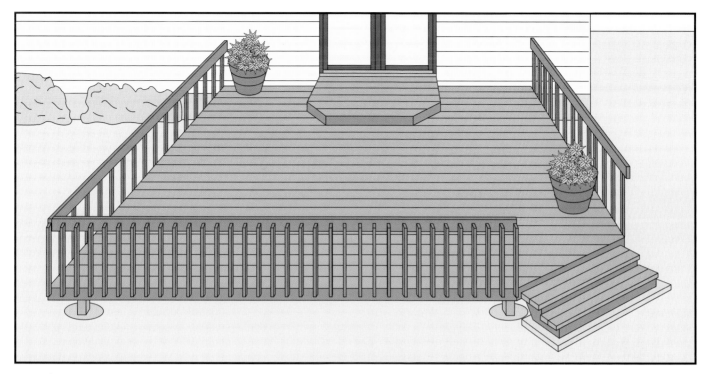

Easy improvements.

The deck above has the same basic shape as the rectangular one opposite, but slight modifications make it more appealing. One corner is cut off at an angle *(pages 40-42)* and the stairs exit that corner. A platform *(pages 84-85)*—also with cut-off corners—serves as a landing in front of the door to the house and interrupts the flat expanse of the deck surface.

A GALLERY OF LAYOUTS

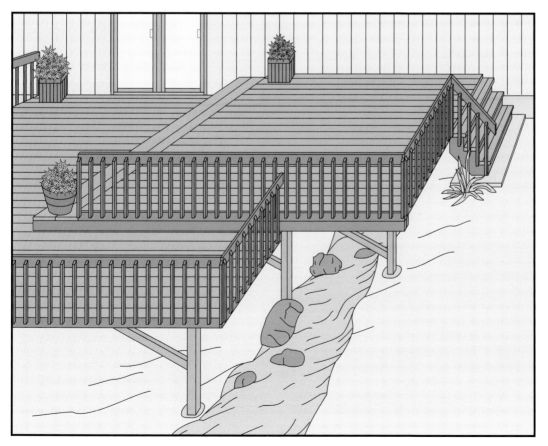

A hillside deck.

Sloping ground is no deterrent to building an attractive deck. Where the yard rises sharply along the house, a two-level deck such as the one at left can mirror the terrain. More levels can be added to cover a very hilly lot. To build a multi-level deck, construct the upper level first, then attach the lower ones sequentially *(pages 86-87)*.

A WOODED RETREAT

The deck in this photograph is built on rocky terrain that slopes away from the house. To adapt to the changes in ground height, the deck was built in two levels with broad steps between them. The lower section extends beyond the side of the house to keep open the view of the woods from the glass doors. A set of steps links the lower deck to a wooded pathway, and built-in benches provide permanent seating under the canopy of trees.

A wraparound design.
A deck that wraps around the corner of a house such as the one at left can extend the deck and create a cozy area sheltered by the house. Such a deck requires minor changes in the basic rectangular design *(pages 108-112)* and the standard decking pattern *(page 52)*.

A low-level deck.

In some cases you may want to build a deck directly on the ground *(page 31)*. In the example above, the lower-level framing incorporates an opening *(pages 43-45)* for a garden pool. An upper level, which rests directly on the lower one *(pages 84-85)*, is situated away from traffic passing through the door, creating an ideal space for activities such as dining.

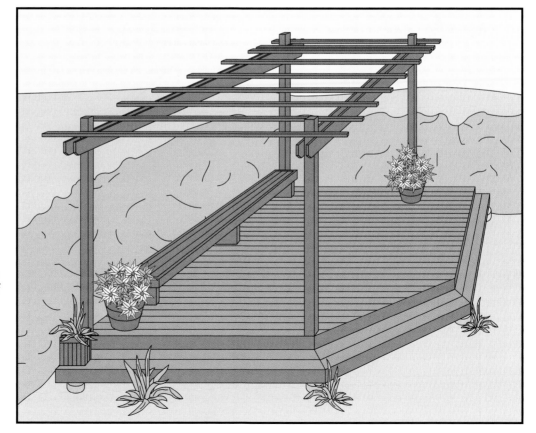

A freestanding deck.

A freestanding deck *(page 38)* is framed slightly differently from one that is attached to a house. You can build such a deck next to the house, or set it in a corner of the yard to serve as a quiet retreat away from activity. The example at right has a cut-off corner *(pages 40-42)*, a broad step *(pages 88-89)*, a backless bench *(pages 136-138),* and an overhead *(pages 160-165).*

A second-story deck.

A high deck is built in much the same way as one at a low level, but the posts must be braced to make it strong and stable *(pages 92-107)*. If you want to access the yard, you must add a long staircase. In the design above, the stairs change direction halfway down to prevent them from extending too far out into the yard. If you are considering building a second-story deck, keep in mind that it will create heavy shade on any windows underneath it.

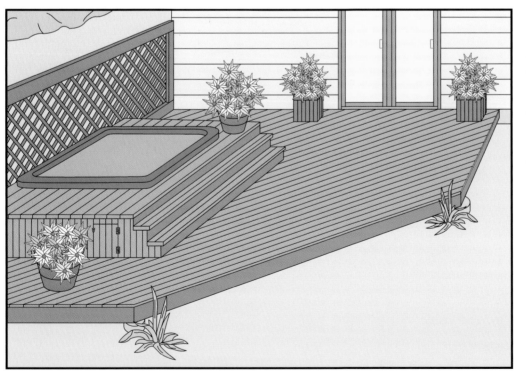

A deck with a hot tub.

An opening can be framed in a deck to accommodate a hot tub *(pages 90-91)*. In this example, the tub is set on a higher level that has a skirt around it to hide the the base of the tub. A screen is placed behind the tub for privacy and to shield bathers from wind.

Considering the Details

Details such as the decking pattern and stair and railing construction have a great influence on the style of a deck. Straight decking is the simplest to install, but you can dress up a deck with a variety of other patterns. You can also incorporate accessories such as benches, planters, screens, and overheads.

In designing these details, choose elements that will harmonize with the house and blend well with each other.

For example, stair treads and bench seats of 2-by-2s with picture-frame trim *(pages 65-66)* make a good match, but avoid combining too many elements. If you choose an elaborate decking pattern, keep benches and railings simple. Information on these details is presented in Chapters 3 and 5. Following the basic building methods shown there, you can adapt any of the styles to create your own.

A DECK THAT MATCHES THE HOUSE

Carefully chosen details can make a deck look like an integral part of the house. The dark oak stain on the deck in the photograph blends with the Tudor-style trim of the house, and the slope of the overhead echoes the house roof. To emphasize the country-cottage look, the railings feature a heart-shaped motif. Railing posts are topped with decorative finials.

Not only do the materials you choose for your deck establish its appearance, they also, to a large extent, determine the life span of the structure.

The Understructure: The posts, beams, and joists of a deck should be made of lumber that has been pressure-treated with a preservative and an insecticide—typically chromated copper arsenate (CCA)—to withstand rot and insects. The woods most commonly available with this preparation are southern pine and Douglas-fir. Pick lumber that is rated No. 2 or better. Consult the dealer to find out whether you need to brush preservative onto cut ends and drilled holes to maintain the warranty.

Decking, Stairs, and Railings: For these highly visible parts of the deck,

pressure-treated lumber is the most economical choice; however, some people prefer the appearance of the more expensive redwood or cedar. Grades of cedar and redwood that are composed of all heartwood—the darker wood from the center of the tree—are naturally resistant to rot and insects. Lower grades require a protective finish *(pages 208-209)*.

Decking boards are typically 2-by-4s or 2-by-6s; for a less massive look, you can buy special 5/4 decking with rounded edges, referred to as "radius-edge decking." Nonwood products are also available *(below)*.

Hardware and Fasteners: All deck hardware and fasteners—framing anchors, nails, screws, and bolts—must be weather resistant. Galvanized fasteners are the most common choice, but deck screws

with an additional resin coating last even longer.

Concrete: To build post footings and slabs at the bottom of stairs and ramps, it is simplest to buy sacks of premixed concrete: dry ingredients to which you add only water. About $2\frac{1}{2}$ cubic feet—enough for one shallow footing—can be mixed by hand in a wheelbarrow *(opposite)*. If the footings are deep, you can rent an electric mixer that can handle up to 6 cubic feet. For a large project with many deep footings, consider having the concrete delivered by a ready-mix truck.

⚠ **CAUTION** *Pressure-treated wood contains toxic chemicals. Always wash your hands thoroughly after handling it, and do not burn it.*

ALTERNATIVES TO WOOD

Deck boards of solid vinyl or wood/plastic composites will not warp, crack, or rot, and they are virtually maintenance-free. Vinyl deck boards *(right)* are available in a range of solid colors and snap into place on metal rails fastened to the deck framing. Wood composite decking resembles real wood and is fastened with nails or screws like ordinary lumber. Railing systems of either material can generally be purchased with the deck boards.

TOOLS
Wheelbarrow

Bucket
Mason's hoe
Square shovel

MATERIALS

Premixed concrete

SAFETY TIPS

Wet or dry, concrete is caustic—wear gloves, goggles, and a dust mask when mixing it.

MIXING CONCRETE BY HAND

1. Mixing in the water.

◆ Empty the premixed dry concrete ingredients into a wheelbarrow and, with a mason's hoe, create a hollow in the middle of the material.

◆ Slowly pour about three-quarters of the required quantity of water into the depression *(right)*.

◆ Push the dry ingredients into the water, mixing until all the water has been absorbed. Then, turn the concrete over two or three times with the hoe.

◆ Add water a little at a time until the mixture completely coats all the coarse aggregate; leave any unused water in the bucket until you have adjusted the consistency *(Step 2)*.

2. Testing the consistency.

◆ Smooth the surface of the mixture with the back of a square shovel.

◆ Jab the edge of the shovel into the concrete to form grooves. If the surface is smooth and the grooves are distinct, the concrete is ready to use *(left)*. If the surface roughens or the grooves are indistinct, add a small amount of water. If the surface is wet or the grooves collapse, add a small amount of dry ingredients.

◆ Retest the batch until the consistency is correct. Then, note the quantity of dry ingredients and water used for subsequent batches.

Building the Understructure

Beneath its smooth decking and attractive railings, a deck is supported by a sturdy system of joists, beams, and posts. This understructure must be carefully laid out so that the finished deck is square and level, and it is engineered to carry the weight of the building materials as well as the furnishings and the people who use the deck.

Engineering a Deck   **18**

Calculating Lumber Sizes and Spacings

A Solid Foundation   **21**

Defining the Layout
Attaching a Ledger to Flat Siding
Fastening to Overlapping Siding
Setting Posts in Concrete
Using Metal Post Bases

Putting Up Beams   **28**

Preparing the Posts
The Standard Method of Placing Beams
Alternate Techniques
Bracing Posts

Installing Joists   **34**

An Attached Deck
A Freestanding Deck
Adding Blocking

Decks with Distinctive Shapes   **40**

A Cut-Off Corner
Building Around an Obstruction

The key to a solid and long-lasting deck is a well designed frame, or understructure. Carefully calculating the spacing and size of the framing members is an essential part of the planning process and can help you save on materials and labor. Most decks are framed in a similar manner—a grid of posts supports the beams, and the beams support a network of joists. As described below and opposite, a deck can be attached to a house or held up by posts on all sides.

Spans and Spacing: In planning a deck, you will need to determine the length and size of the framing members, and how far apart to space them. Make your calculations using the charts on page 20, which give figures for southern pine and Douglas-fir graded No. 2 or better—the two most economical lumber options.

Compute the information for the joists first, then proceed to the data for the beams and the posts. Keep in mind that the spacing between the beams equals the distance the joists can span from beam to beam, and that post spacing is the same as beam span. Since the size and the spacing of one element affects the size and the spacing of the others, you probably will need to work back and forth between the charts to determine the ideal arrangement. As you make your calculations, you may discover that more than one set of figures is appropriate—you usually have a choice between a smaller number of large structural members or a larger number of small ones.

Digging holes and casting concrete footings for the posts are generally the most time-consuming and costly parts of the job, so it is best to minimize the number of posts and beams where possible. The final design will be determined not only by the allowable spans and spacings, but also by any special layout requirements of the deck shape and decking pattern (pages 40-45, 52-57 and 84-89).

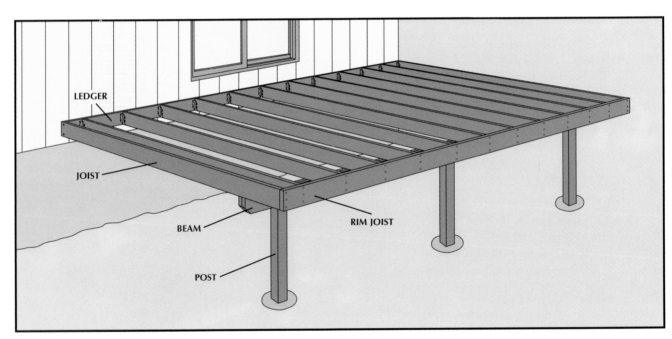

LEDGER

JOIST

BEAM

RIM JOIST

POST

Framing an attached deck.

On an attached deck, one side is held up by a ledger fastened to the house; the other side is supported by a beam sitting on a row of posts set in concrete footings. The joists hang from the ledger and rest on the beam, and a rim joist caps the ends of the joists. When the house has overlapping siding such as clapboard, a section of the siding is cut away to provide a flat surface on which to attach the ledger, and flashing is installed over the ledger to keep water from infiltrating the house wall.

In the framing design above, the beams are cantilevered—they project beyond the posts. The joists also project beyond the beams and posts. With this structure, the posts are recessed somewhat under the deck, so that slight inaccuracies in their positions will be hidden. In addition, cantilevering the joists and beams allows the distance from one support to the next to be reduced.

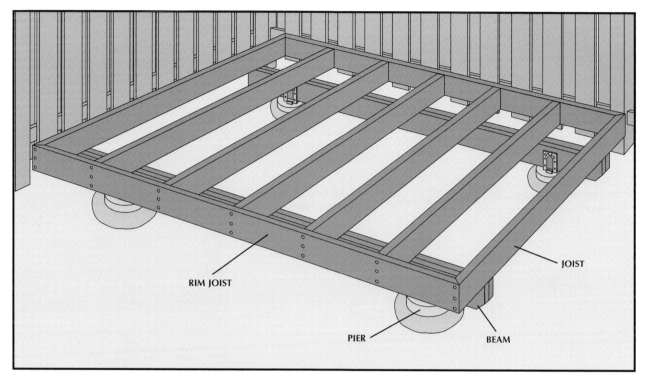

RIM JOIST

JOIST

PIER

BEAM

A freestanding deck.

This design is essentially the same as the one for an attached deck (opposite), except that both sides of the frame are supported by beams. The example shown above is low to the ground, so the beams sit directly on concrete piers; a higher freestanding deck would be supported by posts.

While this design is intended for structures set away from the house—such as a deck in a corner of a yard—it is also practical for a deck next to a house that has overlapping siding, since the siding will not have to be cut away to accommodate the ledger of an attached deck.

A DECK WITH A FLUSH BEAM

An alternative to cantilevering joists is to place them on the same plane as the beam (right). An advantage of this design is that the area underneath is more accessible for storage because there are no beams below the joists; but the design is also a good choice for a ground-level deck since it can be set lower than a deck with cantilevered joists. One drawback is that, to align correctly, the posts must be positioned more accurately than for a deck with cantilevered joists. The design illustrated at right is for an attached deck—a freestanding structure would have at least two flush beams.

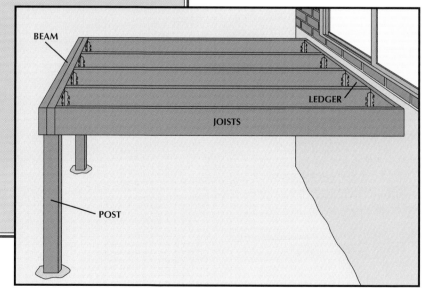

BEAM

LEDGER

JOISTS

POST

CALCULATING LUMBER SIZES AND SPACINGS

Determining joist size and spans.

The spacing of the joists is determined by the selection of decking lumber. Decking of 2-by-6s and 2-by-4s can span joists spaced 24 inches apart—or 16 inches if the decking is laid diagonally—while 5/4 decking must be supported by joists spaced every 16 inches—or 12 inches if laid diagonally. In the chart at right, the columns under the joist spacings indicate the joist span—which equals the beam spacing—for the different joist sizes. By increasing the size of the joist lumber, the span is increased, potentially cutting down on the number of beams and posts. For instance, if you plan to use diagonal 2-by-4 decking, the joist spacing is 16 inches, giving you the choice of 2-by-6 joists that can span 9 feet, 5 inches; 2-by-8 joists that can span 12 feet, 5 inches; etc. In addition, you can increase the length of joists that you use by cantilevering them up to one third of their total permissible span.

MAXIMUM JOIST SPAN

Joist Size	Joist Spacing		
	12"	16"	24"
2 x 6	10'4"	9'5"	7'10"
2 x 8	13'8"	12'5"	10'2"
2 x 10	17'5"	15'5"	12'7"
2 x 12	20'0"	17'10"	14'7"

MAXIMUM BEAM SPAN

Beam Size	Joist Span/Beam Spacing									
	4'	5'	6'	7'	8'	9'	10'	12'	14'	16'
2 x 6s (2)	7'	6'	—	—	—	—	—	—	—	—
2 x 8s (2)	9'	8'	7'	7'	6'	6'	—	—	—	—
2 x 10s (2)	11'	10'	9'	8'	8'	7'	7'	6'	6'	—
2 x 12s (2)	13'	12'	10'	10'	9'	8'	8'	7'	6'	6'

Selecting beam size and spans.

Once the joist spans/beam spacing are determined, use the chart above to figure the sizes and spans of the beams, and thus the post spacing. The figures given are for beams constructed of two pieces of 2-by lumber fastened together, but you can substitute 4-by lumber of the same width. Round up the figure for the joist span/beam spacing to the next interval: For instance, if the joist span is 9 feet, 5 inches, follow the column for a 10-foot joist span; if two 2-by-10s are to be used, the beam span would be 7 feet. Increasing the size of the beams will allow you to increase the beam span, and thus reduce the number of posts needed. Like joists, beams can be cantilevered up to one third of their span.

MAXIMUM POST HEIGHTS

Post Size	Load Area in Square Feet					
	36'	48'	60'	72'	84'	96'
4 x 4	10'	10'	10'	9'	9'	8'
6 x 6	17'	17'	17'	17'	17'	17'

Determining post size and height.

To calculate the load area that each post will have to support, first multiply the joist span by the beam span. Using the chart at left, you can then determine the size of posts required and the maximum height they can extend. For instance, on a deck with a joist span of 9 feet, 5 inches, and a beam span of 7 feet, the load area would be almost 66 square feet. Round this figure up to the next increment, 72 feet. For this load area, you can use 4-by-4 posts for a deck up to 9 feet high. For a higher deck, you must use larger posts or space them closer together. Choose 6-by-6 posts only when 4-by-4s are inadequate.

The stability of a deck depends much on the strength of its foundation, which is built in the first stage of construction. Before you begin, make sure the lot is properly graded to prevent water from pooling around the posts.

Layout: An attached deck *(page 18)* is laid out with one or more string lines parallel to the house that represent the rows of posts *(below)*. A freestanding deck *(page 19)* also employs string lines, with the first one taking the place of the house. For a deck that is not rectangular, a special layout of post locations may be needed *(pages 40-45, 84-89)*.

Ledgers: On flat siding such as wood panels or brick veneer, a ledger is secured by bolts through the siding and into the house framing *(pages 22-23)*. With overlapping siding such as vinyl or clapboard, a section must be removed so the ledger can lie flat against the sheathing *(page 24)*. For a wall of solid brick, concrete, or concrete block, use masonry anchors to fasten the ledger in place.

Foundations: Decks in a freezing climate must be supported on concrete footings that extend 8 inches below the frost line. Posts can generally be sunk directly into the footings *(page 25)*, but some codes require

that they be set in metal bases cast into the footings *(pages 26-27)*. Post bases are also needed for a low-level deck where beams rest directly on the footings. In a frost-free climate, posts can be supported by precast concrete pier blocks *(page 27)*.

When a deck plan includes continuous posts for an overhead or railing *(page 33)*, use post lumber that is long enough to extend the height of the railing or overhead.

⚠ **CAUTION** *Before digging footing holes, establish the location of underground utilities such as electric, water, and sewer lines.*

 TOOLS

Mason's line
Maul
Chalk line
Plumb bob
Powdered chalk
Carpenter's level (4')
Circular saw
Electric drill

Hammer
Socket wrench
Wood chisel
Tin snips
Caulking gun
Post-hole digger
Shovel
Concrete tools
Utility knife

 MATERIALS

1 x 2s, 1 x 4,
   2 x 2s, 2 x 4
Pressure-treated
   lumber for ledgers
   and posts
Exterior plywood ($\frac{1}{2}$")
Wood preservative
Roofing felt
Post bases

Framing-anchor nails
Galvanized nails ($3\frac{1}{2}$")
Galvanized lag screws
   ($\frac{3}{8}$" x $3\frac{1}{2}$") and
   washers
Metal flashing
Silicone sealant
Concrete mix
Fiber form tubes

 SAFETY TIPS

Wear goggles when using power tools or hammering. Add gloves to work with concrete or metal flashing. Put on a dust mask when cutting pressure-treated wood; wash your hands thoroughly after handling the wood.

DEFINING THE LAYOUT

1. Starting the layout.

◆ Make a mark on the wall representing one end of the deck—in this example, an attached deck with cantilevered joists that ends at the corner of the house.
◆ From the mark, measure along the wall the amount of the planned beam overhang to position the outside of the corner post and tap a nail partway into the wall at this point.
◆ Measure an additional 6 feet along the wall and tap in a second nail.

◆ Tie a length of mason's line longer than the deck's planned width to the first nail and the other end to a 2-by-2 stake. Mark this cord 8 feet from the wall.
◆ Tie a length of mason's line to the second nail and mark it at 10 feet.
◆ Working with a helper, pull the lines taut and maneuver them until the marked points meet *(right)*, then drive the stake into the ground with a maul.
◆ Repeat the process at the other end of the deck.

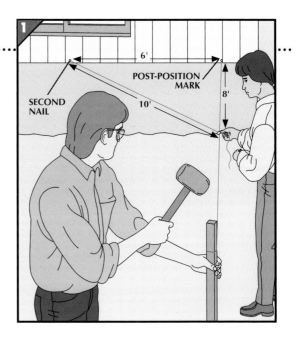

Labels in illustration: POST-POSITION MARK, SECOND NAIL, 6', 10', 8'

2. Locating the posts.

◆ For every planned row of posts, mark both string lines with masking tape where the outside faces of the posts will lie.

◆ Put up another string line—with a stake at each end—parallel to the house and crossing the first two lines at the marked points. Add string lines in the same way for any additional rows of posts that will be located underneath the deck.

◆ With a plumb bob, transfer the points where the string lines cross to the ground and mark each point with powdered chalk.

◆ Measure along the string lines to place any additional posts and mark these points on the ground *(right)*.

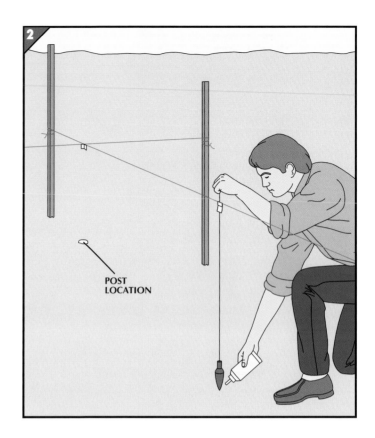

POST LOCATION

ATTACHING A LEDGER TO FLAT SIDING

1. Locating the ledger.

◆ Make a mark for the top of the ledger 3 inches below the door threshold—or, if you are planning to add a platform to the deck *(pages 84-85)*, lower the ledger accordingly.

◆ Cut a straight 2-by-6 to the length of the deck, minus 3 inches to allow for the joists that will cover the ends of the ledger.

◆ With a helper, hold the ledger against the house with the top edge in line with the mark you just made. Place a 4-foot carpenter's level on top of the board and level it.

◆ Make a mark along the top of the ledger near each end *(left)*, then remove the ledger and snap a chalk line between the marks.

For a very large deck requiring more than one ledger board, instead of holding up the boards, establish the ledger height with a water level.

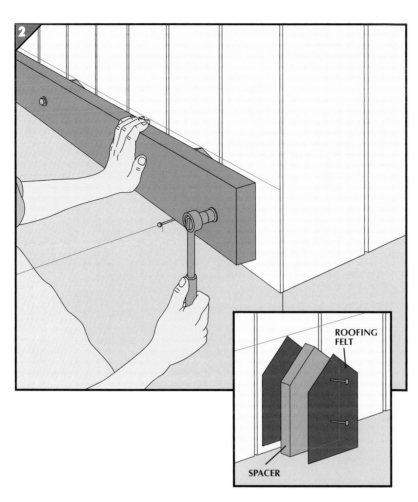

ROOFING FELT

SPACER

2. Installing the board.

◆ From $\frac{1}{2}$-inch exterior plywood, cut pointed spacers 3 inches wide and the height of the ledger board; soak them in wood preservative overnight. For each spacer, cut two pieces of roofing felt of the same shape and sandwich the spacer between the two layers of felt.

◆ Position a spacer 2 inches in from the mark indicating the edge of the deck, with its tip just below the ledger-location line; tack the spacer to the wall with two $3\frac{1}{2}$-inch galvanized common or spiral-shank nails *(inset)*. Fasten additional spacers every 2 feet along the chalk line.

◆ With a helper, lift the ledger into place, aligning it with the chalk line and centering it between the marks indicating the edge of the deck. Tack the ledger to the spacers.

◆ At each spacer location, drill a $\frac{3}{8}$-inch clearance hole through the ledger and the spacer, then drive a $\frac{3}{8}$- by $3\frac{1}{2}$-inch lag screw fitted with a flat washer through each hole *(left)* and into the framing of the house *(box, below)*.

◆ Cover the lag-screw heads with silicone sealant.

FASTENING TO VARIOUS KINDS OF FRAMING

For a ledger to provide solid support to a deck, it must be attached securely to the house framing. If the deck falls above floor height, simply locate wall studs and fasten the ledger to them with lag screws. In most cases where the deck is the same height as the floor, the ledger can be fastened with lag screws to the solid wood of the floor joist at the side of the house *(near right)*. Some houses, however, are built with I-beams or trusses, which must be reinforced before a ledger can be attached. To do so, you must first expose the inner sides of the I-beam or truss where the ledger will sit. Cut away the ceiling in the room below, making an opening about 2 feet wide along the proposed location of the ledger.

For an I-beam, reinforce the beam inside and outside with boards the full length of the ledger *(center, right)*: Measure the distance between the flanges of the I-beam and select 2-inch boards to fit. Working through holes in the ceiling, tack them to the plywood web. Outside,

cut away the siding to expose the web, then secure the boards to it with carriage bolts and nail the strip of siding back in place. Attach the ledger to the assembly with lag screws.

For a truss, strengthen a section at least as long as the ledger with boards that match the height of the truss *(far right)*: Attach the boards to the truss with 3-inch nails and fasten the ledger to these boards with carriage bolts.

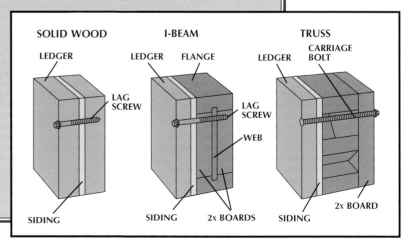

SOLID WOOD I-BEAM TRUSS

LEDGER LEDGER FLANGE LEDGER CARRIAGE BOLT

LAG SCREW LAG SCREW

WEB

SIDING SIDING 2x BOARDS SIDING 2x BOARD

FASTENING TO OVERLAPPING SIDING

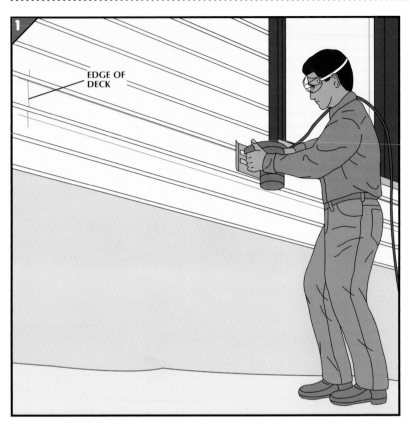

EDGE OF DECK

1. Cutting away the siding.

◆ Mark the top of the ledger board as on page 22, Step 1, allowing an extra 3 inches for the joists that will cover its ends. Also snap a chalk line for the bottom of the ledger, plus 3 inches.

◆ With a carpenter's level, extend the marks indicating the edges of the deck so that they cross both horizontal lines.

◆ Set the blade of a circular saw to the siding depth (for aluminum siding, equip the saw with a metal-cutting blade) and cut along the top and bottom lines (left).

◆ Tack a 1-by-4 along a vertical end mark to create a flat surface for the saw to ride on. Adjust the saw-blade depth and make the vertical cut, letting the saw's base plate ride on top of the 1-by-4; then repeat the cut at the other end of the outline.

◆ Complete the corners with a wood chisel—or tin snips for aluminum.

◆ Work the section of siding away from the wall sheathing, using a pry bar with a wood block under it for leverage, if necessary.

2. Installing flashing.

◆ With tin snips, cut enough strips of 7-inch-wide metal flashing to span the opening in the siding, then bend each one lengthwise 4 inches from an edge.

◆ Push the 4-inch leg of one piece of flashing under the siding, cutting slots for any siding nails.

◆ Continue to install strips of flashing to fill the opening, overlapping the strips by about 2 inches (right).

◆ Fasten the ledger to the sheathing as you would to flat siding (page 23), but without spacers.

◆ Bend the flashing down over the face of the ledger with a hammer and a block of wood.

◆ With silicone sealant, caulk the screw holes, the joints between pieces of flashing, the joint between the flashing and siding, and the joint between the bottom of the ledger and the siding.

FLASHING

SETTING POSTS IN CONCRETE

1. Making the footings.
◆ Remove the string lines.
◆ With a post-hole digger, dig a hole at each chalked post location (right), making the holes 10 inches across at the top, widening to 16 inches at the bottom; and 24 inches deep or 8 inches below the frost line, whichever is deeper. Since footings must rest on undisturbed soil, do not backfill the holes with loose earth.
◆ Mix concrete (page 15) and pour 8 inches of it into each hole.
◆ Allow the concrete to harden up to 48 hours.

BRACE

POST

2. Setting the posts.
◆ Retie the string lines.
◆ Cut a post long enough to extend above the ground by a few inches more than its final height. If the deck plan includes continuous posts for a railing or overhead (page 33), use uncut posts at least as long as the required height.
◆ Set the post in the hole with its uncut end down, and position it at the intersection of the strings. Fasten a 1-by-2 brace to one side of the post with a single nail, then drive a stake into the ground within reach of the brace.
◆ Have a helper plumb the post with a carpenter's level, then nail the brace to the stake, backing up the stake with a maul (left). Plumb and brace an adjacent side of the post, then set and plumb the remaining posts in the same way.
◆ Fill the holes with concrete to within a few inches of the lip.
◆ After the concrete has set for at least 24 hours, remove the braces and pack the hollows with earth, sloping the surface away from the posts.

FIBER FORM TUBE

1. Inserting fiber tubes.

◆ Dig a hole and pour a footing for each post *(page 25, Step 1)*.

◆ With a handsaw, cut an 8-inch-diameter fiber form tube long enough to reach the bottom of the hole and extend 2 inches above the ground. Insert the tube in the hole *(above)* and center it. Fill in around the outside of the tube with about a foot of earth to stabilize it.

◆ Cut and insert the remaining tubes.

◆ If you will be setting beams directly on the piers, put two to three shovelfuls of concrete into each tube, then level the tubes *(Step 2)*. Otherwise, fill all the tubes with concrete and smooth the top of each one with a scrap piece of 2-by-4, then proceed immediately to Step 3.

2. Leveling the tubes.

◆ Set a straight board across an adjacent pair of tubes and place a 4-foot carpenter's level on top of the board. Note which tube is higher. Continue checking adjacent tubes in the same way until you locate the highest one.

◆ Placing the board and level on the highest tube and an adjacent one, pull up on the lower tube until the board is level *(above)*. Continue to adjust the tubes so that each is level with one you have previously leveled.

◆ Add concrete to fill all the tubes, then smooth the top of each by pulling a scrap piece of 2-by-4 across the top of the tube.

TRICKS OF THE TRADE

Pier and Footings in One

Instead of shoveling concrete for the wide footing into each hole, then inserting and filling the tubes to form the piers, you can cast the footings and piers in one shot. Cut a tube to run from 8 inches above the bottom of the hole to 2 inches above the surface. Nail opposite sides of the tube to two 2-by-4s. Set the tube in the hole suspended from the 2-by-4s and center it. With the 2-by-4s held in place with small stakes, the concrete can be poured.

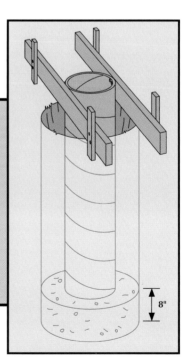

8"

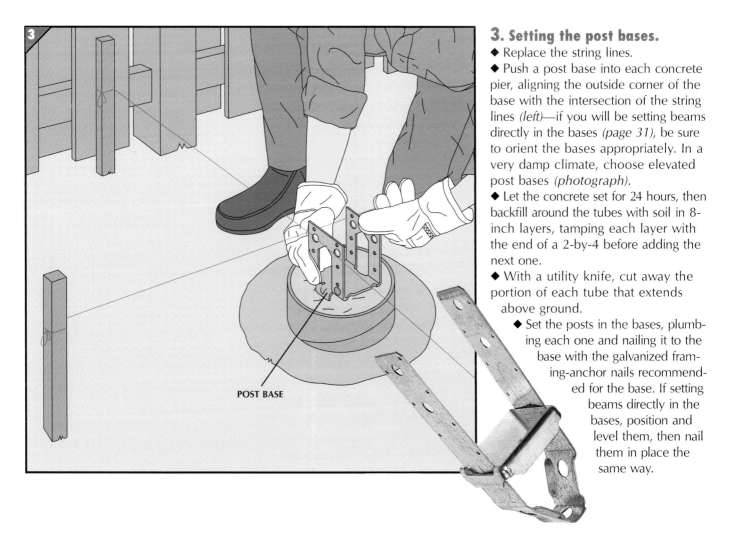

POST BASE

3. Setting the post bases.

◆ Replace the string lines.

◆ Push a post base into each concrete pier, aligning the outside corner of the base with the intersection of the string lines *(left)*—if you will be setting beams directly in the bases *(page 31)*, be sure to orient the bases appropriately. In a very damp climate, choose elevated post bases *(photograph)*.

◆ Let the concrete set for 24 hours, then backfill around the tubes with soil in 8-inch layers, tamping each layer with the end of a 2-by-4 before adding the next one.

◆ With a utility knife, cut away the portion of each tube that extends above ground.

◆ Set the posts in the bases, plumbing each one and nailing it to the base with the galvanized framing-anchor nails recommended for the base. If setting beams directly in the bases, position and level them, then nail them in place the same way.

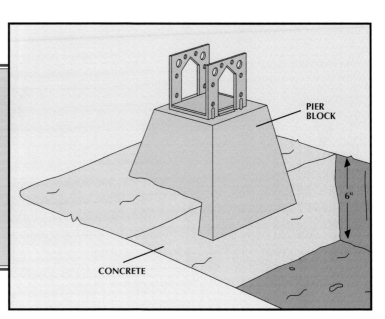

PIER BLOCK

6"

CONCRETE

PIER BLOCKS FOR A WARM CLIMATE

In a climate that does not experience frost, deck posts can be supported with precast concrete pier blocks that contain post bases. To set each block, pour a 6-inch-thick concrete pad on undisturbed soil a few inches larger all around than the block, then simply press the block 2 inches down into the wet concrete.

Once the foundation is in place, the beams can be installed. On an attached deck *(page 18)* they run parallel to the house, while on a freestanding deck *(page 19)* you can set them in either direction.

Lumber: Beams can be cut from 4-by lumber. This size gives a solid look to the deck, and allows the beam to sit squarely on top of the posts. If pressure-treated lumber this thickness is not available in your area, you can make a built-up beam by fastening together a pair of 2-by boards.

Attaching Beams: The standard method for attaching a beam to posts is with metal connectors *(opposite, Step 1)*. For a built-up beam, however, you will need to use adjustable post caps since the combined thickness of the boards is $\frac{1}{2}$ inch less than a 4-by-4 post. On a ground-level deck, beams can be set directly in post bases cast into piers *(page 31)*. For

posts cut from 6-by-6s, notch them to receive the beam *(page 32)*. An alternative method is to sandwich two beams around a post *(page 32)*. Though slightly weaker than beams seated on the posts, this design permits you to extend posts upward to support railings or overheads *(page 33)*. It also simplifies the job of cutting the posts to height.

Before fastening the beams to the posts, make sure that the ends of the assembly are aligned *(page 30, Step 2)*.

Bracing Posts: Cross braces between the posts and beams add rigidity to the deck *(page 33)*. Bracing requirements vary depending on local building codes, but in general it is a good idea to use bracing on a freestanding deck more than about 3 feet high, an attached deck higher than about 4 feet, or any deck that projects a long distance from the house.

 TOOLS

Carpenter's level
Chalk line
Combination square
Carpenter's square

Circular saw
Handsaw
Reciprocating saw
Electric drill
Hammer
Wrenches

 **MATERIALS**

Pressure-treated lumber for beams and braces
Cedar shims
Post caps
Framing-anchor nails
Common nails ($3\frac{1}{2}$")

Galvanized spiral-shank nails (3", $3\frac{1}{2}$")
Galvanized carriage bolts ($\frac{1}{2}$" x 6", 7") and washers
Galvanized lag screws ($\frac{3}{8}$" x 4") and washers

 SAFETY TIPS

Put on goggles when hammering or using power tools. Wear a dust mask when cutting pressure-treated wood; wash your hands thoroughly after handling the wood.

PREPARING THE POSTS

1. Marking the end posts.

For a deck with a ledger, have a helper set one end of a straight piece of lumber on top of the ledger. Rest the other end against an end post, then level the board and mark the post along its bottom edge *(right)*.

◆ Measure down the post the height of a joist and the height of a beam, then make a mark at this point to indicate the top of the post *(inset)*. For a 6-by-6 post or a split beam *(page 32)*, measure down only the height of a joist.

◆ Mark the other end post in the same way.

For a freestanding deck, measure up from the ground to mark one post, then transfer the measurements to the other posts with a water level.

TOP OF JOIST
TOP OF BEAM
TOP OF POST

2. Marking intermediate posts.

◆ Tap a nail into the face of one end post, level with the post-height mark, and hook the end of a chalk line over the nail. Unwind the chalk line and hold it level with the post-height mark on the other end post. Snap the line to mark the intermediary posts *(right)*.

◆ With a combination square, draw a line around all the faces of each post level with the post-height mark.

◆ Unless you will be installing a split beam *(page 32)*, cut off the top of the posts along the marked lines with a circular saw.

THE STANDARD METHOD OF PLACING BEAMS

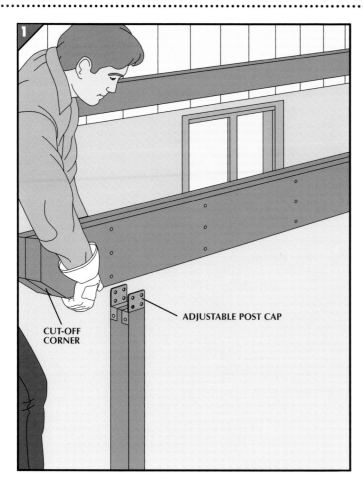

CUT-OFF CORNER

ADJUSTABLE POST CAP

1. Seating the beams.

◆ With galvanized framing-anchor nails, fasten a post cap to the top of each post. Use standard caps for a solid 4-by beam, adjustable caps set 3 inches apart for a built-up beam of 2-bys.

◆ Cut a 4-by beam to the desired length; or, make a built-up beam: Fasten together two pieces of 2-by lumber the length of the deck, driving 3-inch galvanized spiral-shank nails in rows of three at 16-inch intervals. Turn over the assembly and nail in the same pattern, positioning rows to fall midway between those on the opposite side.

◆ On each end of the beam, make marks 2 inches from a corner on the end and the bottom, then draw a diagonal line joining them. Cut along the line with a circular saw.

◆ Working with a helper, sit the beam in the post caps with the cut-off corners at the ends facing down *(left)*.

2. Nailing the beam.

◆ Adjust the position of the beam to allow for the correct amount of overhang at each end.

◆ To check that the ends of the beam line up with the ends of the ledger, tack a long straight board to the ledger and set it on the beam. Square the board to the ledger with a carpenter's square and adjust the beam until the end of it is flush with the outside face of the squared board.

◆ Fasten the post caps to the beam with framing-anchor nails (right).

BEAM

POST

SPLICING BEAMS

For a large deck, you may have to splice lumber to make a long-enough beam. For a beam built of two 2-bys, simply stagger the joints between the two faces when joining the pieces, being sure that joints fall over a post (right). For a solid 4-by beam, locate the joint over a post and tie the pieces together with a length of metal strapping nailed across the joint on each side of the beam near the top.

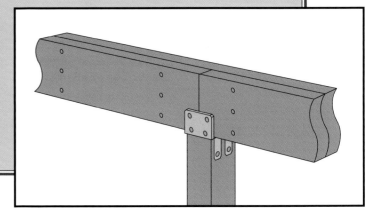

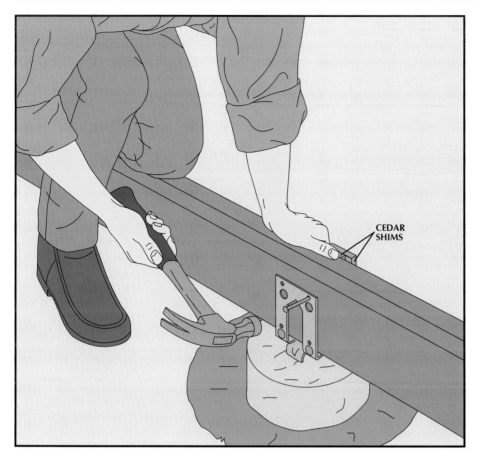

CEDAR SHIMS

Beams for a low deck.

◆ Working with a helper, set the beam directly into the post bases. If you are using a built-up beam *(page 29, Step 1)*, trim a pair of cedar shims to the height of the beam and insert them on the inner side of the beam between it and the post bases.

◆ Measure the beam to ensure that it overhangs each end pier by the same amount. As described opposite, Step 2, use a long straight board and a carpenter's square to align the ends of the beam and a ledger or of two beams.

◆ Fasten the beams to the bases with galvanized framing-anchor nails *(left)*.

DECKING OVER A PATIO

If you want to convert a patio to a deck, you can do it by placing pressure-treated sleepers across the patio, spaced the same distance apart as joists, and laying decking on the sleepers. If the patio is sloped to shed rainwater and the surface is even and in good condition, simply fasten the sleepers to it with glue made for attaching wood to concrete outdoors, then lay the decking in the same way as you would on joists *(pages 48-56)*. For an uneven surface, shim the sleepers with cedar shingles at the low spots, then fasten the sleepers and shims to the patio with glue and masonry anchors.

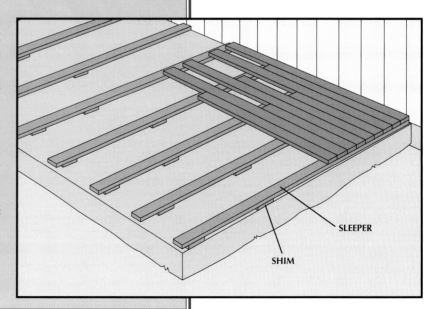

SLEEPER

SHIM

Attaching to 6-by-6 posts.

◆ With a combination square, mark the top of each post for a notch 3 inches deep and as high as the width of the beam lumber you are using—locate the notch on the side of the post facing away from the house.

◆ Set the blade of a circular saw to the maximum cutting depth and cut along the lines, then finish the cuts with a handsaw.

◆ Measure the beam to ensure that it overhangs each end post by the same amount. As described on page 30, Step 2, use a long straight board and a carpenter's square to align the ends of the beam and the ledger or the ends of two beams.

◆ Toenail the beam to each post with $3\frac{1}{2}$-inch galvanized spiral-shank nails.

◆ Drill two $\frac{1}{2}$-inch offset holes through the beam and each post, then install $\frac{1}{2}$- by 6-inch carriage bolts in the holes *(right)*.

A split beam.

◆ Cut two 2-bys to length to form the beam. Working with a helper, lift one piece into place against the posts with its top edge aligned with the marked lines, checking that the appropriate amount extends past each end post.

◆ Tack each end of the beam to the post with a partially-driven $3\frac{1}{2}$-inch common nail. Fasten the second board to the opposite face of the posts in the same way *(left)*.

◆ As described on page 30, Step 2, use a long straight board and a carpenter's square to check that the ends of the beam line up with the ends of the ledger or other beam.

◆ Drill two $\frac{1}{2}$-inch holes through the beam and each post, then install $\frac{1}{2}$- by 7-inch carriage bolts in the holes and pull out the nails.

◆ Unless the posts will support a railing or overhead *(opposite)*, cut them off flush with the top of the beam using a reciprocating saw—the joists will hide the rough ends.

POST-HEIGHT MARK

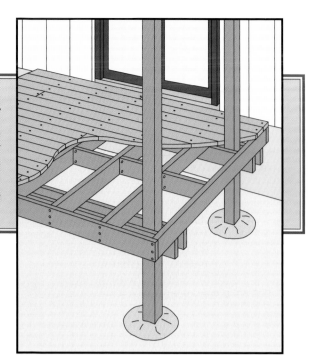

CONTINUOUS POSTS FOR AN OVERHEAD

One advantage of attaching split beams to posts *(opposite)* is that the posts can extend upward to provide solid support for a railing or an overhead. If you design your deck in this manner, you may want to adjust the amount that the beams and joists are cantilevered so that the posts will fall close to the outside edges of the deck.

BRACING POSTS

Attaching the braces.
◆ For posts between 3 and 8 feet tall, cut 2-by-4 braces 3 feet long, making parallel miter cuts at the ends. For taller posts, cut braces from 2-by-6 stock.
◆ Set one end of the brace against the beam and center the lower end on the post. Tack each end in place with a partially-driven $3\frac{1}{2}$-inch nail.
◆ For all but the end posts, attach a second brace, leaving a $\frac{1}{8}$-inch gap between it and the first brace *(left)*.
◆ Add braces to the opposite side of the posts and beams in the same way.
◆ Drill $\frac{1}{2}$-inch clearance holes through the ends of the braces and install $\frac{1}{2}$- by 7-inch carriage bolts, then pull out the nails.

For split beams, 2-by-4 braces fit between the boards making up the beam: Bevel both ends of each brace, tack the brace in place, then fasten it to the beam with a $\frac{1}{2}$- by 7-inch carriage bolt and to the post with a $\frac{3}{8}$- by 4-inch lag screw *(inset)*.

Installing Joists

The next phase of the building process is to install joists, which form the framework on which the decking is laid. For an attached deck *(below)*, joists are fastened to the ledger with joist hangers; their other ends rest on the beam and are joined by a rim joist. On a freestanding deck, whose joists are supported by beams at both ends, the end and rim joists are installed first, then the intermediate joists are laid *(page 38)*.

Special Techniques: Most lumber used for deck framing has a slight curve or "crown." Before you install the joists, sight down their edges to detect the curve and lay them crown-up. On a well-crafted deck, the end grain of the framing members is concealed as much as possible. In the design on these pages, the end joists hide the ends of the ledger. If railing posts will cover the joints between the rim and end joists, you can butt the members together, leaving the end grain exposed. Otherwise, bevel the joints *(page 38)* or hide them with a beveled fascia that matches the decking *(page 50)*.

Blocking: Some local codes require blocking *(page 39)* to keep joists from twisting; it is generally placed directly over an inner beam and at the midpoint of joists spanning more than 8 feet. It is also wise to place blocking behind the end joists wherever a railing post will be added.

 TOOLS

Tape measure
Combination
  square
Chalk line
Hammer
Circular saw
Hand plane
Caulking gun

 **MATERIALS**

Pressure-treated lumber for
  joists and blocking
Joist hangers
Multipurpose framing
  anchors
Rafter ties
Framing-anchor nails
Galvanized spiral-shank
  nails $(3\frac{1}{2}")$
Silicone sealant

 SAFETY TIPS

Protect your eyes with goggles when hammering or sawing. Add a dust mask when cutting pressure-treated wood and wash your hands thoroughly after handling the wood.

AN ATTACHED DECK

1. Installing the end joists.
◆ Cut an end joist a few inches longer than the planned width of the deck.
◆ Set the joist in place with one end resting on the outer beam and the other against the end of the ledger.
◆ With $3\frac{1}{2}$-inch galvanized spiral-shank nails, fasten the end joist to the ledger so the upper edges are flush *(right)*.
◆ Where you have cut away siding, seal the joint between the end joist and the siding with silicone sealant.

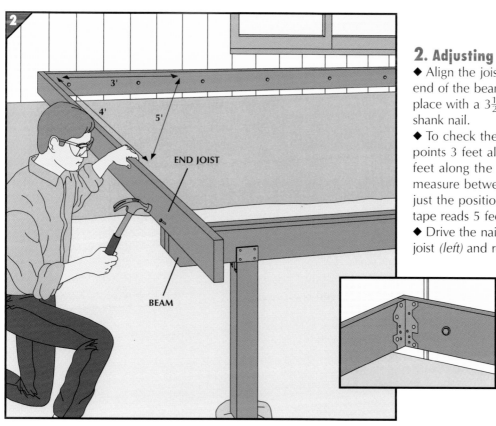

2. Adjusting for square.

◆ Align the joist's outer face with the end of the beam and tack the joist in place with a $3\frac{1}{2}$-inch galvanized spiral-shank nail.

◆ To check the joist for square, mark points 3 feet along the ledger and 4 feet along the joist. Stretch a tape measure between the marks and adjust the position of the joist until the tape reads 5 feet.

◆ Drive the nail all the way into the joist *(left)* and reinforce the inside corner at the ledger with a galvanized multipurpose framing anchor *(inset)*.

◆ Install the end joist on the opposite side in the same manner.

3. Marking the joist locations.

◆ Starting from one end joist, measure along the ledger and mark joist locations at the appropriate spacing *(chart, page 20)*. The last joist location may fall closer to the end of the ledger than the standard distance.

◆ With a combination square, draw a vertical line on the face of the ledger in line with a mark *(right)*, then draw an X on the side of the line where the joist will be attached.

◆ Outline the remaining joist locations, then mark the top face of the outermost beam in the same way, beginning the layout at the same end that you did for the ledger.

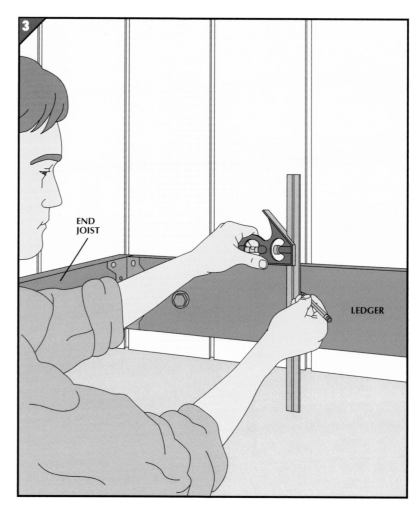

4. Installing joist hangers.

◆ Position a joist hanger on the ledger at the first location line so the opening falls over the X.

◆ Set a scrap piece of joist lumber in the hanger and adjust the height of the hanger so the block is flush with the top of the ledger.

◆ With galvanized framing-anchor nails, fasten the joist hanger on the side next to the line. Squeeze the hanger snug around the block of wood and nail the opposite side. Install joist hangers at the remaining location lines in the same way *(right)*.

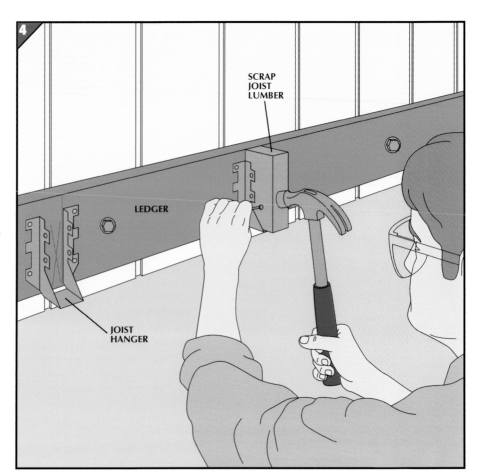

SPLICING JOISTS

If you are building a large deck, you may not be able to purchase joist stock long enough to span the distance from the ledger to the out- ermost beam. In this case, splice joists togeth- er over a beam by overlapping them 12 inch- es and nailing them together with 3-inch galvanized spiral-shank nails *(right)*. Be sure to take into account the staggered layout when marking the joist locations on the ledger and beams. In the case of a deck with three or more beams, avoid placing all the splices over the same beam.

Since an overlapping splice on an end joist would be visible, butt the joist sections end- to-end instead and reinforce the splice with a 1-foot length of joist lumber nailed across the inner side of the joint.

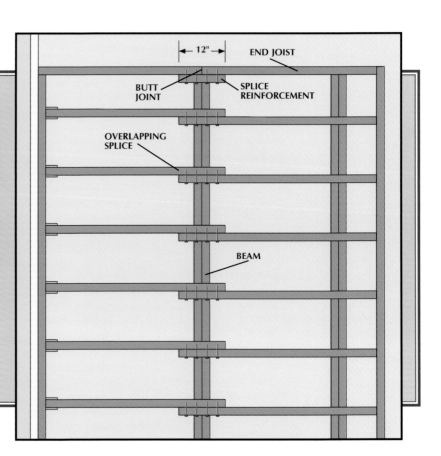

5. Trimming the joists.

◆ Set a joist a few inches longer than the planned width of the deck into the joist hanger next to the end joist and fasten it in place with galvanized framing-anchor nails.

◆ Install the remaining joists in the same way.

◆ Align a joist with its mark on the beam and toenail it in place, or attach it with a rafter tie *(photograph)* where required by code.

◆ Fasten the remaining joists to the beam in the same way.

◆ Along each end joist, measure from the house the planned width of the deck less 1½ inches and make a mark.

◆ Tap in a nail at one of the marks and slip the end of a chalk line over the nail. Stretch the line to the mark on the other end joist and snap the line *(left)*.

◆ With a combination square, transfer the mark on each joist to the face of the joist, then trim the joists along the lines with a circular saw.

6. Adding the rim joist.

◆ Cut a rim joist to the length of the deck, or splice one to fit *(page 38, box)*. Working with a helper, hold it in place against the ends of the joists flush with the outer sides of the end joists and fasten it to one of the end joists with three galvanized 3½-inch spiral-shank nails.

◆ Have your helper raise or lower the rim joist so it is flush with the next joist, then nail it in place. Continue fastening the rim joist to the end of each joist, raising and lowering it as needed *(right)*.

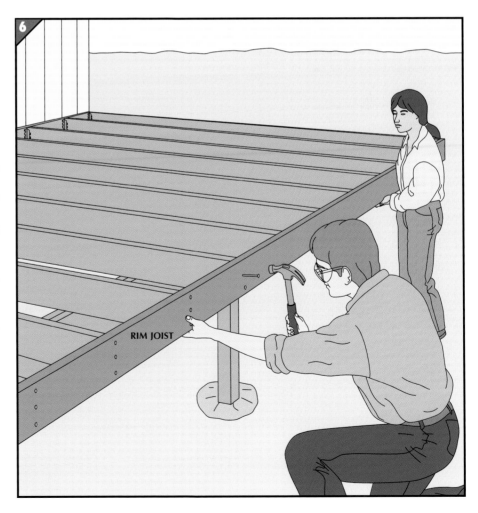

RIM JOIST

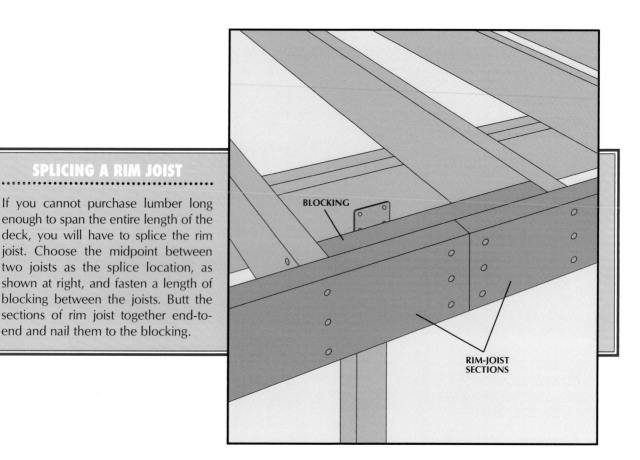

BLOCKING

RIM-JOIST SECTIONS

A FREESTANDING DECK

Installing the framing.
◆ Cut two end joists to length, beveling the ends.
◆ Position one piece across the beams so it over-hangs them by the same amount at both ends.
◆ Cut two rim joists, beveling the ends to fit the end joists. Working with a helper, lift the rim joist into place and fasten each beveled corner with three nails. Install the second rim joist in the same way.
◆ Measure the deck diagonally from corner to corner; if the diagonals are not equal, tap the frame with a hammer to square it.
◆ Toenail the end joists to the beams with $3\frac{1}{2}$-inch galvanized spiral-shank nails.
◆ Round the frame's beveled corners slightly with a hand plane.
◆ Mark the joist locations on the rim joists as you would on a ledger *(page 35, Step 2)*.
◆ Cut the intermediate joists and lift each one into place, align it with the marks, and fasten it to the rim joists with three nails *(right)*. Toenail the joists to the beam or install rafter ties if required by code *(page 37, Step 5)*.

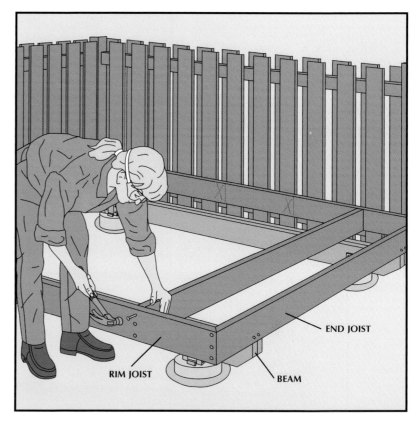

END JOIST

RIM JOIST

BEAM

ADDING BLOCKING

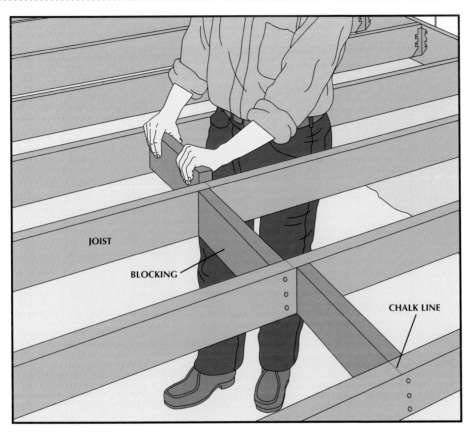

JOIST

BLOCKING

CHALK LINE

Fitting in blocking.

◆ If codes require blocking *(page 34)*, cut a piece to fit between each pair of joists from lumber of the same size.

◆ Snap a chalk line across the joists in the middle of the deck or over a beam, as the code indicates.

◆ Fit the blocking between the joists, placing consecutive pieces on opposite sides of the chalk line *(left)*, and fasten it to the joists with three $3\frac{1}{2}$-inch galvanized spiral-shank nails at each end.

BLOCKING FOR RAILINGS

Where an intermediate railing post *(dashed lines)* will be attached to an end joist *(page 69)*, it is a good idea to reinforce the joist with blocking. Cut a length of blocking and fasten it between the joists as described above, placing it about 4 inches from the planned railing-post location.

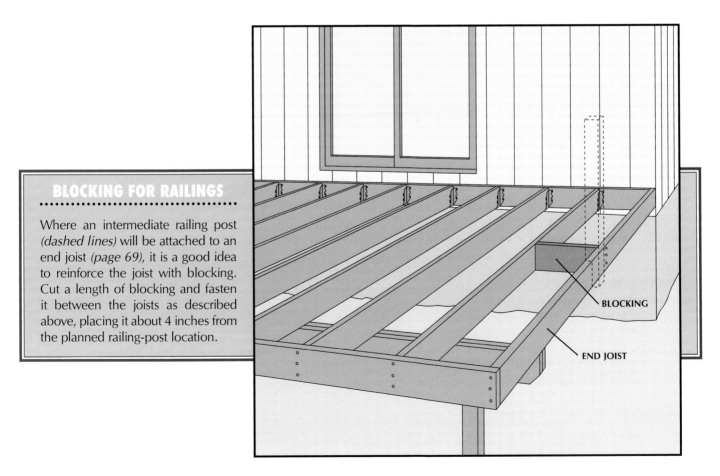

BLOCKING

END JOIST

Although a rectangular deck is the easiest type to build, altering this shape can add visual interest. Variations include cutting the corners at an angle or incorporating a natural element of the landscape such as a tree or rock.

A Cut-Off Corner: You can create a small angled corner by cutting the end and rim joists short and linking the two sides with a board. For a large angle, you'll need to cut one or more of the intermediate joists and add a short beam to support them *(below)*. This frame can also be used to make a deck with curved corners *(pages 55-56)* by laying the deck slightly differently.

Natural Features: Rather than removing trees or rocks that lie within the perimeter of the deck, you can leave them in place to integrate the deck with its surroundings and enhance its natural charm. To do so, you must first frame an opening in the substructure *(pages 43-45)*; the decking can then be cut to follow the shape of the object *(page 57)*.

 TOOLS

Tape measure
Mason's line
Maul
Chalk line
Combination square
Circular saw
Reciprocating saw
Electric drill
Hammer
Socket wrench
Hand plane
Post-hole digger
Shovel
Concrete tools

 **MATERIALS**

2 x 2s
Materials for casting footings and setting posts
Pressure-treated lumber for ledgers, posts, beams, joists, and other framing
Post caps
Multipurpose framing anchors
Joist hangers
Framing-anchor nails
Galvanized lag screws ($\frac{3}{8}$" x $3\frac{1}{2}$") and washers
Galvanized spiral-shank nails ($3\frac{1}{2}$")
Galvanized common nails (3")

 SAFETY TIPS

Put on goggles when using a power tool or hammering. Wear a dust mask to cut pressure-treated lumber and wash your hands thoroughly after handling the wood.

A CUT-OFF CORNER

Anatomy of an angled corner.
In this design, the rim and end joists, as well as two intermediate joists, are cut at an angle and linked with a short rim joist beveled to fit the angle. The end post of the main beam is set back farther than usual from the edge of the deck and the corner is buttressed by a short extra beam set on two posts.

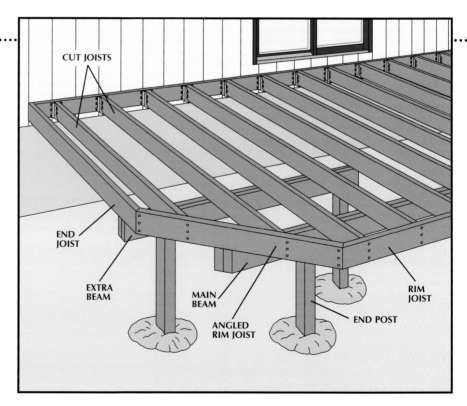

CUT JOISTS

END JOIST

EXTRA BEAM

MAIN BEAM

ANGLED RIM JOIST

END POST

RIM JOIST

1. Cutting end and rim joists.
◆ Cast footings and set posts and beams *(pages 21-33)*, placing the end post of the main beam far enough from the edge of the deck to accommodate the corner and adding a short beam to support the joists to be cut short.
◆ Install the joists and rim joist *(pages 34-38)*, but omit the intermediate joists that will be shortened.
◆ Mark the end joist at the desired distance from the corner and the rim joist at the same measurement.
◆ Set the blade of a circular saw to $22\frac{1}{2}°$ and trim the end joist at the mark *(left)*—angle the cut so the outside face of the joist is longer than the inside one.
◆ Bevel the rim joist in the same way.

2. Trimming the main beam.
◆ Measure the distance between the beveled ends of the rim and end joists and cut a short length of rim joist to fit, angling the ends at $22\frac{1}{2}°$.
◆ Have a helper hold the joist in place, and mark where it crosses the main beam *(right)*. Remove the angled rim joist and, with a combination square, transfer the cutting line to the faces of the beam. With a reciprocating saw, trim the beam along the lines.
◆ Fit the angled joist back in place and nail it to both the end and rim joists with three $3\frac{1}{2}$-inch galvanized spiral-shank nails.
◆ Round the beveled corners slightly with a hand plane.

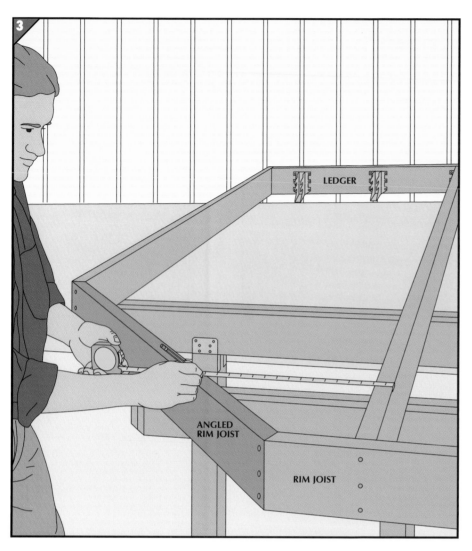

3. Locating the cut joists.

◆ Hook a tape measure over the last full-length joist, positioning it parallel to the rim joist and across the angled rim joist at a point equal to the joist spacing; mark the angled joist at this location *(left)*.

◆ Record the location of the remaining joists on the angled rim joist in the same way.

◆ Measure the distance between each joist hanger on the ledger to the corresponding mark on the angled rim joist and cut a joist to fit, beveling one end at a 45° angle.

◆ Install the cut joists, fastening them to the joist hangers with galvanized framing-anchor nails and to the angled rim joist with three $3\frac{1}{2}$-inch galvanized spiral-shank nails.

LEDGER

ANGLED RIM JOIST

RIM JOIST

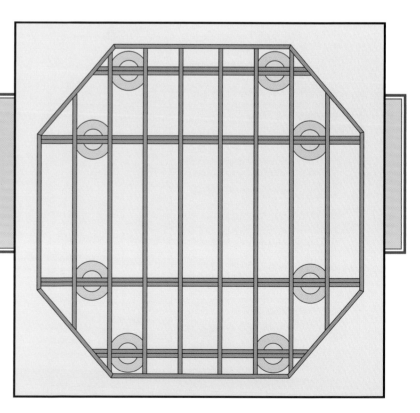

AN OCTAGONAL DECK

By angling all four corners of a square free-standing deck, you can create an octagonal design *(right)*. For the framing, use the methods for building a standard deck, but set additional posts and beams to support the shortened joists at the corners.

BUILDING AROUND AN OBSTRUCTION

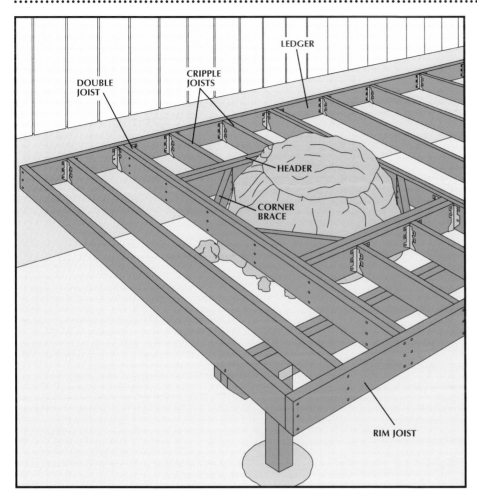

LEDGER

CRIPPLE JOISTS

DOUBLE JOIST

HEADER

CORNER BRACE

RIM JOIST

A reinforced opening.

An opening in a deck that accommodates an obstruction is framed in a specific way to support the joists that must be shortened. First, the joists at each side of the opening are doubled and headers made of doubled joist lumber are fastened to them. Cripple joists are then fastened with joist hangers between the headers and the ledger and rim joist, and the decking is laid over the frame.

Decking can overhang this framing by a maximum of 4 inches. If the opening is large and round—such as for a tree or boulder (*left*)—the deck boards may need to extend by more than 4 inches in some places. In this case, you will need to install corner braces to support the ends of the deck boards. When you frame around a tree, leave a gap of at least 5 inches between the decking and the trunk to give the tree room to grow.

A TREE AS A CENTERPIECE

An enormous oak was growing right in the middle of the planned location of this deck. Instead of cutting down the tree, the owners simply built the deck around it. Plenty of room was left between the deck and the tree to allow for growth, and benches (*pages 136-143*) were added to take advantage of the shade.

1. Hanging double joists.

◆ Install a ledger and set posts and beams as you would for an ordinary deck *(pages 21-33)*.

◆ Lay out joist locations along the ledger and install joist hangers *(pages 34-36)*; use double-joist hangers where the double joists will fall. Transfer the joist locations to the beam.

◆ Install the single joists, omitting those that would cross the obstruction, then add the rim joist.

◆ For each double joist, cut two pieces of joist lumber to length and nail each pair together with rows of three 3-inch galvanized common nails spaced every 16 inches.

◆ Lift the double joist into place and fasten it to the joist hanger with galvanized framing-anchor nails *(right)* and to the rim joist with three $3\frac{1}{2}$-inch galvanized spiral-shank nails. Toenail the double joist to the beam.

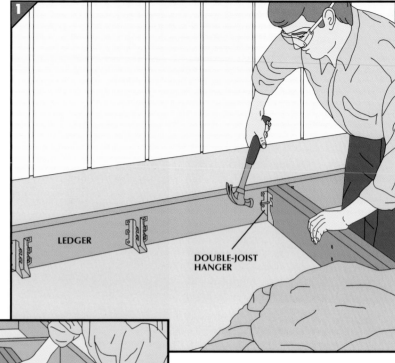

LEDGER

DOUBLE-JOIST HANGER

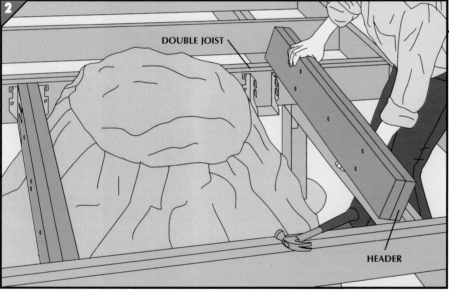

DOUBLE JOIST

HEADER

2. Fitting in the headers.

◆ Install two double-joist hangers on each double joist at the planned locations of the headers.

◆ From lumber the same size as the joists, cut two pairs of boards to serve as headers between the double joists. Nail each pair together with three 3-inch galvanized common nails spaced every 16 inches.

◆ Lift each header into place *(left)* and fasten it to the joist hangers at each end.

3. Filling in with cripple joists.

◆ Measuring from one of the single joists, mark the locations of the cripple joists on the rim joist and headers, spacing them the same distance apart as regular joists. Install joist hangers at these locations on the headers.

◆ Cut cripple joists to fit between the ledger and the first header, fit each one in place, and fasten it at both ends to the joist hangers with galvanized framing-anchor nails.

◆ Cut cripple joists to fit between the other header and rim joist. Fit each one in place and fasten it at one end to the joist hanger with galvanized framing-anchor nails and at the other end to the rim joist with three $3\frac{1}{2}$-inch galvanized spiral-shank nails *(right)*.

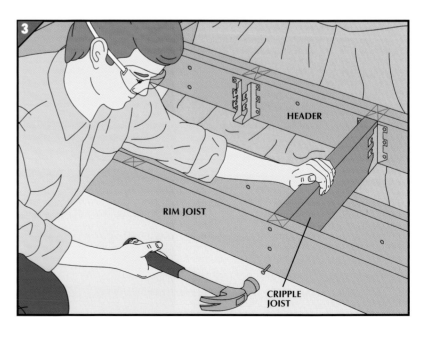

HEADER

RIM JOIST

CRIPPLE JOIST

4. Adding corner braces.

◆ From joist lumber, cut four corner braces to fit between the headers and double joists, beveling both ends at 45° angles.

◆ Fit one brace into place and fasten it to the frame at each end with three nails. Fasten the remaining corner braces in the same way *(right)*.

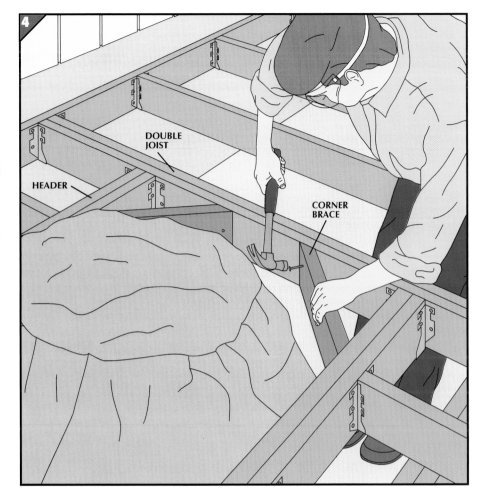

FRAMING A WINDOW WELL

To prevent a deck from blocking light to a basement window, you can frame an opening around the window. To do so, attach the ledger to the wall in two sections, one on each side of the window. Frame the opening with double joists—located at the standard joist spacings—and a header at the desired distance from the window. In the example shown here, the double joist to the left of the window has one length of lumber cut $1\frac{1}{2}$ inches longer than the other so that it can be nailed to the end of the ledger next to the window; the other length is secured to the ledger with a multipurpose framing anchor. Because the joist spacing is standard, the double joist on the right side is several inches past the opening, requiring a cripple joist to be fastened to the end of the ledger and to the header.

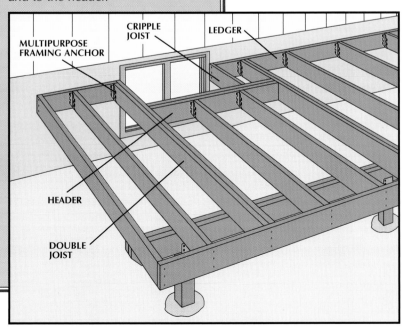

3

Decking, Railings, and Stairs

Once the deck structure is framed, you can put down the deck boards and add railings and stairs. Decking and railings can define or complement the style of the deck, while the placement and size of stairs establishes traffic patterns. Gates also add safety and charm.

Laying Decking   **48**

A Basic Pattern
Adding a Fascia
Using Invisible Fasteners
Decking that Meets at a Corner
A Picture-Frame Design
Cutting a Curve
Fitting Around an Obstacle
Building a Trap Door

Stairs and Ramps   **60**

Making and Installing the Stringers
Closing the Risers and Adding Treads
Picture-Frame Treads with Open Risers
A Wheelchair Ramp

Railings and Gates   **69**

Shaping the Posts
Attaching to the Deck
A Colonial Railing
A Traditional Alternative
A Gate for a Colonial Railing
A Traditional Gate

The decking pattern is an important element in the style of the deck. The simplest design is to run the boards perpendicular to the joists; you can modify this style by combining boards of various widths. Other alternatives are to lay the decking diagonally across the joists or add a picture frame *(pages 53-54)*—but avoid busy patterns, particularly on a small structure. For a wraparound deck *(pages 108-112)*, miter the ends that meet at the corner *(page 52)*. Decking at an angled corner *(pages 40-42)* can follow the line of the angle, or be cut on a curve *(pages 55-56)*. When you have built a frame around an obstacle *(pages 43-45)*, you can scribe the decking to fit closely around the object *(page 57)*.

Fastening Decking: Decking can be anchored to the framing with galvanized screws or nails. Another option is to fasten the boards with invisible clips *(pages 50-51)*. Nails are fast to drive, but likely to work loose over time—to minimize popping of nails, use the spiral-shank variety. Renting a pneumatic nailer will speed the work, but if you plan to drive the nails by hand, recess the heads with a nail set.

If you will be adding an overhead *(pages 160-165)*, omit the end boards until the overhead is built.

Finishing Touches: After the decking is laid down, you can trim it flush with the edges of the deck's framing or leave a 1-inch overhang. For a flush installation, hide the ends of the boards with a fascia *(page 50)* or add a cap installed after the railing posts are in place *(page 73, box)*. If you are using redwood or cedar decking, you can make the fascia of the same wood to hide the rougher framing lumber. If you do not plan to cap the decking, round over exposed edges with a router to prevent chipping, being sure to stay clear of the fasteners.

A trap door is a handy feature *(pages 58-59)* that allows access to items stored or located under the deck such as outdoor faucets.

 TOOLS

Circular saw
Saber saw
Handsaw
Hammer
Pry bar

Electric drill
Chalk line
Combination square
Hand plane
Wood chisel
Mallet

 **MATERIALS**

Decking and fascia lumber
Pressure-treated 2 x 2s and blocking
Plywood scraps ($\frac{1}{8}$", $\frac{1}{4}$")

Galvanized spiral-shank nails (3", $3\frac{1}{2}$")
Invisible deck clips
Framing-anchor nails
Deck screws ($2\frac{1}{2}$")
Butt hinges
Recessed drawer pull

 SAFETY TIPS

Protect your eyes with goggles when using a power saw or hammering. Wear a dust mask to cut pressure-treated wood and wash thoroughly after handling the lumber.

A BASIC PATTERN

Fastening boards.
◆ Cut a straight board to the deck's finished length—or plan a splice *(opposite)*—and place it along the house, offsetting it from the wall with spacers of $\frac{1}{8}$-inch plywood.
◆ Fasten the board to each joist with two $3\frac{1}{2}$-inch galvanized spiral-shank nails.
◆ Continue with boards a few inches longer than the deck, positioning them with plywood spacers and leaving an overhang at both ends. To fasten a bowed board, place its convex edge along the previous board and have a helper pry the end into line while you nail it *(right)*.
◆ Lay the decking until you are a few boards from the edge of the deck; then, measure the remaining space. If the boards won't fit without ripping them, cut the last two or three equally or finish with a wider board, rather than end with one very narrow board.
◆ At each end of the deck, snap a chalk line across the decking, fasten a straight board as a saw guide *(page 52, Step 1)*, and trim the ends of the decking with a circular saw.

SPACER

Decking Spacers

An alternative to using pieces of $\frac{1}{8}$-inch plywood to keep deck boards apart as you install them is to make spacers out of nails and small wood blocks. Simply drive a $3\frac{1}{2}$-inch nail partway through each block and slip the nail between decking boards so the block sits on the surface *(right)*.

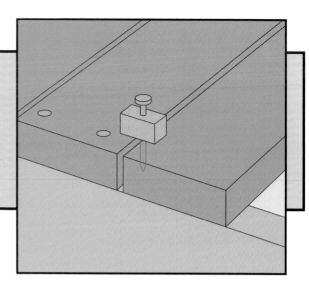

Splicing boards.

◆ For boards that are too short to span the deck's entire length, lay them end-to-end and locate the joint over a joist.

◆ Place a spacer between the spliced boards and the adjacent board, then butt the board ends tightly together.

◆ Drill two pilot holes at an angle through each board and into the joist under the splice.

◆ Drive a nail into each hole *(left)*. If you will be making several splices, locate them over different joists so the joint lines are staggered.

A DECK WRENCH

If you are laying decking without a helper, the tool in the photograph at right will help you straighten bowed boards. The jaw of the tool fits over the joist and the cam lies along the decking; pulling on the handle straightens the board and locks the tool in position while you nail the board in place.

ADDING A FASCIA

Trimming the deck.
◆ Cut three lengths of 5/4 stock to fit as fascia boards around the perimeter of the deck—four pieces for a free-standing deck—beveling the ends to meet at the corners.
◆ Fasten the boards to the end and rim joists so the upper edges are flush with the surface of the decking, driving five 3-inch galvanized spiral-shank nails at each corner *(right)* and two more nails every 2 feet in between.
◆ Round the beveled corners slightly with a hand plane.

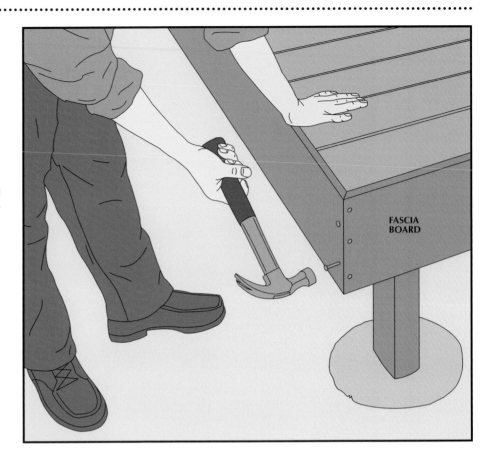

FASCIA BOARD

USING INVISIBLE FASTENERS

1. Fastening the first board.
◆ Fasten a straight board along the wall of the house as for an installation with nails *(page 48)*, but drive only one nail through the face of the board into each joist as close to the wall as possible.
◆ Drive a second nail at an angle through the outer edge of the board into each joist *(left)*.

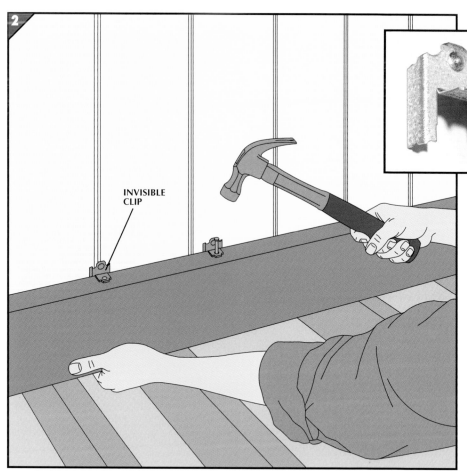

INVISIBLE CLIP

2. Attaching the clips.

◆ Lay the second board on edge across the joists.

◆ Place an invisible clip *(photograph)* on the edge of the board about 2 inches from an end joist and tap the clip with a hammer, driving the teeth into the wood.

◆ Fasten the clip to the board with a galvanized framing-anchor nail.

◆ Secure a clip to the board for every joist, offset about 2 inches from the joist location *(left)*.

3. Installing the boards.

◆ Lay the board flat so the clips sit a few inches from the first board, offsetting them from the joists.

◆ Place a wood block against the outer edge of the second board near one end and tap the block with a hammer *(right)* to drive the boards together and force the clips under the first board. Work along the length of the board until the entire edge is snug against the first.

◆ Nail the outer edge of the second board to the joists as you did for the first board.

◆ Install the remaining boards in the same way, then trim their ends.

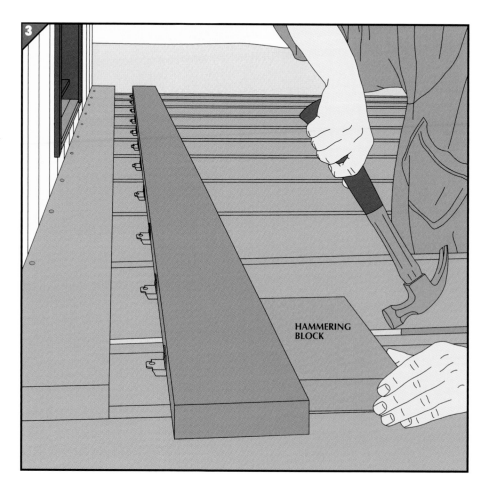

HAMMERING BLOCK

DECKING THAT MEETS AT A CORNER

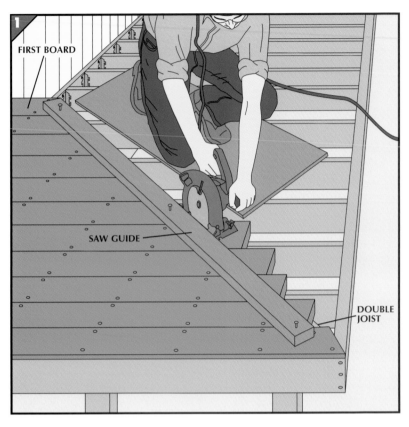

FIRST BOARD

SAW GUIDE

DOUBLE JOIST

1. Decking the first section.

On a wraparound-deck frame, the decking is mitered to meet over the double joist at the corner. To create the understructure for this simple wraparound deck, follow the building instructions on pages 21 to 27 and the set-up and design instructions on pages 108 to 112.

◆ Fasten the first board of one of the sections *(page 48)*, cutting one end flush with the end joist and mitering the other to align with the middle of the double joist.

◆ Finish laying the decking on the first section, spacing the boards $\frac{1}{8}$ inch apart and splicing short ones end-to-end *(page 49)* so each board overlaps the double joist. Avoid driving any nails along or beyond the seam in the double joist.

◆ Tack a straight board to the decking as a saw guide, positioning it so the saw will trim the boards in line with the joint in the double joist.

◆ Working on a sheet of plywood, miter the ends of the deck boards *(left)*.

2. Decking the second section.

◆ Position the first board of the second section *(right)* and fasten it as described in Step 1, butting its end against the end of its counterpart in the first section of the deck.

◆ Miter one end of each remaining board, then nail them down, butting the ends between the two sections along the corner double joist.

A PICTURE-FRAME DESIGN

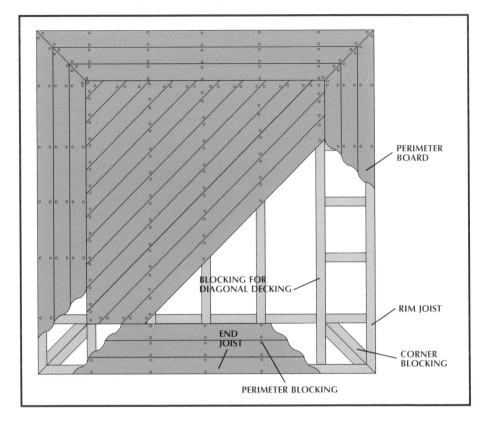

PERIMETER BOARD

BLOCKING FOR DIAGONAL DECKING

RIM JOIST

END JOIST

CORNER BLOCKING

PERIMETER BLOCKING

Diagonal decking with a frame.
On the deck at left, a center section of decking laid diagonally is framed by perimeter boards meeting at mitered corners. On an attached deck, you can omit the perimeter boards along the house.

To support this pattern of decking, the understructure must have end joists spaced 16 inches center-to-center from the adjacent joists. For 2-by-6 deck boards, the intermediate joists are laid at 16-inch intervals; 12 inch-intervals for 5/4 decking. Parallel to the rim joists and 16 inches inside them, blocking supports the ends of the diagonal deck boards. Blocking is also installed along the end joists to hold up the perimeter boards. Corner blocking is fashioned in a similar manner as the corner joist on a wraparound deck *(page 118)*.

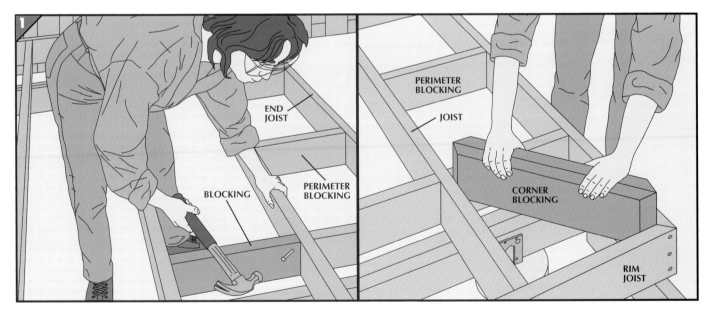

END JOIST

BLOCKING

PERIMETER BLOCKING

PERIMETER BLOCKING

JOIST

CORNER BLOCKING

RIM JOIST

1. Adding the blocking.
◆ Build a deck frame *(pages 18-38)*, spacing the joists as described above.
◆ For every 16 inches of end-joist length, cut a piece of joist lumber to fit as perimeter blocking between each end joist and the adjacent joist. Install the blocking at 16-inch intervals, driving three $3\frac{1}{2}$-inch galvanized spiral-shank nails per end.
◆ Cut blocking for the diagonal decking to fit between each pair of intermediate joists 16 inches from the rim joists

and fasten each piece in place, face-nailing one end and toenailing the other *(above, left)*.
◆ At each corner of the deck, measure the distance between the angles formed by the end and rim joists, and by the first piece of perimeter blocking and the first intermediate joist. Cut two lengths of blocking to length, beveling both ends of each piece. Fasten the blocks together so they form points at both ends, then slip the corner blocking into place *(above, right)*, and fasten each end with three nails.

2. Laying the diagonal boards.

◆ Set a short board diagonally across the joists, aligning its outer edge with the inner tip of the corner blocking. With a combination square, angle the board at 45° to the joists.

◆ Fasten the board with two nails to the blocking and the first intermediate joist; avoid driving a nail near the outer face of the joist—you will be trimming the decking along the joist later.

◆ Continue laying decking diagonally, using boards long enough to overhang the first intermediate joist and the blocking *(right)* and spacing the boards $\frac{1}{8}$ inch apart. Fasten them to the joist and blocking.

◆ When you are a few boards away from the opposite corner, rip the last pieces to width as needed to align them with the tip of the corner blocking.

◆ Trim the decking *(page 52, Step 1)* in line with the outer sides of the blocking and the first intermediate joists.

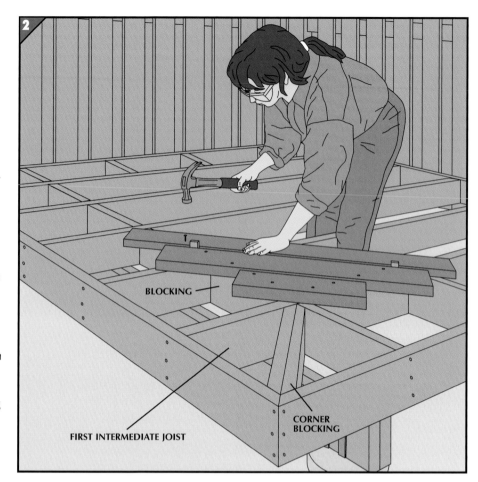

BLOCKING

CORNER BLOCKING

FIRST INTERMEDIATE JOIST

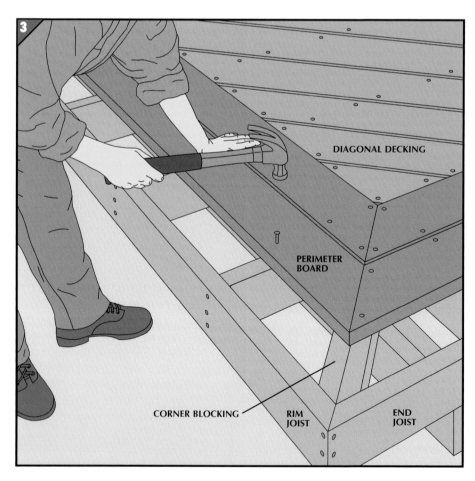

DIAGONAL DECKING

PERIMETER BOARD

CORNER BLOCKING

RIM JOIST

END JOIST

3. Laying the perimeter boards.

◆ Cut four lengths of deck boards to fit around the perimeter of the diagonal decking, mitering the ends at 45° so the joints will align with the corners. If you want the last boards to sit flush with the outer sides of the end and rim joists rather than overhang them by $\frac{3}{4}$ inch, trim $\frac{1}{4}$ inch from the width of each piece.

◆ Set one of the perimeter boards in place, aligning its ends with the joints in the corner blocking and butting it against the diagonal decking.

◆ Fasten the board to every joist and length of blocking it crosses; nail the ends to the corner blocking.

◆ Install the three remaining boards, butting the mitered ends together.

◆ Lay two more rows of perimeter decking in the same way *(left)*.

CUTTING A CURVE

A deck with rounded corners.
A deck with curved corners is built on a frame with angled corners *(pages 40-42)*. Cut long enough to overhang the end and angled rim joists, the deck boards are then trimmed straight along the end joist and in a curve along the angled joist.

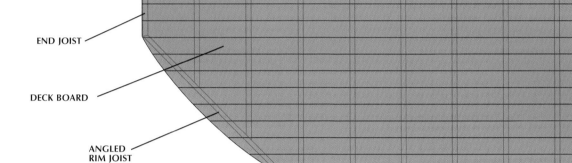

END JOIST

DECK BOARD

ANGLED
RIM JOIST

ANGLED
RIM JOIST

1. Drawing the curve.
◆ Frame a deck with an angled corner *(pages 40-42)* for each corner you wish to curve.
◆ Lay the deck boards *(pages 48-49)* so they overhang the end joist and the angled rim joist by a few inches.
◆ Drive a nail partway into the decking directly above each outside end of the angled rim.
◆ Set a length of $\frac{1}{4}$-inch plywood a foot or two longer than the distance between the nails on edge so one side is against the nails and trace a straight line along the molding.
◆ Pull back on the plywood so the middle is about $2\frac{1}{2}$ inches behind the marked line, then trace a curved line along the piece *(left)*.

2. Cutting the decking.

◆ Trim the ends of the deck boards flush with the outer face of the end joist.
◆ Cut along the curved line with a saber saw *(right)*.

A DECK WITH MULTIPLE CURVES

The ground-level deck in the photograph at right is built with a series of curves that help the deck blend into its setting. The structure is built with angled corners *(pages 40-42)* and the deck boards cut on a curve. To lay out such curves, you can use a garden hose, filled with water to keep it from kinking, and pin it in place with a nail driven to one side at the ends of each curve. Trace the curves on the decking and trim the boards with a saber saw, as described above. The decking can over- hang the understructure by a maximum of 4 inches. This deck features a fascia *(page 50)* made of flexible benderboard.

FITTING AROUND AN OBSTACLE

NOTCH

1. Laying the decking.
◆ Fasten the decking, starting at the house wall *(pages 48-49)*.
◆ As you lay the decking around the obstacle, trim the boards to size and cut notches so you can place them within a few inches of the obstruction *(left)*—if the obstacle is a tree, leave a space of about 5 inches around it so it has room to grow.

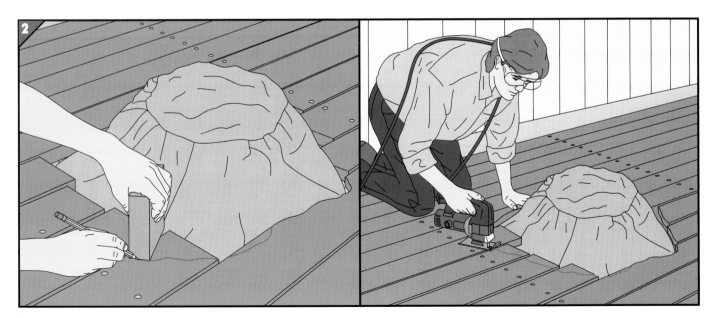

2. Cutting the decking around the obstruction.
◆ Set a 2-by-4 block on the decking—use a 2-by-6 if the obstruction is a tree—with an edge against the obstacle and mark a line along the opposite edge, following the perimeter of the obstruction with the block and pencil *(above, left)* until you have scribed a line around it.
◆ With a saber saw, cut into the end of a board to the scribed line, then continue sawing along the line *(above, right)*.

BUILDING A TRAP DOOR

1. Cutting the decking.

◆ Outline the door on the decking between two joists, aligning the marks with the joists' inner faces and making the outline no longer than the width of four deck boards.

◆ Cut along the lines with a circular saw, starting with a technique known as a plunge cut: Hold the saw with only the front of the base plate on the decking and the blade clear of the surface. Retract the blade guard with the lever, align the blade with one of the marks near one end, turn on the saw and slowly lower the blade into the wood until the base plate is flat, then advance the saw to the opposite end of the line *(right)*.

◆ Saw along the other line in the same way, then complete the ends of the cuts with a handsaw.

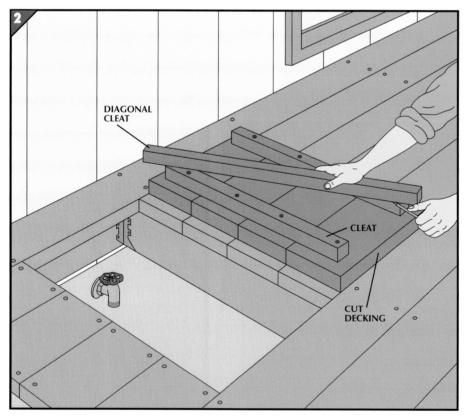

DIAGONAL CLEAT

CLEAT

CUT DECKING

2. Making the door.

◆ Place the cut boards alongside the opening, ends aligned, lining up their edges with the decking below.

◆ Cut two 2-by-2 cleats 2 inches shorter than the combined width of the cut boards. Position the cleats 2 inches in from the edges, centered across the width and leaving 1 inch on each end, then fasten them to each board with a $2\frac{1}{2}$-inch coated deck screw.

◆ Measure the diagonal between the cleats, then cut a third cleat a few inches longer than the distance. Place it across the cleats, aligning its edges with the corners, and mark its underside along the inner edges of the cleats *(left)*.

◆ Trim the diagonal cleat to length and fasten it to the deck boards so the cut ends butt against the straight cleats.

3. Preparing the opening.
◆ Cut two 2-by-2 cleats to the same length as the opening and fasten one to a joist adjoining the opening, flush with the top edge, with $2\frac{1}{2}$-inch deck screws spaced every 8 inches *(left)*.
◆ Fasten the second cleat to the other joist in the same way.

If you want to use the space as a storage compartment, drill pilot holes for two galvanized hooks into each joist just below the cleats and twist a hook into each hole, then hang a plastic-coated wire basket of the right size on the hooks *(inset)*.

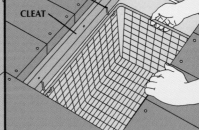

4. Hinging the door.
◆ Place the door in the opening, setting it on the cleats, and position two 3-inch galvanized butt hinges across the seam between the edge of the door nearest the house and the deck.
◆ Mark the screw holes, remove the hinges, drill a pilot hole for the screws provided at each mark, and screw in the hinges *(right)*.
◆ Center a recessed drawer pull *(photograph)* on the door near the opposite end and outline its faceplate on the surface.
◆ With a wood chisel, cut a mortise within the outline equal in depth to the thickness of the faceplate, then fasten the pull in place with the screws provided.

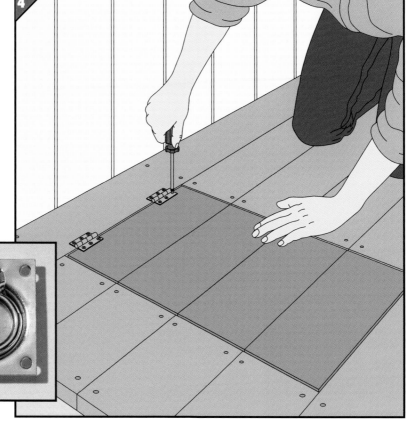

Stairs and Ramps

When a deck is more than three steps above ground level, you will need to build a flight of stairs if you want convenient access to the yard. You can also use stairs to link two deck levels. On a low-level deck, you may want to add a ramp for wheelchair access or for rolling heavy items onto the deck or into the house.

Design and Materials: The stairs on these pages are supported by three notched stringers *(pages 61-63)* made of 2-by-12s; choose lumber that is as straight and knot-free as possible. The stringers are attached to the end or rim joist and rest on a concrete slab—for a flight of more than three steps, the stringers are fastened to the slab as well.

The treads are typically made of the same lumber as the deck, but you can use boards of different widths for decorative effect. The risers can be enclosed *(page 64)* or left open, and the ends of the treads can overhang the stringers or be cut flush with them. If you choose to cut the treads flush, you can conceal the ends of the treads and risers with face boards, but to do so you will have to attach the stringers to the deck in a different way *(page 63, box).* For a more elaborate style of stairs, you can make the treads from 2-by-2s and hide the end grain *(pages 65-66).* Plan the proportions of the steps as described below.

Adding a Ramp: A ramp for a wheelchair requires a gradual slope—a rise of no more than 1 vertical inch for every horizontal foot. Because of the potential length of a straight ramp, it is practical only for low-level decks. To keep the structure from jutting out too far into the yard, build a landing at deck level and run the ramp along one side of the deck *(pages 67-68).* Make the ramp 42 inches wide and the landing 42 inches square.

 TOOLS

Carpenter's level (4')
Carpenter's square
Circular saw
Handsaw
Powdered chalk
Hammer
Electric drill
Pointed shovel
Concrete tools

 **MATERIALS**

Pressure-treated
  2 x 6s, 2 x 8s, 2 x 12s, 1 x 8s, 4 x 4s
Pressure-treated
  5/4 stock
Materials for casting concrete piers
Wood shims
Post caps
Multipurpose framing anchors
Angle irons
Galvanized spiral-shank nails ($3\frac{1}{2}$")
Galvanized framing-anchor nails
Deck screws (1", $2\frac{1}{2}$")
Masonry screws ($1\frac{1}{2}$")

 SAFETY TIPS

Put on goggles when using a power tool or hammering. Add a dust mask to cut pressure-treated wood and wash your hands thoroughly after handling it.

Stair dimensions.

While there is some flexibility in stair design, certain aspects of the construction are governed by building codes. The unit rise—measured from the surface of one step to the next—must fall between 6 and $7\frac{1}{2}$ inches. For your stairs, choose a figure that divides evenly into the total rise—the vertical distance between the deck surface and the slab at the bottom of the stairs. The unit run, measured from the face of one riser to the next, can be from 10 to 16 inches. Choose a figure that will accommodate the tread materials you plan to use without ripping boards; for closed-riser steps, allow for

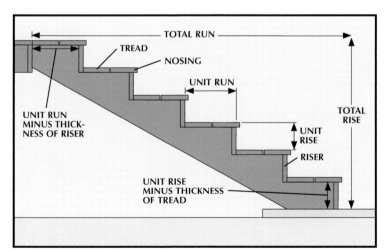

a slight nosing that extends past the front of each riser. For example, a $10\frac{1}{2}$-inch unit run will accommodate treads made of two 2-by-6s with a $\frac{1}{8}$-inch gap between them and a $\frac{5}{8}$-inch nosing. Since

there is no tread at the bottom of the stairs or riser at the top, you'll need to trim the thickness of a tread off the bottom of the stringers and the thickness of a riser off the back of the top of the stringers to make the top and bottom steps the same height and depth as the others. As you determine the rise and run for your project, keep in mind that steps with a shorter rise and deeper run are more comfortable to climb but will extend farther from the deck. You can make the flight of stairs 36 to 48 inches wide.

TOTAL-RUN MARK

1. Measuring the total rise.

To determine the total rise of the stairs on ground that may slope, you need to measure the drop from the deck surface to the spot where the slab for the foot of the stairs will be placed.

◆ Measure the vertical distance between the deck surface and the ground, then divide the figure by an ideal unit rise of 7 inches. Round the result up to the next whole number to get the number of treads, then multiply this figure by the desired tread depth to determine the total run. Mark this distance with tape on a straight board.

◆ While a helper holds the board level on the deck with the tape at the edge, measure from the bottom edge of the board at the end to the ground to determine the total rise *(left)*. Make a chalk mark at this point.

◆ Adjust the unit rise to a figure that will divide evenly into this measurement.

2. Casting the slab.

◆ Make a chalk mark on the ground 15 inches in front of the one marked in Step 1 and another 15 inches behind it.

◆ Dig a hole 6 inches deep, about 1 foot wider than the stairs, between the second and third chalk marks. In poorly draining soil, make the hole 12 inches deep and lay a compacted 6-inch bed of gravel.

◆ Cut four 1-by-4s to fit around the inside of the hole as a form to contain the concrete you will pour. Nail the form together, then fasten two more 1-by-4s to the outer faces of the two longer pieces, flush with the top edges, to hold the form at the right height; slip shims under them as needed to level it *(right)*.

◆ Fill the form with concrete and, with a straight board, strike the surface flush with the top of the form. Smooth the concrete with a wood float and let the slab cure overnight.

FORM BOARDS

3. Cutting the stringers.

◆ With masking tape, mark the unit rise on the short arm of a carpenter's square and the unit run on the long arm.

◆ Set the square against a 2-by-12 so the tape marks are flush with the same edge of the boards. Mark the first unit run.

◆ Move the square along the 2-by-12 and mark the first unit rise and the next run *(right)*. Continue outlining the steps along the length of the board until you have marked the last unit run. Then, draw one additional rise.

◆ Square off the top and bottom of the layout.

◆ Draw a second line for the bottom of the stringer, subtracting the thickness of a tread. For closed-riser steps, make a second line for the top of the stringer, subtracting a riser's thickness *(inset)*.

◆ Cut the stringer with a circular saw, then finish the cuts with a handsaw.

◆ Use the first stringer as a template to lay out and cut out the other two.

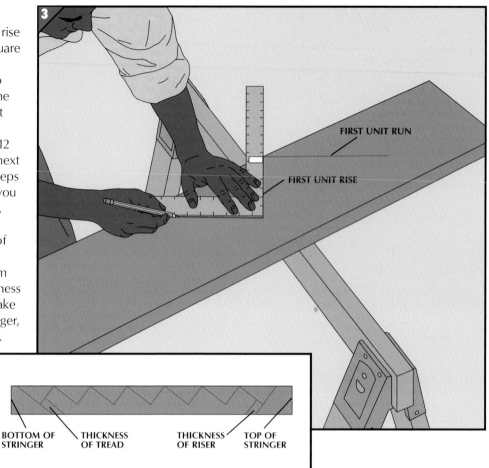

FIRST UNIT RUN

FIRST UNIT RISE

BOTTOM OF STRINGER | THICKNESS OF TREAD | THICKNESS OF RISER | TOP OF STRINGER

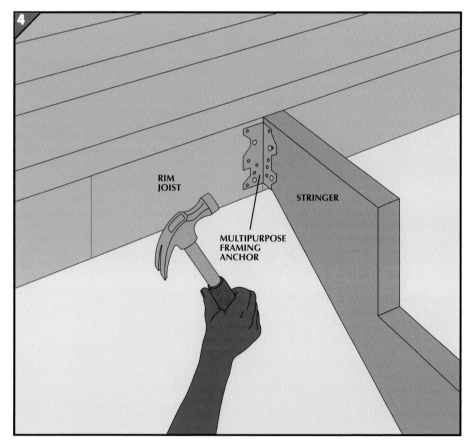

RIM JOIST

STRINGER

MULTIPURPOSE FRAMING ANCHOR

4. Fastening at the top.

◆ Draw three plumb lines on the edge of the deck's rim or end joist to indicate the tops of the stringers.

◆ Set an outer stringer in place against the deck so its top is flush with the top of the rim or end joist and the face is flush with the plumb line. Drive three $3\frac{1}{2}$-inch galvanized spiral-shank nails through the back of the joist into the end of the stringer.

◆ Fasten the inside face of the stringer to the deck with a multipurpose framing anchor and galvanized framing-anchor nails *(left)*.

◆ Fasten the remaining two stringers to the deck in the same way.

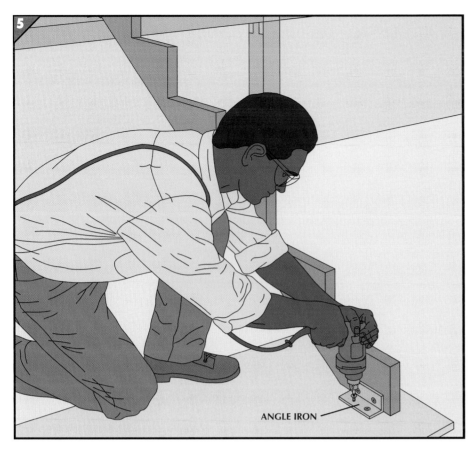

ANGLE IRON

5. Anchoring to the slab.
◆ Adjust the bottom of the stringers so they are the same distance apart as at the top.
◆ Set an angle iron against the inside of one of the outer stringers and mark the screw holes on the concrete slab.
◆ Remove the angle iron and, with an electric drill and masonry bit, drill a pilot hole for a $1\frac{1}{2}$-inch masonry screw at each mark.
◆ Replace the angle iron and fasten it to the slab with masonry screws *(left)*, then fasten it to the stringer with 1-inch coated deck screws.
◆ Fasten the bottoms of the other two stringers in the same way.

AN ALTERNATIVE STAIR ATTACHMENT

If you prefer the stairs to begin one step down from the deck, you can attach the stringers as shown below. Also use this method if you want to cover the ends of the treads and risers with face boards. Lay out the stringers as shown opposite, Step 3, but with one less riser since the rim or end joist will serve as the top riser. Splice a length of 2-by-6 blocking to the bottom of the rim or end joist, attaching it on the back with vertical cleats. Measure down one unit rise from the top of the end or rim joist to position the stringers and attach them with multipurpose framing anchors as shown opposite, Step 4. Then, cut the ends of two 2-by-12s at the same angle as the top and bottom of the stringers and fasten the face boards to the outer stringers every 8 inches with galvanized spiral-shank nails.

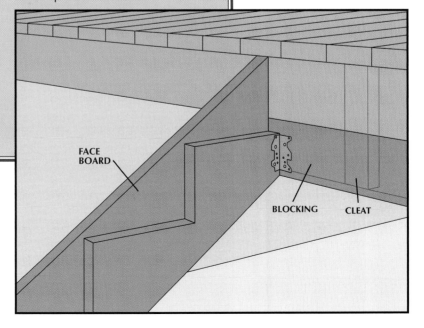

FACE BOARD

BLOCKING   CLEAT

1. Installing risers.
◆ Measure the distance between the outside faces of the two outer stringers at the bottom of the stairs and cut a 2-by-8 to length. Rip the board to the height of the first vertical section of the stringers.
◆ Set the riser against the stringers and fasten it to each stringer with three $2\frac{1}{2}$-inch coated deck screws.
◆ Cut the remaining risers, ripping them to match the unit rise, and install them in the same way *(left)*.

RISER

2. Adding the treads.
◆ For each unit run, cut a tread to the same length as the risers—here, each tread is made of two 2-by-6s.
◆ Starting at the bottom step, set the first 2-by-6 in place across the stringers against the riser and fasten it to each stringer with three screws.
◆ Attach the second board in the same way about $\frac{1}{8}$ inch from the first.
◆ Install the remaining treads *(right)*.

$\frac{1}{8}$" GAP

TREAD

1. Fastening the 2-by-2s.
◆ Make each tread by cutting seven 2-by-2s to a length equal to the distance between the outside faces of the two outer stringers.
◆ Set the 2-by-2s on the bottom step of the stringers, placing them so they are evenly spaced and the front piece is flush with the front of the stringers.
◆ Drill a pilot hole for a $2\frac{1}{2}$-inch coated deck screw where each 2-by-2 crosses a stringer *(left)*, then drive the screws.

TRICKS OF THE TRADE

Cutting 2-by-2s Quickly

To quickly cut 2-by-2s for stair treads to exactly the same length, cut them in groups. Align one end of the 2-by-2s and clamp them together with two bar clamps. With a carpenter's square, mark a line across the 2-by-2s at the desired length. Then, cut them all at once with a circular saw *(right)*.

2. Framing the treads.

◆ Beginning with the second tread, cut three pieces of 5/4 stock to wrap around the front and sides of the tread, beveling both ends of the front piece and the front end of the side pieces at 45°; bevel the back end of the side pieces at 60°.

◆ Attach a side piece to one of the stringers with two screws near each end so the top edge is flush with the surface of the tread. Then, fasten the front piece to each stringer with two screws. Finally, add the other end piece *(right)*.

◆ Round the beveled frame corners slightly with a hand plane.

◆ Frame the remaining steps in the same way, omitting the top and bottom steps. Once the stair-railing posts have been installed *(page 77)*, frame the top and bottom steps, cutting the end pieces to fit around the posts.

60° BEVEL CUT

SIDE PIECE

INCORPORATING A LANDING

A high deck will require a very long flight of stairs. If you run them straight out, they will likely extend quite far into the yard or onto the lower level of the deck. To avoid this situation, you can incorporate one or more landings along the run. In the design shown here, the landing at the highest level allows the stairs to begin their descent parallel to the edge of the deck; the second landing partway down provides a pause in the flight. You can also use a landing to change the direction of the stairs. Build a landing in the same way as a small freestanding deck *(page 38)* and attach the stairs to it as you would to a deck.

A WHEELCHAIR RAMP

Framing for a sloping ramp.

The ramp at right consists of three sections: a landing and two sloping modules with joists running along their length. The landing is set on two beams placed at the same height as the deck beams. A middle beam, partially buried, supports the bottom of the middle module and the top of the end module. An end beam, completely buried, is located at the end of the ramp. The joists of the end module are partially buried so their top edge meets a concrete slab at ground level at the end of the ramp. The number and length of the modules and the height of their beams depends on the height of the deck and the required slope *(page 60)*, but the modules should be equal in length and no longer than 8 feet.

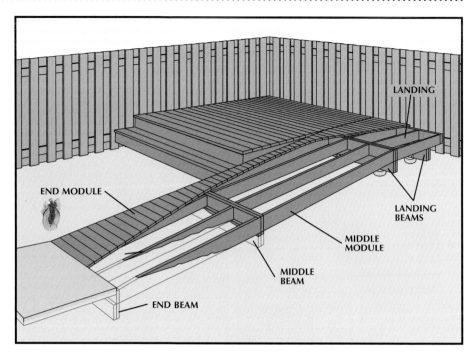

1. Setting the beams.

◆ Set up stakes and run two string lines parallel to the deck and at the same height as the deck surface: one 1 foot away from the deck and the second 3 feet away.

◆ Dig a trench at each buried-beam location, then cast cylindrical piers to support all four beams *(page 26)*, measuring down from the string line and moving the fiber-form tubes up and down to the appropriate height.

◆ Set post bases into the piers *(page 27)*, then fill the trenches with gravel up to the top of the piers.

◆ Make beams *(page 29)* 42 inches long, sit them in place *(above)*, and fasten them to the post bases *(page 31)*.

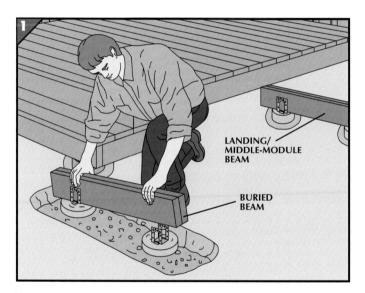

2. Building the landing.

◆ Construct a frame 42 inches square with four joists capped by two rim joists, fastening each joist with three $3\frac{1}{2}$-inch galvanized spiral-shank nails.

◆ Place the frame on the beams with an end joist against the deck and the outer face of one rim joist aligned with the center of the beam it will share with the middle module.

◆ Nail the end joist to the deck *(above)* and toenail each of the joists to the beams.

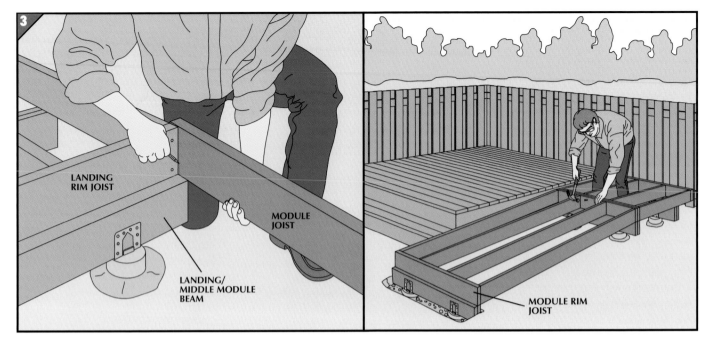

3. Installing the middle module.

◆ Holding a middle-module joist against the side of the landing platform with the other end resting on the middle beam, make a mark across the joist in line with the end of the landing's rim joist *(above, left)*.

◆ Cut the joist along the line, then trim the other end to length at the same angle.

◆ Use this joist as a template to mark and cut the remaining joists for both the middle and end modules.

◆ Cut the module rim joists 42 inches long, then assemble the middle module as you did the landing.

◆ Position the assembly on its beams, then fasten it to the landing platform with galvanized 3-inch nails spaced every 8 to 10 inches *(above, right)*.

◆ Toenail the module to the middle beam.

4. Installing the end module.

◆ Dig a shallow, progressively deeper trench for each end-module joist.

◆ Cut rim joists and assemble the end module as you did the middle one, then place it on the middle and end beams.

◆ Fasten the end module to the middle one and toenail it to the end beam.

◆ Fill in around the joists and beams with soil *(right)*.

◆ Cast a concrete slab 42 inches square at the end of the ramp *(page 61)*, its finished surface at a height that allows a smooth transition to the ramp.

◆ Install decking boards across the joists *(pages 48-49)*.

Railings and Gates

Decks higher than three steps generally require a railing, as do ramps and stairs with more than two risers. An important safety feature, the railing can also define the style of the deck *(below and page 79).*

Design Considerations: Per building codes, the handrail must be at least 36 inches above the deck surface, and gaps—such as between spindles or under the bottom rail—cannot exceed 4 inches. For a deck with 2-by-6 framing, buy 4-foot-long 4-by-4 posts. Otherwise, cut posts

long enough to extend from the bottom of the rim or end joist to 42 inches above the deck surface. For a solid look, notch the posts and bolt them to the outside of the rim and end joists *(pages 70-72).* You can make the railings appear to be a more integral part of the deck by cutting through the decking boards and attaching the posts to the inside of the rim and end joists or by installing continuous posts *(page 33).*

Stairs and Gates: Design a stair railing to match the deck railing as

closely as possible *(pages 77 and 79).* The handrail must be a type that is easy to grasp, set from 34 to 38 inches high—as measured from the back of the step's tread to the top of the handrail. Spindles can be spaced up to 4 inches apart; the gap below the bottom rail must not allow a 6-inch sphere to pass through. A gate at the top of the stairs is a sensible addition if the deck will be used by small children *(pages 80-81).*

 TOOLS

Tape measure
Combination square
Carpenter's level (4')
C-clamps
Circular saw

Power miter saw
Router
Wood chisel
Mallet
Pry bar
Electric drill
Socket wrench

 MATERIALS

Pressure-treated
  1 x 2, 2 x 2s,
  4 x 4s
Pressure-treated
  2 x 6 or colonial-
  style handrail

Deck screws
  ($1\frac{1}{2}$", 2", $2\frac{1}{2}$")
Galvanized lag
  screws ($\frac{3}{8}$" x 3",
  5") and washers
Butt hinges (3" x 3")
Swiveling caster
Locking gate latch

 SAFETY TIPS

Protect your eyes with goggles when using a power tool or hammering. Wear a dust mask when cutting pressure-treated wood; wash your hands thoroughly after handling it.

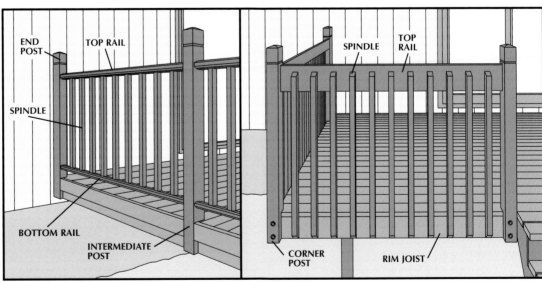

Two railing styles. The railings at right illustrate two different architectural styles. The colonial railing *(near right)* features commercial milled handrail stock with 2-by-2 spindles linking top and bottom rails; the assembly is set between 4-by-4 posts. Such a railing can span distances of up to 5 feet—10 feet if a support block is added in the middle of the span *(page 76).* If you plan to add a built-in bench *(pages 136-139),* substitute an intermediate post for the support block.

More difficult to climb than the colonial style, a traditional railing *(far right)* is a good choice for families with young children. This style has only a top rail, made either of ordi-

nary 2-by-6 lumber or commercial milled 2-by-6 handrail stock. The spindles are attached to the handrail about $1\frac{1}{2}$ inches below the top, and to the outside face of the rim and end joists flush with the bottom. Intermediate posts are not required unless the deck will have a built-in bench along the railing; in this case, set posts every 5 feet for extra support.

SHAPING THE POSTS

Adding a chamfer and dado.
◆ With a combination square, draw two sets of lines all the way around each post, one $\frac{1}{2}$ inch from the top end and the second 3 inches away.
◆ Set the blade of a power miter saw to 15° and cut all four faces of the post in line with the $\frac{1}{2}$-inch mark, forming a special bevel known as a chamfer.
◆ Clamp the post to a work surface, then equip a router with a $\frac{1}{2}$-inch straight bit. Adjust the depth to $\frac{1}{2}$ inch, align the bit with the 3-inch mark on the post, and position a wood block on the post flush against the router base. Screw the block to the post as a guide so its edges are perpendicular to the sides of the post, then cut a channel known as dado across the surface, feeding the router with its base against the guide.
◆ Remove the guide, rotate the post 90°, and reposition the guide to rout dadoes across the post's remaining three sides *(right)*.

Instead of cutting chamfers and dadoes in the posts, you can top them with a decorative post cap such as the one in the photograph.

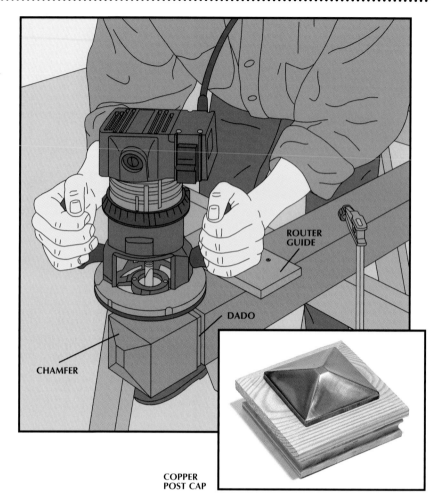

ROUTER GUIDE

DADO

CHAMFER

COPPER POST CAP

ATTACHING TO THE DECK

1. Notching the end posts.
◆ With a pencil and a combination square, outline a 2-inch-deep notch on one face of each end post at the bottom end, sizing its height to reach from the bottom of the end joist to the top of the decking.
◆ Cut along the lines with a circular saw *(right)* and clear out the waste piece with a pry bar.
◆ Clean up the cut with a mallet and a wood chisel.

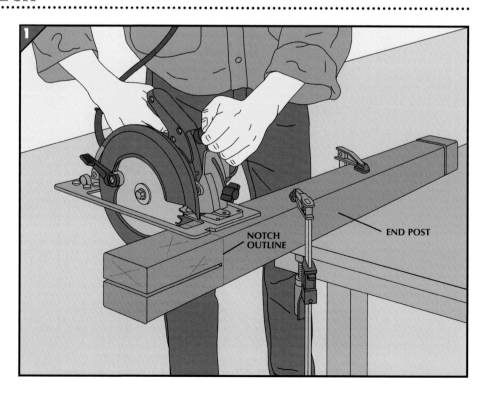

NOTCH OUTLINE

END POST

END POST

END JOIST

2. Installing the end post.

◆ Position the end post next to the house so the notch hugs the decking and the end joist.

◆ While a helper steadies the post, drill a pilot hole for a $\frac{3}{8}$- by 3-inch lag screw through the post and into the joist near the top edge, then fit a washer on the lag screw and drive it in.

◆ Have your helper plumb the post with a carpenter's level, then drive a second lag screw a few inches below the first *(left)*.

NOTCHING DECKING THAT OVERHANGS

Where the deck boards overhang the end joists, you will have to notch the decking to install the end posts. At each post location, mark a notch as wide as the post in line with the outer face of the end joist. Cut out the notch with a wood chisel and a mallet.

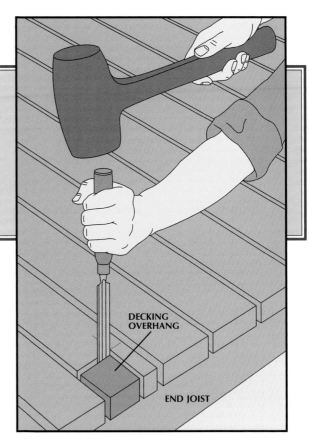

DECKING OVERHANG

END JOIST

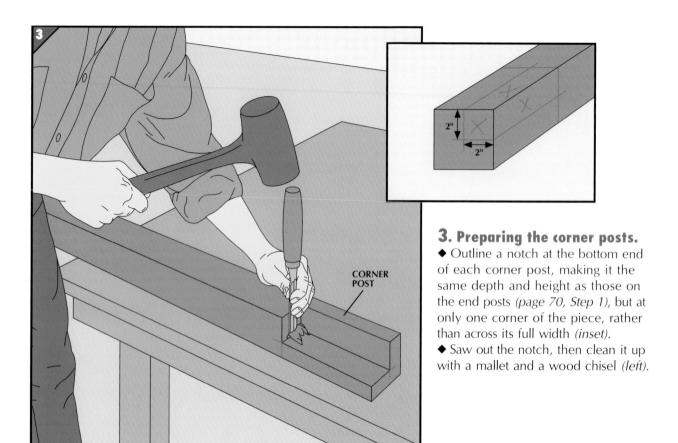

3. Preparing the corner posts.
◆ Outline a notch at the bottom end of each corner post, making it the same depth and height as those on the end posts *(page 70, Step 1)*, but at only one corner of the piece, rather than across its full width *(inset)*.
◆ Saw out the notch, then clean it up with a mallet and a wood chisel *(left)*.

4. Installing the corner post.
◆ Position the corner post, fitting its notch at the corner of the deck. Then, while a helper checks the post for plumb on two adjoining sides, fasten it to the rim and end joists with two 2½-inch coated deck screws driven through each face. Tighten the screws alternately to keep the post plumb *(right)*.
◆ Fasten the post to the deck framing with lag screws as in Step 2, locating the screws on the two outer faces of the pieces; offset the screws so they won't hit each other.

TOP STAIR-RAILING POST

STRINGER

RISER

5. Installing stair-railing posts.

◆ Notch a railing post for the top of the stairs as you would an end post *(page 70, Step 1)*.

◆ Position the post at the junction between one stair stringer and the deck, resting the top of the notch on the decking. Fasten the post in place *(page 71, Step 2)*.

◆ Place an unnotched post on the concrete slab at the bottom of the stairs, butting it against the stringer 2 inches back from the first riser. While a helper steadies and plumbs the post, drill pilot holes and fasten the post to the stringer with two $\frac{3}{8}$- by 5-inch galvanized lag screws and washers *(left)*.

◆ Install posts on the other side of the stairs in the same way.

If you have installed picture-frame steps, finish framing them *(page 66, Step 2)*.

CAPPING THE DECK EDGES

If the deck boards are flush with the outer sides of the end and rim joists, you can install a cap to conceal the decking. From the same type of wood used for the decking, cut a length of 5/4-by-4 stock to fit as a cap between each pair of railing posts. Fit the cap between two posts so its top edge is flush with the surface of the decking, then fasten it in place with $2\frac{1}{2}$-inch galvanized spiral-shank nails spaced every foot, driving them alternately into the joist and the decking.

CAP

JOIST

POST

A COLONIAL RAILING

1. Laying out the spindles.
◆ Cut two lengths of handrail and one filler strip to fit between each pair of posts.
◆ Wedge the lower rail and the strip between the posts so they are side by side on the deck, and mark the middle of each piece.
◆ Cut a piece of spindle stock as a spacer, making it as long as the desired spindle spacing. Center it on-end on the mark and outline the center spindle on the rail and filler strip.
◆ Mark the edge of the next spindle by holding the spacer on one side and aligning an end with one of the center-spindle lines. Outline the spindle's other edge, then continue to lay out spindle locations until you have marked the last one at the post.
◆ Go back to the center-spindle outline and lay out the spindle locations between it and the opposite post *(right)*.

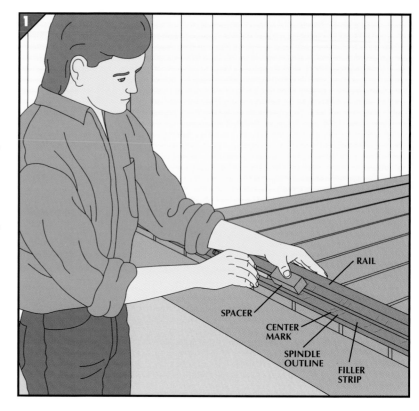

RAIL

SPACER

CENTER MARK

SPINDLE OUTLINE

FILLER STRIP

2. Cutting the spindles.
◆ Measure up from the decking and mark the position of the top of the upper rail *(left)*, then set a scrap of rail with a piece of filler strip *(inset)* at the mark and outline the bottom of the upper rail.
◆ Starting at the height of the bottom of the lower rail, lay out the position of the lower rail *(dashed lines)* using the same method, but omitting the filler strip.
◆ Measure the distance between the bottom of the top rail and the top of the bottom rail, then cut a spindle to length for each outline you made in Step 1. You can cut several pieces at once as described on page 65.

TOP OF UPPER RAIL

TOP OF LOWER RAIL

BOTTOM OF LOWER RAIL

RAIL

FILLER STRIP

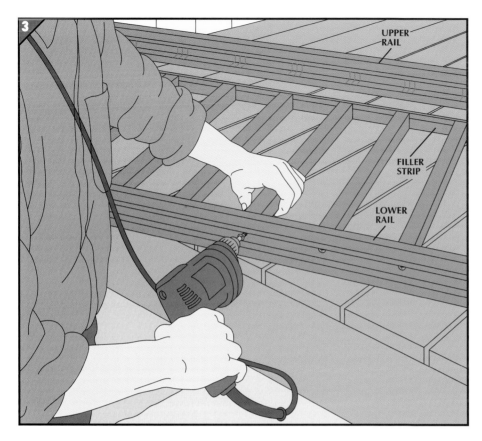

3. Assembling the railing.

◆ Drill a pilot hole for a $1\frac{1}{2}$-inch coated deck screw through the filler strip at each marked spindle outline.

◆ Fasten the spindles to the filler strip.

◆ Attach the lower rail to the opposite end of the spindles in the same manner *(left)*.

4. Adding the upper rail.

◆ Turn the top rail upside down and set the assembly on top of it, fitting the filler strip into the groove in the rail and aligning the ends of the pieces.

◆ Drill a pilot hole for a 2-inch coated deck screw through the filler strip and into the handrail every 8 to 10 inches, then drive the screws *(right)*.

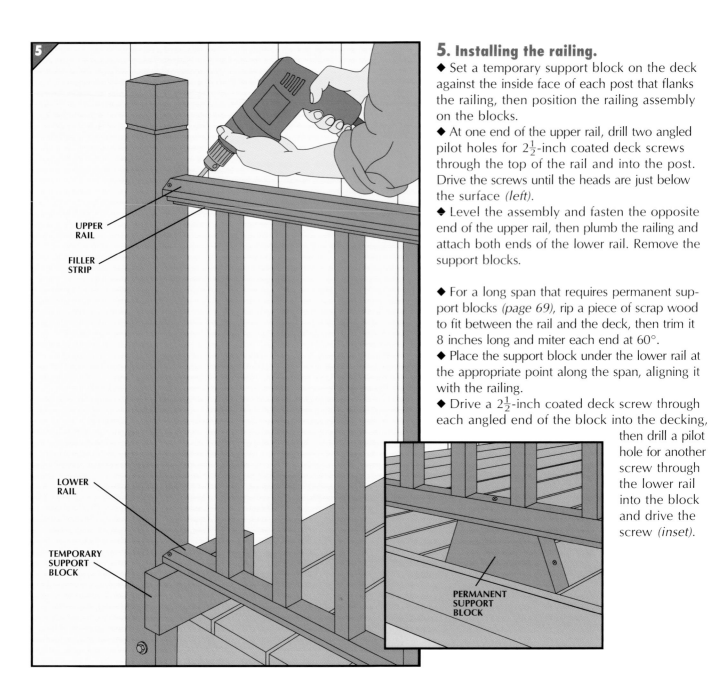

UPPER RAIL

FILLER STRIP

LOWER RAIL

TEMPORARY SUPPORT BLOCK

PERMANENT SUPPORT BLOCK

5. Installing the railing.

◆ Set a temporary support block on the deck against the inside face of each post that flanks the railing, then position the railing assembly on the blocks.

◆ At one end of the upper rail, drill two angled pilot holes for $2\frac{1}{2}$-inch coated deck screws through the top of the rail and into the post. Drive the screws until the heads are just below the surface *(left)*.

◆ Level the assembly and fasten the opposite end of the upper rail, then plumb the railing and attach both ends of the lower rail. Remove the support blocks.

◆ For a long span that requires permanent support blocks *(page 69)*, rip a piece of scrap wood to fit between the rail and the deck, then trim it 8 inches long and miter each end at 60°.

◆ Place the support block under the lower rail at the appropriate point along the span, aligning it with the railing.

◆ Drive a $2\frac{1}{2}$-inch coated deck screw through each angled end of the block into the decking, then drill a pilot hole for another screw through the lower rail into the block and drive the screw *(inset)*.

PREFABRICATED RAILINGS

An alternative to building your own railing is to buy prefabricated railing assemblies, such as the ones at right. The sections are fastened between railing posts in the same manner as the custom-made railings on these pages.

RAILING-HEIGHT MARK

HANDRAIL

POST

6. Fastening the stair railing.

◆ Lay a handrail on the steps and mark it where it meets the inside of each stair post *(inset)*. Adjust a power miter saw to the angle of the marks, then cut the rail to length.
◆ Cut another rail and a filler strip to the same length, beveling the ends at the same angle as the first rail.
◆ Cut spindles to the same height as those on the deck, beveling the ends at the angle of the rails.
◆ Assemble a railing section *(page 75, Steps 3 and 4)*, then place the section between the posts. Measuring from the back of an upper step, position the assembly so the hand-rail is at the correct height. Mark the upper post along the top of the rail.
◆ With a helper holding the railing assembly between the posts so the top of the handrail is even with the mark on the upper post, position the bottom end of the assembly so the handrail is at the same height relative to a lower step. Mark the lower post along the top of the rail *(left)*.
◆ With the railing section even with the marks, drill pilot holes for two $2\frac{1}{2}$-inch coated deck screws through the un-derside of the bottom end of the handrail and into the post. Drive the screws. Fasten the top end of the handrail by driving the screws through the top of the handrail.
◆ Plumb the assembly, then fasten both ends of the bottom rail in the same way.

A TRADITIONAL ALTERNATIVE

1. Laying out the spindles.

◆ Cut a 2-by-6 or a section of milled 2-by-6 railing to fit between a pair of posts.
◆ Lay out the location of the spindles *(page 74, Step 1)* along the top edge of the railing, then with a combination square, mark a line along the railing $1\frac{1}{2}$ inches from the top edge.
◆ Cut spindles to reach from the bottom of the rim or end joist to within $1\frac{1}{2}$ inches of the required height of the railing—at least 35 inches above the deck, beveling both ends at 45°. You may be able to buy spindles of the right length with the ends already beveled.
◆ Drill two pilot holes for $2\frac{1}{2}$-inch coated deck screws through each spindle about 1 inch from the ends.
◆ Position the first spindle on the handrail within its outline and its top even with the line on the handrail, then screw it in place *(right)*.
◆ Fasten the last spindle to the opposite end of the handrail in the same way.

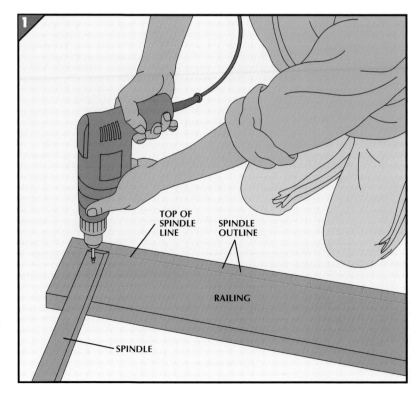

TOP OF SPINDLE LINE

SPINDLE OUTLINE

RAILING

SPINDLE

END SPINDLE

RIM JOIST

2. Mounting the railing.

◆ Place the railing assembly between the posts. With a helper holding one end spindle flush with the bottom of the rim or end joist, adjust the other end spindle so it is plumb and flush with the bottom of the joist.

◆ Fasten each spindle to the joist *(left)*.

◆ Plumb one of the end spindles, then drill two angled pilot holes for $2\frac{1}{2}$-inch coated deck screws through the face of the handrail and into the post at the same end. Then, drive the screws.

◆ Fasten the opposite end of the handrail in the same way.

3. Filling in the spindles.

◆ Secure the top of a spindle to the handrail at the second spindle location. Then, position the bottom of the spindle using the spacing block, and fasten the spindle to the joist.

◆ Continue adding spindles in the same way *(right)*. After installing four or five, fasten the top of the next one, then plumb it before attaching the bottom.

◆ Install the remaining spindles, plumbing every fourth or fifth one.

SPACER

HAND-RAIL

STRINGER

4. Attaching the stair railing.

◆ Cut a 2-by-6 or a length of milled 2-by-6 railing as you would a colonial handrail (page 77, Step 6), but align the ends of the rail with the outer sides of the posts.

◆ Position the handrail as described on page 77, Step 6, and, working with a helper, fasten the rail to the post with two $2\frac{1}{2}$-inch coated deck screws at each end (left).

◆ Lay out the spindle locations on the rail (page 74, Step 1), then cut the spindles to reach from the bottom of the stringer to $1\frac{1}{2}$ inches below the top edge of the handrail, cutting both ends to match the angle of the rails and beveling them at 45 degrees.

◆ Drill a pilot hole for a deck screw 1 inch from each end of the spindles.

◆ Fasten the spindles to the stringer and handrail (opposite, Step 3).

DISTINCTIVE RAILINGS

The primary restrictions in designing a deck railing are that the plan meet all code requirements and the railing be supported by an adequate number of posts to prevent it from flexing and sagging. Following these guidelines, you can choose among any number of styles to complement your deck. Two distinctive railings are featured in the photographs below. The one at left has vertical slats of alternating 2-by-2s and 1-by-4s, and the pattern along the top augments the Japanese motif. The railing at right represents the style known as Craftsman. Its heaviness is softened by the sweeping curve of the handrail. This particular structure has continuous posts (page 33).

A GATE FOR A COLONIAL RAILING

1. Assembling the gate.

◆ Build the gate in the same way as a railing section *(pages 74-75)*, but with two spindles side by side at each end. Size the gate to fit between the posts at the top of the stairs with a $\frac{1}{4}$-inch gap on each side.

◆ Make two vertical braces of 1-by-4 stock: Cut them to fit between the rails and rip them to the same width as the doubled spindles.

◆ Lay the gate down inside-face up and attach the 1-by-4s to the end spindles with $1\frac{1}{2}$-inch coated deck screws, aligning the edges of the pieces *(right)*.

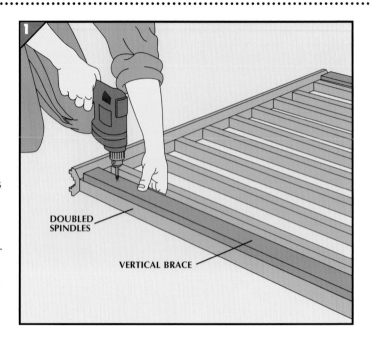

DOUBLED SPINDLES

VERTICAL BRACE

2. Bracing the gate.

◆ Fasten a 1-by-2 brace diagonally between the vertical ones so it runs from the top of the gate's latch side to the bottom of the hinge side. Drive a $1\frac{1}{2}$-inch coated deck screw through the brace into every other spindle and into each vertical brace *(left)*.

◆ Position one leaf of a 3- by 3-inch butt hinge on the hinge-side of the gate, locating it 4 inches from the top and so the gate will swing onto the deck. Mark the screw holes, remove the hinge, drill a pilot hole for a screw at each mark, then fasten the hinge to the gate.

◆ Attach a second hinge 4 inches from the bottom of the gate.

◆ Cut a filler strip 8 inches long and position it on the bottom rail at the latch side of the gate.

◆ Drill a pilot hole for a deck screw through the filler strip at each spindle location, then drive the screws.

◆ Fasten a swiveling caster to the filler strip near the latch edge *(inset)*.

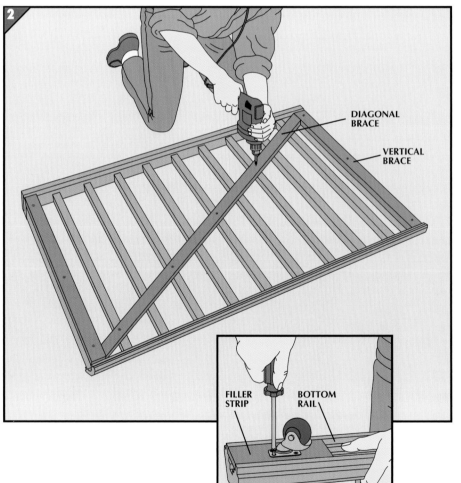

DIAGONAL BRACE

VERTICAL BRACE

FILLER STRIP

BOTTOM RAIL

3. Hanging the gate.
◆ Position the gate between the stair posts, have a helper hold it level, then mark the free screw holes of the top hinge on the post *(left)*.
◆ Fasten the hinge leaf to the post, then attach the bottom hinge.

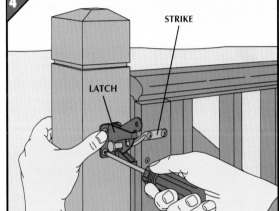

4. Adding the latch.
◆ Position the strike 3 inches from the top on the latch-side vertical brace of the gate, mark its screw holes, drill pilot holes, and fasten the strike in place.
◆ Engage the strike with the latch, then close the gate.
◆ Mark the latch's screw holes and screw it to the post *(right)*.

A TRADITIONAL GATE

Assembling the gate.
◆ Cut a 2-by-6 handrail and a length of 2-by-4 to fit between the stair posts, with a $\frac{1}{4}$-inch gap on each side.
◆ Lay out spindle locations *(page 74, Step 1)* on both pieces, adding marks for double spindles at each end.
◆ Cut spindles to reach from the bottom of the 2-by-4 to $1\frac{1}{2}$ inches below the top of the handrail when the gate is assembled, then fasten the spindles to the two pieces as described on page 78, Step 3.
◆ Cut two 2-by-4s to the planned height of the gate, beveling the ends, and cut them 3 inches wide as vertical braces.
◆ With $2\frac{1}{2}$-inch coated deck screws, fasten the braces to the inside face of the gate assembly flush with the outer edges.
◆ Add a diagonal 2-by-2 brace *(opposite, Step 2)*, then add a caster, hang the gate, and install a latch as for a colonial gate.

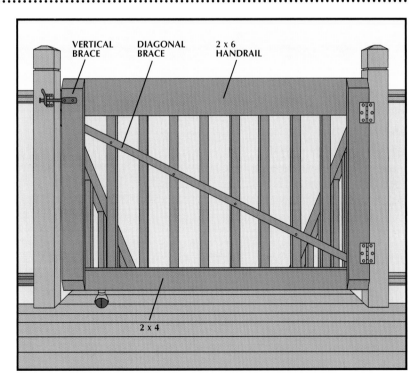

4

Rustic Decks and Elegant Porches

The outdoor additions described in this chapter range from a second-story deck to a wraparound porch with a hip roof anchored to the house. These ambitious structures can challenge an experienced carpenter, yet all are within your reach if you plan ahead, take your time, and proceed in the orderly fashion described on the following pages.

Framing Multilevel Decks   **84**

Adding a Platform
Stepping Down from House Level
Side-by-Side Decks
A Transition Step
Steps for a Low-Level Deck

Incorporating a Hot Tub   **90**

Decks for the Second Story   **92**

Erecting the Posts
Cutting through Siding
Hanging a Ledger Board
Notching Posts and Constructing a Frame

Custom Details for a Second-Story Deck   **102**

Variations on the Rectangle
Adding a Stairway
Building to Fit the Space
Slanted Railings for a Deck

Spacious Porches with a Choice of Views   **108**

Constructing a Ledger Board
Planning and Pouring Footings
Building Brick Piers
Weatherproofing the Ledger
Assembling the Substructure
Laying Floorboards

The All-Important Stairway   **120**

Skirts to Hide a Crawlspace

A Hip Roof for a Wraparound Porch   **122**

The Correct Height for a Rafter Plate
Supports for the Roof
Cutting and Installing Common Rafters
Adding Hip and Jack Rafters
Sheathing and Shingles
Side Enclosures and Soffit Supports

Ceilings and Railings   **132**

Adding one or more deck levels can smooth the transition between the yard and house or add interest to an otherwise ordinary design. Distinct levels can also be used to define areas for specific activities, such as dining or sun bathing.

A Platform: The simplest way to add a level is to build a platform and fasten it on top of the joists of the main deck *(below and opposite)*. Since this design uses more lumber than most other methods, it is best for platforms of modest size, such as a landing in front of a door or a step between two deck levels.

A Lower Level: A second deck can be hung from the front of the main deck to allow one or more steps between levels *(page 86)*. Alternatively, place the lower level at the side of the deck by using a split beam attached to the posts of the main deck *(pages 86-87)*.

Steps Between Levels: To link levels, you can make the transition with one or more stacked platforms *(page 87)*. Plan the drop between the levels to be an even multiple of the height of the platforms. When made of 2-by-6 lumber, each step will be 7 inches high if you are using 2-by-4 decking, $6\frac{3}{4}$ inches high with 5/4 decking. Lay decking *(pages 48-54)* on the main deck before you install the platforms so the bottom step will be the correct height.

To make a transition from a low-level deck to the ground, build one or more steps the length of the deck *(pages 88-89)*. For the steps to be the correct height, plan the height of the deck when you are laying the foundation *(pages 26-27)* so that the vertical rise of each step will be no higher than about 7 inches when the deck boards are in place. Otherwise, you may need to rip boards to keep the rise of the steps equal.

 TOOLS

Tape measure
Combination
  square
Mason's line
Chalk line

Circular saw
Maul
Hammer
Electric drill
Wrenches
Post-hole digger
Concrete tools

 MATERIALS

2 x 2s
Materials for casting
  footings and
  setting posts
Pressure-treated
  lumber for ledgers,
  posts, beams, joists,
  and other framing
Post caps
Multipurpose
  framing anchors

Joist hangers
Framing-anchor
  nails
Galvanized lag
  screws ($\frac{3}{8}$" x 4")
  and washers
Galvanized carriage
  bolts ($\frac{1}{2}$" x 6", 7")
  and washers
Galvanized spiral-
  shank nails ($3\frac{1}{2}$")
Galvanized common
  nails (3")

SAFETY TIPS

Goggles protect your eyes when you are using a power tool or hammering.

ADDING A PLATFORM

1. Assembling the platform.

◆ Assemble a frame of the desired size from four pieces of 2-by-6 lumber, butting them together or beveling the corners. Fasten the corners with $3\frac{1}{2}$-inch galvanized spiral-shank nails.
◆ Fill in the frame with joists spaced the same distance apart as the deck joists, nailing them to the sides of the frame so they will run at right angles to the house.
◆ If the house has flat siding, install spacers along the wall *(page 23)* where the platform will rest. For overlapping siding, remove a section the length of the platform *(page 24)*.
◆ Position the frame on top of the main deck *(right)*, setting one of the sides flush against the wall.

2. Fastening the platform.
◆ Fasten the back of the platform to the house wall through the spacers with galvanized $\frac{3}{8}$- by 4-inch lag screws and washers *(left)* as for a ledger *(pages 23-24)*.
◆ Toenail the front of the platform to each joist that it crosses with a $3\frac{1}{2}$-inch galvanized spiral-shank nail.

3. Adding a support joist.
When the platform extends past a joist at either end and leaves more than 4 inches of space between it and the next joist, add a short joist to support the decking up against the platform at that end.
◆ Cut a piece of joist lumber to fit as blocking between the joists.
◆ Place the blocking a few inches beyond the front edge of the platform between the joists straddled by the end of the platform, then nail the blocking to the joists.
◆ With galvanized framing-anchor nails, fasten a joist hanger to the deck ledger about 4 inches beyond the edge of the platform.
◆ Cut a support joist long enough to fit between the deck ledger and the blocking, then fasten it to the joist hanger with framing-anchor nails and to the blocking with three spiral-shank nails *(right)*.
◆ If necessary, install a support joist on the opposite side of the platform.

SUPPORT JOIST

BLOCKING

STEPPING DOWN FROM HOUSE LEVEL

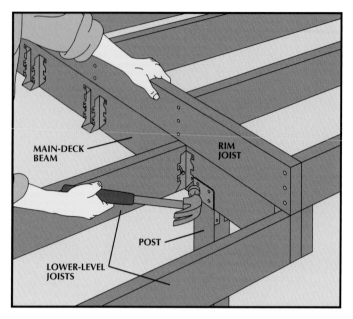

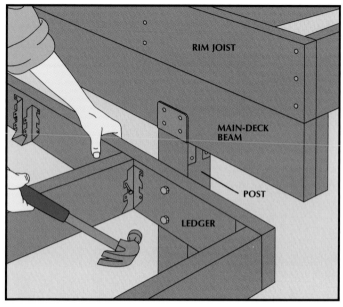

One step down.

◆ Build the main deck *(pages 18-45)*, but align the outer edges of the beam and rim joist.

◆ For a single step down, set the posts and beam for the far end of the lower level, using the beam on the main deck as a ledger for the lower deck.

◆ Install end joists for the lower deck, fastening the attached ends to the outer face of the main-deck beam. Use multipurpose framing anchors and rest the opposite ends on the lower-level beam.

◆ Attach joist hangers to the outer face of the main-deck beam *(pages 35-36)*, then add the remaining joists *(above)* and complete the lower-level frame *(page 37)*.

Two or three steps down.

◆ Build the main deck in the same manner as for a one-step level change *(left)*, then mark the vertical drop on the main-deck posts, measuring from the top edge of the rim joist.

◆ Position a ledger board across the posts so its top edge is level with the marks.

◆ Drill holes through the ledger and posts, and fasten the ledger to each post with two $\frac{1}{2}$- by 6-inch galvanized carriage bolts and washers.

◆ Attach the joists to the ledger *(above)* and complete the lower-level frame *(page 37)*.

◆ Add one or more transition steps *(opposite)*.

SIDE-BY-SIDE DECKS

1. Attaching the beam.

◆ Build the upper deck *(pages 18-45)*, then lay out the lower deck and set its posts, counting the last post of the upper level as the first post of the lower one.

◆ At the house wall, mark the top of the lower ledger, measuring from the upper ledger a distance equal to the planned vertical drop between the decks.

◆ Install a ledger for the lower level at the mark, spacing it as shown in the inset so the end joists of the two decks will lie alongside each other.

◆ Tack a split beam between the posts *(page 32)* of the lower deck.

◆ Drill holes for two $\frac{1}{2}$- by 7-inch galvanized carriage bolts through the beam into each post *(right)* and tighten the bolts.

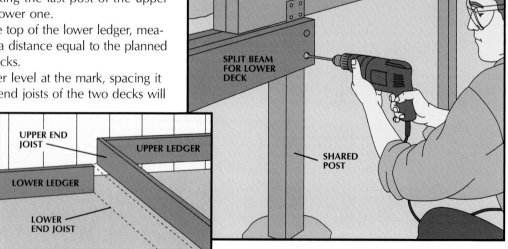

2. Adding joists.
◆ Install an end joist for the lower deck, positioning it alongside, but not under, the end joist of the upper deck *(left)*.
◆ Fasten the remaining joists *(pages 35-37)*.

A TRANSITION STEP

Installing the platform.
◆ Build a two-level deck and install the decking *(pages 48-54)* on the lower level.
◆ Construct a platform *(page 84, Step 1)*, place it on the lower deck, and fasten it to the beam or posts of the upper deck with $\frac{3}{8}$- by 4-inch galvanized lag screws and washers.
◆ Toenail each joist of the platform to the decking with $3\frac{1}{2}$-inch galvanized spiral-shank nails spaced every 16 inches *(right)*.

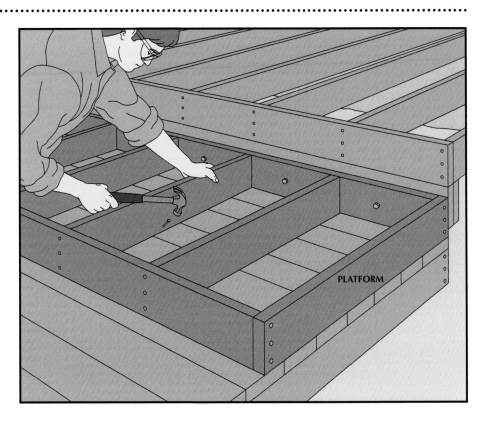

STEPS FOR A LOW-LEVEL DECK

RIM JOIST

FACE BOARD

1. Positioning the face board.
◆ Frame a low-level deck *(page 38)*, planning its finished height so that each step will be about 7 inches high when the decking is in place.
◆ Run a string line parallel to and $11\frac{1}{4}$ inches from the rim joist—with this distance, the step will be two deck boards in width—and mark locations for piers at least every 10 feet along it.
◆ Cast piers at the marks as described on page 26,

Step 1, but set the tops of the tubes at ground level instead of 2 inches above it and level them by raising any that are too low.
◆ From 2-by-6 lumber, cut a face board the length of the deck.
◆ Set the face board on the piers parallel to the rim joist and measure at several points to position its outer face $11\frac{1}{4}$ inches from the rim joist *(above)*.

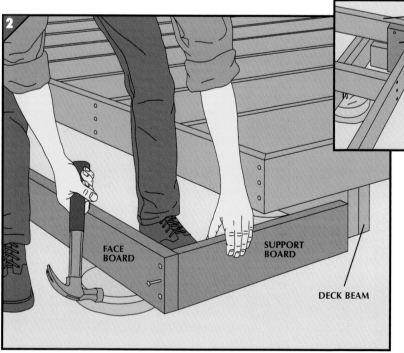

END JOIST

CLEAT

SUPPORT BOARD

FACE BOARD

SUPPORT BOARD

DECK BEAM

2. Installing face-board end supports.
◆ Measure the distance between the face board and the deck beam, then cut two 2-by-6s to this length as end supports.
◆ Holding a support board level between the face board and the beam at one end of the deck, fasten it to the face board with three $3\frac{1}{2}$-inch galvanized spiral-shank nails so the top edges of the pieces are flush *(left)*, then toenail the board to the beam.
◆ Measure from the top edge of the deck's end joist to the bottom edge of the support board, cut a 2-by-6 cleat to this length, and fasten it to the inner faces of the boards *(inset)*.
◆ Install the other end support at the opposite end of the face board in the same way.

3. Adding support boards.
◆ For every second deck joist, cut a support board to the same length as the end supports.
◆ Fasten each board to the beam and face board as in Step 2, aligning the piece with a deck joist *(left)*.

FACE BOARD   SUPPORT
                    BOARDS

WRAPAROUND STEPS

If you want to build a transition step all the way around a deck *(photograph)*, support the section that runs along the rim joist as shown opposite and above, but cast an additional pier where the face boards of both steps meet at the corner; bevel the ends of the face boards at 45°. To support the step that parallels the deck joists, hang wood cleats from the end joist *(opposite, Step 2 inset)*, then butt the support boards against the cleats and fasten them with nails. For a drop that exceeds one step, you can erect a series of steps by building the bottom step in the same manner as the platform described on page 87, then stacking the steps on top of it.

Incorporating a Hot Tub

Adding a hot tub to a deck can increase your enjoyment of the outdoor living area. You can make the tub the centerpiece of the deck, or you can design a special area or add another level in order to accommodate the unit.

The easiest type of hot tub to install is a portable unit. Completely self-contained, such a model requires no special plumbing. After the tub is set into place in the deck, it is filled with water from a garden hose and plugged into an appropriate outdoor electrical outlet *(opposite)*.

Supporting a Hot Tub: Portable units are generally about 3 to 4 feet high. For a customized appearance, you can mount the tub flush with the surface of the deck. To do so, you will need to frame an opening in the deck and build a concrete or wooden platform to support the tub. To keep the tub as low as possible, you can support it on a concrete slab cast slightly above ground level. Excavate 6 inches below the surface and lay a 4-inch bed of gravel, then cast a level 4-inch slab. For a taller deck, you will need to frame a platform under the tub *(below)*. The structural requirements will vary depending on the weight of the unit and soil conditions; have the local building department review your plans before you start.

Accessing the Controls: You may want to hide the hot-tub support by adding a skirt around the deck *(pages 154-159)*. Most portable models have controls or equipment that must be accessed on occasion from the side, so include a door or hinged panel in the skirt.

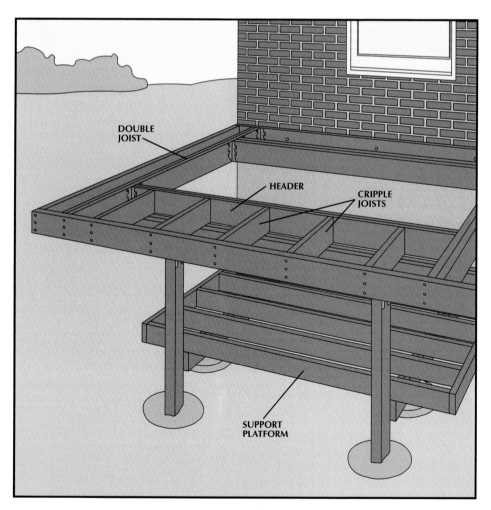

DOUBLE JOIST

HEADER

CRIPPLE JOISTS

SUPPORT PLATFORM

Framing for a hot tub on a support deck.

The hot tub at left is supported on a low wooden platform framed much like a freestanding deck *(page 38)*; however, the footings may need to be slightly larger—often 18 inches in diameter—depending on local codes. In addition, the joists are typically spaced 1 foot apart to support the weight of the unit. The height of the platform will depend on how much of the tub you wish to leave exposed above the main deck.

In this design, the upper deck is framed around the tub with double joists, headers, and cripple joists as described on pages 43 to 45. The opening is about 4 inches larger all around than the unit to allow for the overhang of the decking plus a slight gap. If the tub is round or octagonal, you will need corner braces to support the ends of the deck boards *(page 45)*. Once the unit is in place, you can scribe the boards to match its contours *(page 57)*.

A portable hot tub must be plugged into a nearby outdoor outlet equipped with a ground-fault circuit interrupter (GFCI). Usually, this outlet is wired to a dedicated 20-amp grounded circuit run from the house service panel to the tub; however, the wiring restrictions may vary depending on the tub model and on local codes. Most codes require that the outlet for the tub be located within sight of the tub's access panel. If the panel is under the deck, as in a flush-mounted unit, code may require a second GFCI outlet above the deck for powering radios or other electrical devices.

To run the wiring for a flush-mounted hot tub *(right)*, drill a hole for underground feeder (UF) cable through the house's band joist and the deck ledger. Fish the cable from the service panel through the hole and run it along a deck joist to the outlet location, fastening it with cable clamps at the house and the outlet, and at a minimum of every $4\frac{1}{2}$ feet in between. Attach the cable to the outlet box with a weatherproof connector, then fasten the box to the joist. To wire the GFCI outlet *(inset)*, attach the cable's black wire to the brass terminal labeled "LINE" and the white wire to the silver terminal marked "LINE". Fasten a green jumper wire to the receptacle's ground screw and another to the ground screw of the box, then join the jumpers and the copper wire of the UF cable with a wire cap. Next, drill a hole through the decking and bring a second cable up through it from the service panel. Install a second GFCI outlet on the house wall, protecting the exposed cable with electrical conduit. Finally, seal the hole in the house wall with caulk.

Once the receptacles and the hot tub have been installed, have a licensed electrician complete the installation by hooking up the new circuits to the service panel; bonding the tub to any permanent metal objects within 10 feet of it—such as gutters or fences; and running a separate ground wire from the tub to the service panel if the manufacturer requires it.

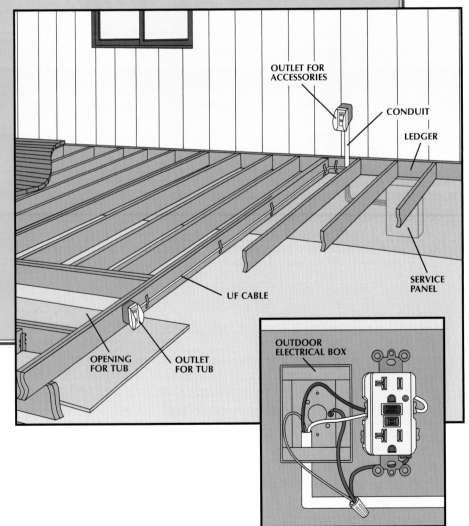

OUTLET FOR ACCESSORIES

CONDUIT

LEDGER

SERVICE PANEL

UF CABLE

OPENING FOR TUB

OUTLET FOR TUB

OUTDOOR ELECTRICAL BOX

Decks for the Second Story

A deck that rises 8 or more feet above the ground shares much with similar structures built nearer the ground. For example, joist spans and spacing *(page 20)* are identical to those for a low-lying deck. Decking is also the same.

Fastened directly to the house like those for low-lying decks, the ledger allows the second-story deck to borrow strength from the larger structure. However, these taller structures require additional rigidity—which they gain from thicker, stiffer posts at the outer edge of the deck.

Design Considerations: The layout of your house is an important factor in planning a high deck. The wall next to the deck must have a door—or a place where a new door can be added. Consider siting the deck with the door close to one end of the deck to allow you to make the most of your outdoor space.

The overall height of the deck is dictated by the level of the framing for the adjacent house floor, to which the ledger is anchored. The deck surface is positioned 3 inches below the door. Any deck higher than a couple of feet off the ground requires a railing.

Structural Concerns: The technique for attaching the ledger varies according to the type of framing members in the house floor. If your house was built before 1970, it probably has a solid band of lumber for securing the ledger. A newer house, however, may have prefabricated framing components that lack the solid wood needed for anchoring the ledger. In such cases, you will need to strengthen the house framing before building the deck.

If your house has an unfinished basement or a crawlspace, look there to identify the type of framing you have. *(Without such accessibility, check with your local building authorities. They may have the builder's plans on file.)* If the boards resting on the foundation are solid lumber—usually 2-by-10 or 2-by-12—the framing will require no reinforcement.

The opposite is true if you see either I-beams or floor trusses *(page 23)*. I-beams look like their name: A cross section shows top and bottom 2-by-3s or 2-by-4s called flanges joined by a web of plywood or flake board about 10 inches high. Floor trusses are equally recognizable. Between the flanges runs a web of short diagonal pieces that form a zigzag pattern.

Building Codes: All the structural elements of your deck are governed by local building codes. Check them well as you plan your deck—before beginning construction. The design shown here conforms to most codes for decks from 8 feet to 3 stories high. Keep in mind that an inspector will want to check the deck framing and any house reinforcements that you make to accommodate the ledger. Leave your work visible until the inspection is completed.

⚠️ **CAUTION** *Before excavating, establish the locations of underground obstacles such as electric, water, and sewer lines, and dry wells, septic tanks, and cesspools.*

TOOLS

Plumb bob	Water level
Measuring tape (25-foot)	Circular saw
	Framing square
Posthole digger	Combination square
Carpenter's level	Drill with $\frac{9}{16}$-inch and $\frac{3}{8}$-inch bits
Chalk line	
Ladders	Hand ripsaw

MATERIALS

Mason's cord
Powdered chalk
Concrete mix
6-by-6s
2-by-8s, 2-by-10s, or 2-by-12s
Lag screws ($\frac{1}{2}$- by $3\frac{1}{2}$-inch)
Carriage bolts ($\frac{1}{2}$- by 6-inch)
Galvanized common nails (3- and $3\frac{1}{2}$-inch)
Framing connectors and nails
Aluminum flashing (7-inch)
Decking

SAFETY TIPS

Wear goggles when hammering nails or sawing. Use a dust mask when sawing pressure-treated lumber, and wash your hands thoroughly after handling it. When you are sawing or drilling an unfastened board, have a helper steady it.

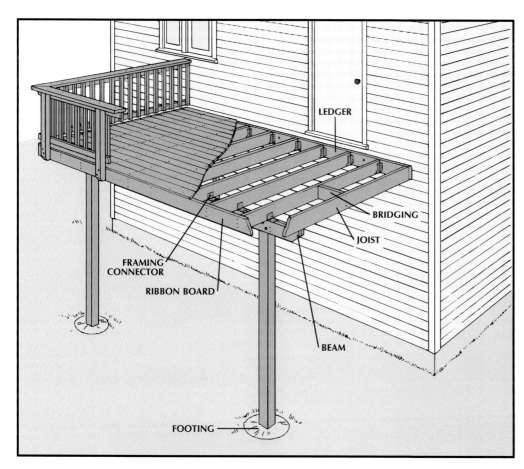

Components of a second-story deck.
This second-story deck is attached to the side of the house by a ledger bolted directly to the house framing. Notched 6-by-6 posts embedded in concrete footings that reach below the frostline support a beam of doubled boards, which is bolted to the posts. The deck's joists are fastened to the ledger with joist hangers and to the beam with nails or framing connectors. A ribbon board covers joist ends. The decking and railing are identical to those shown on the free-standing deck *(pages 48-57 and 69-79)*.

ERECTING THE POSTS

1. Laying out the deck.
◆ Drop a plumb bob from the center of the door threshold and mark a reference line on the foundation. To do so, hold one arm of a framing square against the foundation with the outer edge of the other arm touching the plumb bob string. Mark the foundation at the corner of the square *(right)*.
◆ With this mark as a reference point, measure in each direction along the foundation to establish the width of the deck. Drive stakes at these points.
◆ Cut two pieces of mason's cord at least as long the planned depth of the deck. Tie a string to each stake, then use the squaring technique shown on page 22 to stake the strings at right angles to the house wall.

2. Marking footing positions.

◆ Measuring from the house, mark the beam's outer edge on each string. Stake a third string so that it crosses the first two at these points.

◆ Beginning at a deck-edge string, mark the length of the beam overhang *(page 20),* on the beam string. Drop a plumb bob from that point and spray a chalk mark *(right).* After repeating this process on the other side of the deck, take down the beam string, leaving the stakes in place.

◆ At each chalk mark, dig a hole 16 inches square, extending below the frostline. Pour 8 inches of concrete into each hole. Replace the beam string and allow the concrete to harden up to 48 hours.

DECK-EDGE STRING

BEAM-EDGE MARK

BEAM-EDGE STRING

OUTER STAKE

3. Setting the posts.

◆ Set an uncut post on each footing, with the post corner at the intesection of the deck-edge and beam-edge strings. Pour 4 inches of concrete around the post.

◆ Fasten a 2-by-3 brace, 6 to 8 feet long, to one side of a post with a single nail or screw. Drive a stake into the ground within reach of the brace. While a helper with a 4-foot level holds the post vertical, fasten the brace to the stake. Attach a brace to an adjacent side of the post in the same way, then plumb and brace the other post.

◆ Pack dirt tightly around the posts and allow 24 hours for the concrete to harden.

DECK-EDGE STRING

BEAM-EDGE STRING

CUTTING THROUGH SIDING

1. Marking the width on the wall.
Have a helper hold a long, straight board upright against the wall and touching a deck-edge string. While the helper plumbs the board with a 4-foot level, draw a line on the house from a point several inches above the door threshold and extending more than 1 foot below it. Repeat this step at the other side of the deck.

2. Measuring for the cut.
◆ Mark the planned height of the deck surface on the wall below the threshold, then measure down the thickness of the decking to mark the top edge of the ledger. Pencil a similar mark for the bottom of the ledger.
◆ While a helper holds one end of a water level at the ledger top, hold the other end at the vertical line drawn on the wall in Step 1. Mark the line at the height of the water.
◆ Transfer the height of the ledger bottom by the same means, then repeat the process at the other side of the deck.
◆ Snap chalk lines for the top and bottom of the ledger.

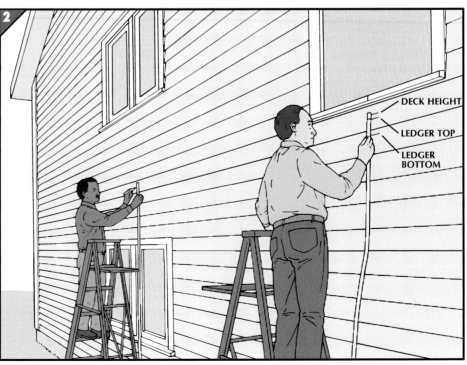

DECK HEIGHT
LEDGER TOP
LEDGER BOTTOM

3. Cutting the siding.

◆ For wood siding, set a circular saw to cut through the siding but no deeper. Begin with a plunge cut *(box, below)* at one end of the area marked for removal. Next, saw along the ledger-top line as far as you can without leaning, then start a similar cut at the ledger-bottom line. Move the ladder and cut along both lines, continuing to the end of the ledger. There, make a vertical cut.

◆ With aluminum siding, follow the same procedure using a metal-cutting blade in the saw. Vinyl siding can be sawed with a blade intended for wood or cut with a utility knife guided by a straightedge.

Beginning a Cut in Siding

TRICKS OF THE TRADE

With your finger off the trigger, retract the blade guard with your thumb. Hold the saw with the back of the blade about 2 inches from the beginning of the cutting line, then rest the front edge of the baseplate on the board and tilt the saw so that the blade is about 1 inch above the line. Grip the saw tightly, switch it on, and pivot the blade slowly into the board. Turn off the saw, and after the blade stops turning, lift it from the cut. Reposition the saw and make another plunge cut to the beginning of the cutting line, and without turning off the saw, push it forward to complete the cut.

  Make vertical cuts from the top down. Restart a saw in a cut 1 inch back from your farthest progress. If you hit a nail, back off and start a new plunge cut beyond it. Later, remove wood around the nail with a knife and pull or cut the nail.

4. Prying off the siding.

◆ Insert the flat end of a pry bar into the lower cut and lift the siding—wood, aluminum, or vinyl—away from the sheathing. Reach under the siding with wire cutters to sever the exposed nails.

◆ If the nails are too thick to cut, place a wood block under the pry bar to gain enough leverage to pull the siding farther from the wall, freeing the nails.

◆ Discard the siding, and hammer the cut ends of the siding nails flush with the sheathing.

5. Installing flashing.

◆ Cut strips of 7-inch-wide flashing to span the ledger opening, allowing for a 3-inch overlap between sections. Make a strip approximately 12 inches long for each end of the ledger.

◆ Bend each strip lengthwise, 4 inches from the edge. Push the 4-inch leg of the flashing under the siding, cutting slots for siding nails you encounter. Cut the end pieces so they can be folded to enclose the top corners of the ledger *(inset)*. Friction will hold the flashing in place until the ledger is installed.

HANGING A LEDGER BOARD

1. Marking joist locations.
◆ Cut four straight pieces of joist lumber to deck width, one for the ledger, one for the ribbon board, and two for the beam. Clamp the pieces together, edges and ends aligned.
◆ With a combination square, mark the edges of the boards at 16-inch intervals, then pencil an X beside each line, away from the starting point.
◆ Unclamp the boards and extend the lines down the face of the one to be used as the ledger board. Install joist hangers as described on page 36, and attach an all-purpose hanger $1\frac{1}{2}$ inches from each end of the ledger.
◆ Starting 6 inches from one end, drill $\frac{9}{16}$-inch holes at 2-foot intervals, staggered as shown here *(inset)*.

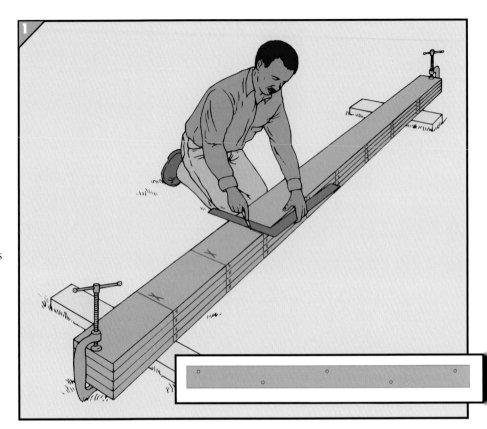

2. Attaching the ledger.
◆ With a helper, lift the ledger into position under the flashing. Drive 3-inch nails at 2-foot intervals to hold the ledger in place.
◆ Fold the flashing over the face and corners of the ledger. To secure the flashing, nail it to the face and ends of the ledger with common nails.
◆ For mounting the ledger to a joist or reinforced I-beam in a house, bore $\frac{3}{8}$-inch holes for $\frac{1}{2}$- by $3\frac{1}{2}$-inch lag screws, using the holes already drilled in the ledger as guides. With trusses, bore $\frac{9}{16}$-inch holes for carriage bolts *(see box, page 23)*.
◆ With silicone sealant, caulk the screw holes, the joints between pieces of flashing, the joint between the flashing and siding, and the joint between the bottom of the ledger and the siding.

NOTCHING POSTS AND CONSTRUCTING A FRAME

1. Marking and cutting posts to height.

◆ With a water level, mark each post at the height of the top of the ledger board. Extend the mark around all four sides of each post.

◆ Trim the posts to height, beginning with a circular saw and finishing the job with a hand saw.

2. Marking post tops.

With a square, mark the top of each post for a beam notch as shown at left, taking care that the notch faces away from the house *(below)*. The width of the notch is always 3 inches, and the depth is equal to the width of the ledger board and beam lumber.

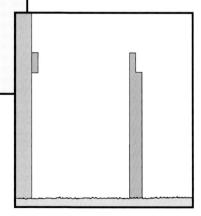

3. Cutting the notches.
◆ With a circular saw set to its maximum depth, cut across the top of the post and the side facing away from the house along the lines drawn in Step 2.
◆ Finish cutting out the notch with a handsaw. A ripsaw with about eight teeth per inch is the most efficient tool for the vertical cut; nearly any saw will do for the small amount of wood remaining in the horizontal cut.

4. Attaching the beam.
◆ Make a beam (pages 28-29) with the boards' marked edges at the top. Set it in the notches of the posts, with equal overhangs. Toenail a 3-inch nail through the bottom of the beam into each post.
◆ On a diagonal across the notch—and at least 2 inches from the top or sides of the post—drill two $\frac{1}{2}$-inch holes through the beam and post. Secure the beam with $\frac{1}{2}$- by 6-inch carriage bolts.
◆ If the deck has more than two posts, drill and bolt the beam to interior posts after tightening the bolts at the ends.

5. Attaching the joists.

◆ Nail a multipurpose framing anchor to one end of a joist. Rest the board on the beam and nail the anchor to the ledger *(right)*.

◆ To install interior joists, place one end on the beam and the other in a joist hanger. Hold the hanger closed, then nail it first to the ledger, then to the joist.

◆ Use the marks atop the beam to align the joists perpendicular to the ledger. Secure each joist to the beam with a right-angle framing connector or with 3-inch nails toenailed through the joist into the beam, two on one side and one on the other.

6. Trimming the joists.

◆ Mark the joist length atop the two end joists, then snap a chalk line between these points across the tops of the interior joists. Use a square to extend the chalk marks down one side of each joist.

◆ Lay a 4- by 8-foot sheet of $\frac{1}{2}$-inch plywood on the joists as a work platform. Kneeling on the plywood, trim the joist ends with a circular saw, always cutting on the same side of the lines to ensure equal joist lengths.

7. Nailing the ribbon board.

◆ With the ribbon board on the ground, hammer three $3\frac{1}{2}$-inch nails into the board as follows: Below each mark made on page 98, Step 1, place one nail 1 inch from the top, one 1 inch from the bottom, and the third midway between the first two. The nail tips should barely protrude from the other side.

◆ With a helper to support one end of the ribbon board, nail it to the other end joist. While the helper raises or lowers the ribbon board to align it, nail it to the next joist and then to the remaining joists in succession.

Custom Details for a Second-Story Deck

Modifications to the structure of a deck allow you to adapt it to your own tastes. A stairway provides access to the yard from a second-story deck, and an angled railing adds a touch of elegance. Joists cut to different lengths allow variations in deck shape. You can even frame a hole to accommodate a favorite shade tree.

Any option you add must conform to building codes, which govern everything from the spacing of stair rails to the method of attaching a bench. Submit plans to local authorities early to avoid last-minute changes at inspection time.

Variations in Technique: Any of these options may call for unusual construction methods. A hole or a cutaway corner, for example, requires adjustments to the framing before the deck is surfaced. The angled railing, on the other hand, is installed in holes cut through the decking. And stairs, whose stringers may be no more than 30 inches apart, should precede deck railings because railing posts at the top of the stairs can help support the deck railing as well.

Building a Landing: Most codes require a landing for stairs higher than 8 feet. Base the height of the landing on a multiple of the unit rise *(page 60)*. A landing must be at least 36 inches square. The distance between landing and deck is determined by the number of risers above the landing multiplied by the unit run—typically about 10 inches. Subtracting 15 inches from the result lets the upper section of the stairs rest on the landing. If the calculations produce an awkward position for the landing, you may want to modify the deck plans.

TOOLS

Carpenter's protractor	Circular saw
T bevel	Framing square
Measuring tape (25-foot)	Drill with $\frac{1}{2}$-, $\frac{3}{8}$-, and $\frac{9}{16}$-inch bits
Plumb bob	Folding rule
Posthole digger	Spade
Carpenter's level	Chalk line
Mortar tub	Hammer
Hoe	Hand ripsaw
Trowel	Ladders
Water level	Combination rule

MATERIALS

Galvanized common nails ($3\frac{1}{4}$-inch)	Joist hangers, single and double
Galvanized finishing nails (2-, 3-, and $3\frac{1}{4}$-inch)	Concrete
	Mason's cord
	1-by-2s
Masonry nails (3-inch)	2-by-6, 2-by-10, and 2-by-12 framing stock
Carriage bolts ($\frac{1}{2}$-inch)	4-by-4 and 6-by-6 posts

VARIATIONS ON THE RECTANGLE

1. Altering the frame.

To shape the corners or edges of a second-story deck, construct the framing as shown on pages 92 to 101, then cut away portions for the profile you want.

◆ For an angled corner, mark the end joist for cutting between the outside corner and the supporting beam, then make a mark on the ribbon board at the same distance from the corner. Cut both boards at the marks you have just made, removing the corner of the frame.

◆ Measure the distance between the outside edges of the cut frame members *(inset),* and transfer this measurement to a length of ribbon-board stock.

CORNER-BOARD LENGTH

2. Closing the cutaway corner.

◆ To make a corner board, cut along the marks with a circular saw set at a 45° angle. Bevel the board so the outer face is longer than the inner one.
◆ Drill pilot holes in the ends of the corner board, then secure it to the end joist and ribbon board with $3\frac{1}{2}$-inch nails.

By cutting the frame elsewhere along the deck edge, you can create different shapes. Shortening a joist near the midpoint of an edge and adding angled ribbon boards creates a notch. Cutting the joists progressively longer from two corners of the deck out to the midpoint of one edge creates a curve *(inset)*.

3. Fitting an angled railing.

◆ After installing decking, add at least two 4-by-4 railing posts to each railing segment *(pages 69-79)*.
◆ Cut top rails slightly long and support a side top rail on nails driven partway into the posts. Hold the corner top-rail under the side rail, and mark the intersection points on both faces of each board.
◆ Take down the rails and connect the points with a line across the edge, then bevel both rails with a circular saw.

SIDE TOP RAIL

CORNER TOP RAIL

ADDING A STAIRWAY

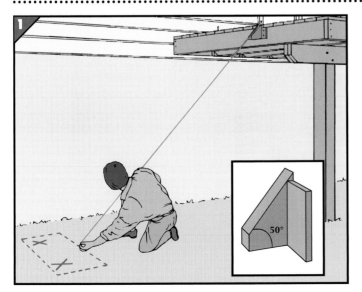

50°

1. Locating the bottom of the stairs.

◆ From a scrap of 2-by-12 lumber, cut a pitch block—a right-angle triangle with a 50° angle at one corner.
◆ Tack the pitch block to the deck where you plan to install a stair carriage *(inset)*. Stretch a string along the edge of the pitch block, and chalk a mark where the string meets the ground. Do the same for the other carriage.
◆ Enclose the chalk marks in a rectangle 6 inches wider and longer than a stair tread, with the front of the rectangle 2 inches in front of the marks *(dotted line)*. Dig a 6-inch-deep hole, pour and finish a slab *(page 61)*, and wait 24 hours before proceeding.

2. Installing the stairs.

◆ Cut 2-by-10 carriages (*page 120*), making the first tread below the stair top $1\frac{1}{2}$ inches deeper than the others. Cut two facing boards, using a carriage as a template for cutting the ends.

◆ Nail the facing boards to the carriages, then nail each assembly to the deck, tops against the underside of the decking (*right*).

◆ Nail the carriages to a 2-by-6 fitted between them on the slab, then drive four 3-inch masonry nails through the 2-by-6 into the slab. Add stair treads to the carriages (*page 64-65*).

FACING BOARD

3. Adding stair-railing posts.

◆ At intervals less than 5 feet, bolt 4-by-4 railing posts to the carriages (*page 73*). Set posts with the bottom edge nearest the deck aligned with the bottom carriage edge. (*At the top of the stairs, the stair railing shares posts with the deck railing.*)

◆ Use a framing square to mark the carriage-post tops for cutting; rest the tongue (*short arm*) on the edge of the facing board and pencil a line along the end of the body (*right*).

4. Attaching the rails.

◆ Tack a 2-by-6 top rail to the posts, edge flush with the post tops. Draw lines across the rail at the outer edges of the top and bottom posts.

◆ Remove the board, cut it along the lines, and attach it with three 3-inch nails into each post.

◆ Mark and cut lower rails in the same manner, allowing gaps of no more than 4 inches between them.

5. Attaching the handrail.

◆ On the top rail, rest a 2-by-6 handrail long enough to extend about 4 inches beyond the bottom stair post.

◆ Mark the edge of the board on both sides of the top post and draw lines at these marks across the face of the handrail board. Between these lines draw another line $3\frac{1}{2}$ inches from the railing edge and parallel to it.

◆ Use these marks as guides for a two-sided notch in the end of the handrail *(inset),* cut so that the end and the outside edge of the handrail fit flush with the top post.

◆ Mark and notch the other handrail in the same way, then nail the handrails to the posts and top rails.

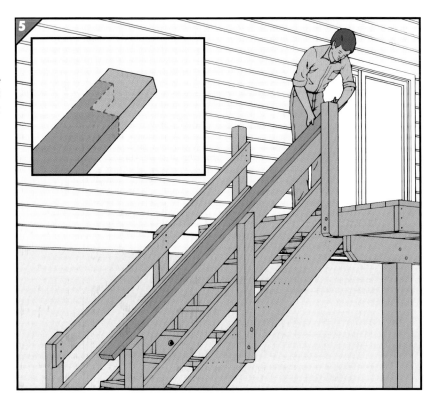

BUILDING TO FIT THE SPACE

A stairway landing.

A landing is a miniature deck with doubled ribbon boards in lieu of a beam, joists spaced at 16-inch intervals, and standard decking. The ledger is anchored to wall studs with lag screws, and notched 6-by-6 posts support the ribbon board. For a freestanding landing, a second pair of posts can substitute for a ledger board, as long as postholes are dug more than 8 inches from the house foundation. The height of a landing is a whole-number multiple of the height of a step.

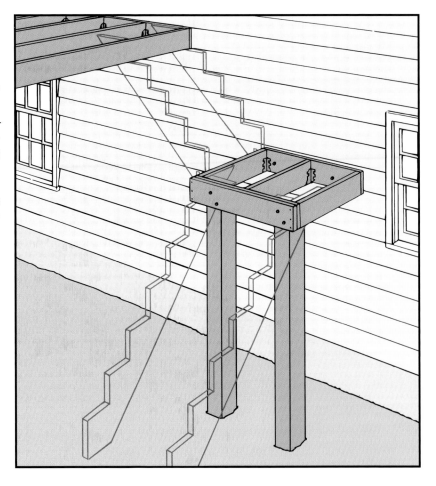

An aperture in a deck.

◆ To frame an opening—around a tree, for example—begin by doubling the joists on both sides of the hole. Double-wide joist hangers are available for this purpose.

◆ Between the doubled joists, insert headers, also made of two thicknesses of joist stock.

◆ For every joist location spanned by the headers, place a partial joist between the header and the ledger board on one side of the opening and, on the other side, between the header and the ribbon board.

◆ After the decking is in place, erect a railing around the opening.

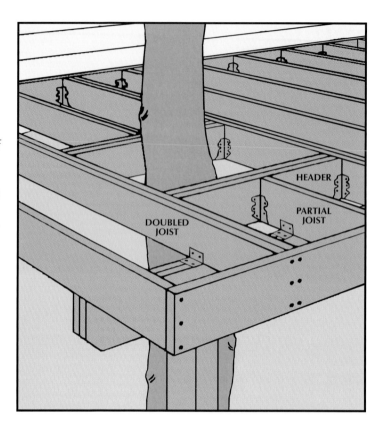

DOUBLED JOIST

HEADER

PARTIAL JOIST

SLANTED RAILINGS FOR A DECK

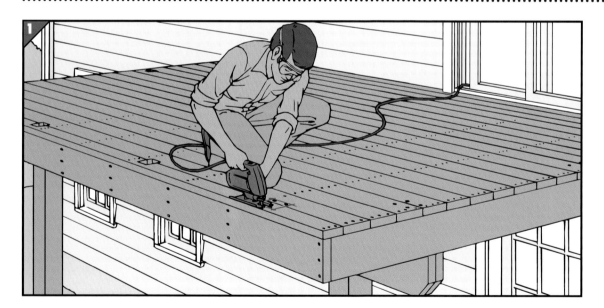

1. Cutting postholes.

◆ On the decking, mark openings $3\frac{3}{4}$ inches wide and $3\frac{7}{8}$ inches long, with the shorter dimension $1\frac{1}{4}$ inch from the deck edge. Position openings within 16 inches of the corners and no more than 5 feet apart. Along the ribbon board, each opening must have one long side adjacent to a joist.

◆ Drill 15° angled holes at the corners of each rectangle, tilting the top of the drill toward the edge of the deck. Saw the long sides with a saber saw set for a vertical cut; on the short sides, set the saw for a 15° cut.

◆ Nail blocking (page 39) next to one edge of each opening along the end joists.

2. Attaching the posts.

◆ Draw a line on each post at the point where the top of the decking will meet it. Drive a large finishing nail halfway into each post above the line and just touching it.

◆ Have a helper hold each post in position with its weight resting on the nail while you drill a $\frac{1}{2}$-inch hole through the post and the deck joist or blocking. However, instead of anchoring the posts in a vertical position, use a carpenter's protractor to slant them at an angle of 15° *(left)*. Insert a carriage bolt, fit a washer, and nut onto the end, and tighten the assembly so the post moves only when tapped with a hammer.

◆ Under the deck, align the inner corner of the post with the bottom of the adjacent joist or blocking. While the helper plumbs the post with a level, drill another hole and insert a carriage bolt. Tighten both bolts, then remove the finishing nail.

◆ Measure 36 inches up from the deck surface on the inner face of each post. Stretch a string between the marks and use it to align the inner faces of the remaining posts as you install them.

◆ Make a cutting mark across each post at the height of the string, then set a circular saw for a 15° cut and trip the post tops level.

3. Adding the rails.

◆ Drive a nail partway into each post $5\frac{1}{2}$ inches from the top to support a 2-by-6 rail.

◆ Butt a rail board against the house, its end extending beyond the deck corner. Set the adjoining rail against the first. Mark the first board where the second touches its lower edge *(left)*. Mark the bottom edge of the second board 3 inches from the end.

◆ With a protractor set at $14\frac{1}{2}$°, extend cutting lines from the marks across the faces of the rails, making the top edges longer than the bottom ones.

◆ Miter the boards along these lines with a circular saw set at 44°, cutting so that the outer face of the board is the longer.

◆ Nail the rails to the posts and to each other, then add more rails, spaced no more than 4 inches apart, in the same manner *(inset)*.

Spacious Porches with a Choice of Views

A porch can improve the appearance and increase the value of your home. The wraparound design shown on the following pages goes best with a large house, but you can easily modify the design to build a porch along one side of a smaller one.

Either structure is a major undertaking. Before you break ground to begin construction, contact your local building authority for a building permit and the required schedule of site inspections.

Planning a Porch: Regardless of the shape you intend for your porch, draw a detailed sketch of the structure, making sure that it satisfies local codes. Position piers so that the concrete footings beneath them will not encounter underground utilities. Ideally, piers and the roof supports above them should frame rather than block doors and windows. If your property slopes more than 3 feet in 8, have a professional excavator level it. Concrete steps or sidewalks may need to be partially demolished.

In most porches, the floor lies one step—6 to $7\frac{1}{2}$ inches—below the threshold of the door into the house. For a wraparound porch, plan wings of equal depth no greater than 10 feet. Doing so will enable you to build a roof with the relatively simple techniques shown on pages 122-133.

Lumber for the Frame: A porch 10 feet deep is supported on joists and beams of 2-by-8s. For narrower structures, consult the chart on page 20. Pressure-treated southern pine is the wood of choice. For every running foot of porch, you'll need 12 to 15 feet of 2-by-8.

Estimating Materials for Piers: Use the depth of your footing *(page 112)* in the formula on page 182 to calculate how much concrete to buy. Dry concrete mix is available in bags or you can buy it from a ready-mix company *(page 190)*.

Build the piers with standard construction-grade cored bricks. Pier height is the finished height of the porch floor, less the thickness of a floor board, the height of a joist, and a small amount to slope the porch for drainage *(page 182)*.

After calculating pier height, use a mason's rule—marked in inches on one side and in courses (rows) of brick on the other—to determine how many courses of brick each pier will require. Add one course to compensate for starting the pier below grade. Multiply the number of rows by the number of bricks in each *(page 113)* and again by the number of piers, then add 5 percent for waste.

Lay the bricks with mortar mix formulated for outdoor use. One cubic foot of mortar will bond 25 to 30 bricks.

Beyond the Basic Structure: Once the floor and stairs are in place, you can add a roof *(pages 122-131)* and a ceiling *(page 132)*, as well as a railing and columns *(page 133)*. When the porch is completed, paint the floor and the stairs with a finish coat made especially for porches and decks.

⚠ **CAUTION** *Before excavating, establish the locations of underground obstacles such as electric, water, and sewer lines, and dry wells, septic tanks, and cesspools.*

 **TOOLS**

Hammer drill	Spade
Circular saw	Posthole digger
Hammer	Mason's trowel
Mason's level	Convex jointer
Plumb bob	Mason's rule
Try square	Utility knife
Framing square	Caulk gun
Water level	Power floor nailer
Power screwdriver	and mallet

 **MATERIALS**

Concrete	Silicone caulk
Bricks	Wood preservative
Mortar	Wood putty
Powdered chalk	Joist hangers
2-by-4s	Joist-hanger nails
1-by-6s	Framing anchors
2-inch framing	Lag screws ($\frac{1}{2}$- by
lumber	4-inch)
1-inch fascia board	Lag shields ($\frac{1}{2}$-inch)
Tongue-and-groove	Masonry drill bit
flooring	($\frac{3}{4}$-inch)
Aluminum flashing	Drill bit ($\frac{9}{16}$-inch)

 SAFETY TIPS

Wear goggles or other eye protection when hammering or using a power saw, a dust mask when cutting pressure-treated lumber, and gloves when working with wet mortar.

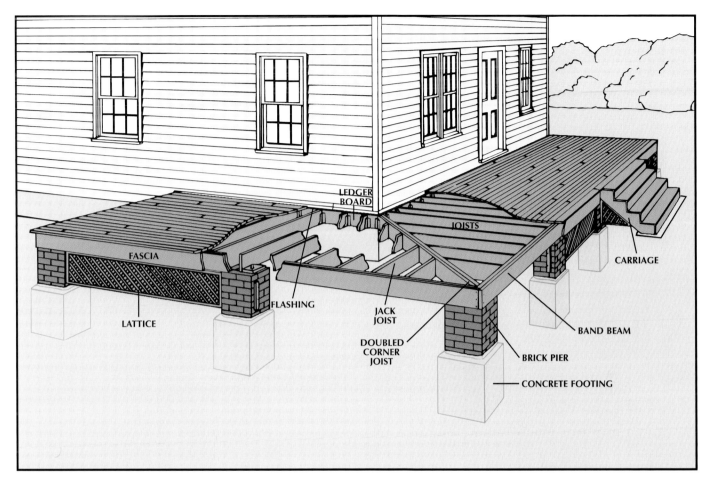

Anatomy of a wraparound porch.

Brick piers built on concrete footings support a doubled band beam at the perimeter of the 8-foot-wide porch shown above. The larger central corner pier bears the additional load carried by a doubled corner joist. A ledger board bolted to the house wall sup-

ports the inner edge of the porch. Flashing prevents water from seeping behind the ledger board. Joists of 2-by-8 lumber between the ledger and the band beam—and shorter jack joists between the band beam and the corner joist—underlie a floor made of $\frac{3}{4}$- by $3\frac{1}{4}$-inch tongue-and-groove

boards. The carriages that support a wide set of steps are fastened at the top to the band beam and rest at the bottom on a shallow concrete footing. A fascia board covers the rough lumber of the band beam, and lattice skirts enclose the crawl space underneath the porch.

CONSTRUCTING A LEDGER BOARD

1. Marking hole positions.

◆ Cut away house siding with a circular saw $\frac{1}{4}$ inch above the planned height of the porch floor *(page 96)*.
◆ From the straightest lengths of joist lumber available, cut ledger-board pieces for each porch wing. Make one ledger board $1\frac{1}{2}$ inches longer than the length of the wing it will support.
◆ Four inches from one end of each ledger board—and every 16 inches thereafter—make a pencil mark on the centerline.
◆ Alternating 2 inches above and below the centerline, drill a $\frac{9}{16}$-inch bolt hole opposite each mark.

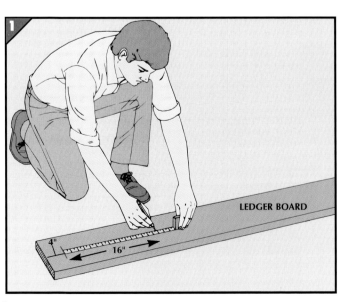

2. Installing the ledger board.

◆ Nail the board to the house wall—level, and $\frac{3}{4}$ inch below the porch-floor height.

◆ For a concrete foundation, bore $2\frac{1}{2}$ inches into the concrete through the lower holes with a hammer drill and a $\frac{3}{4}$-inch masonry bit, then seat expansion shields in the holes with the bit. Other foundation materials require a different approach (box, below).

◆ Fasten the ledger to the concrete with $\frac{1}{2}$- by 4-inch lag screws and washers.

◆ Secure the upper half of the ledger board according to your house framing (page 97).

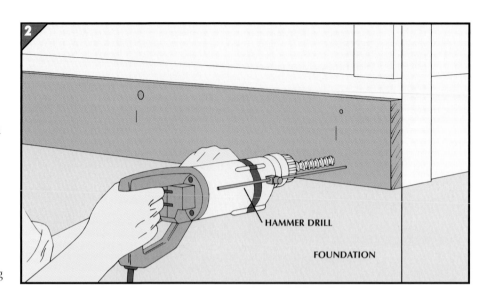

HAMMER DRILL

FOUNDATION

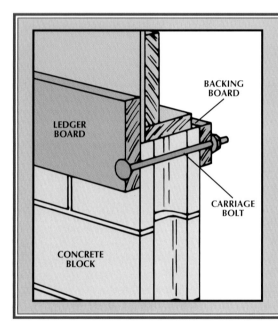

LEDGER BOARD

BACKING BOARD

CARRIAGE BOLT

CONCRETE BLOCK

Dealing with Other Types of Masonry

To attach a ledger board to brick, hollow block, or a veneered surface, bolt it through a backing board on the other side of the foundation. Doing so requires access to the ledger location from inside the foundation—simple enough in an unfinished basement or tall crawlspace, but more challenging in a finished basement.

Proceed by nailing the ledger in place and using ledger bolt holes (page 109) as guides to bore $\frac{3}{4}$-inch holes through the foundation with a hammer drill. Tack a 2-by-4 or wider backing board over the row of holes in the house interior, and use the foundation holes as guides to drill through the backing board. Place a $\frac{1}{2}$- by 12-inch carriage bolt in each hole. Inside the foundation, put a washer and nut on each bolt, and tighten securely.

PLANNING AND POURING FOOTINGS

1. Stakes for batter boards.

◆ Lay out a pattern of five small stakes as rough perimeter, or boundary, markers. Place stakes at the three corners of the porch and at the two points where the house walls, if extended, would intersect the perimeter (dotted lines).

◆ Cut sixteen 2-by-4 stakes about 1 foot longer than porch height for batter boards. Drive pairs of stakes about 2 feet outside the perimeter markers, then remove the markers.

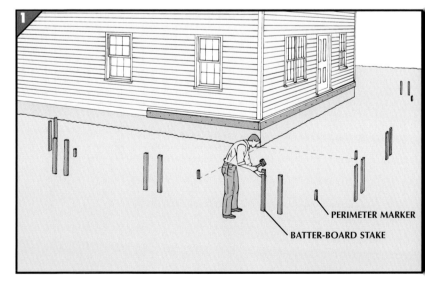

PERIMETER MARKER

BATTER-BOARD STAKE

2. Erecting batter boards.

◆ With a water level, mark the height of the top of the ledger board on the 2-by-4 stakes.

◆ Measure down from this mark a distance equal to the width of the ledger board ($7\frac{1}{2}$ inches for a 2-by-8) plus an amount for drainage—$\frac{1}{8}$ inch for each foot that the porch extends from the house. A mark at this point establishes pier height.

◆ Screw a 1-by-6 batter board to each pair of stakes with the top at pier height, making sure that the board is level.

3. Stringing boundary lines.

◆ Hammer nails partway into the bottom of the ledger, one nail 8 inches from each end and one at the central corner.

◆ Tie two lengths of mason's cord to the corner nail, then use the squaring method described on page 22, Step 1, to align each string perpendicular to a house wall. Where each string crosses a batter board, hammer a small nail and loop the string around it.

◆ To establish the perimeter of the porch (left), adapt the method for squaring a layout shown on page 94. To square the layout, measure the diagonals of the two rectangles and one square formed by the strings. The diagonals of each shape should be equal.

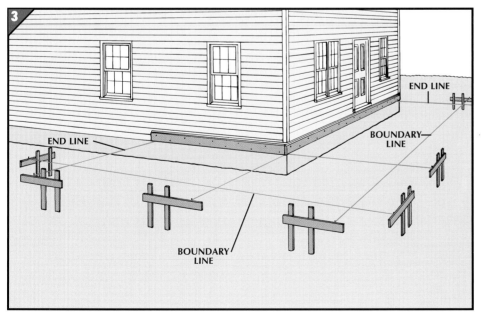

END LINE

END LINE

BOUNDARY LINE

BOUNDARY LINE

PIER
PERIMETER

4. Establishing footing locations.

◆ For footings between corners, mark evenly spaced pier centers on the boundary and end lines of each wing. Space them no farther apart than the maximum span allowed for doubled beams of your joist lumber—9 feet for 2-by-8s *(page 20).* Drop a plumb line 8 inches to either side of each mark and chalk an X as shown at left, then outline a 12- by 16-inch rectangle at each pier position.

◆ For the pier at the end of each wing, drop a plumb bob from the intersection of the boundary and end strings to establish the center of the pier. Chalk an X at that point, then outline a 12- by 16-inch rectangle on the ground, straddling the end line.

◆ Repeat the process at the boundary-line intersection to mark the corner of the pier at the central corner, but chalk a 16- by 16-inch square on the ground.

5. Constructing the footings.

◆ Unhook one end of each batter-board string.

◆ With a spade and a posthole digger, excavate footing holes at least 4 inches larger in each dimension than the outlines chalked on the ground. Dig 24 inches deep or 8 inches below the frostline, whichever is greater, then tamp the soil at the bottom to compact it.

◆ Pour concrete into each hole to a height 3 inches below ground level. Slice through the wet concrete with a spade in order to remove air bubbles and push large pebbles below the surface.

◆ Cover the footings with moist burlap and allow them to set for 24 to 48 hours.

6. Marking footings for piers.

◆ Reattach the boundary lines to the batter boards.

◆ Outline the shapes of the piers on the footings as you did on the ground in Step 4 above, using a try square to make accurate corners. Take down the boundary strings.

BUILDING BRICK PIERS

1. Laying the bricks.

◆ With a mason's trowel, spread a $\frac{3}{8}$-inch layer of mortar inside the pier outline. Furrow the mortar with the point of the trowel. Lay the first course of well-dampened bricks, buttering adjoining surfaces with $\frac{3}{8}$ inch of mortar. *(For a 16- by 16-inch pier, duplicate the pattern that is shown in the top inset at right.)*

◆ Trowel away excess mortar, then level and square the first course before laying the next.

◆ Stagger the joints in succeeding courses as shown in the bottom inset at right. At the end of each course, shape and smooth the joints with a convex jointer.

2. Completing the piers.

◆ When you have laid bricks to a point four or five courses below the planned height of the pier, gauge your progress with a mason's rule and a level set atop a batter board—or reattach the boundary line as a guide. If the distance to build is not an even multiple of the average height per course of the bricks you've already laid, adjust the thickness of the mortar joints on the remaining courses to compensate.

◆ After you have built all the piers, remove the batter boards and stakes.

MASON'S RULE

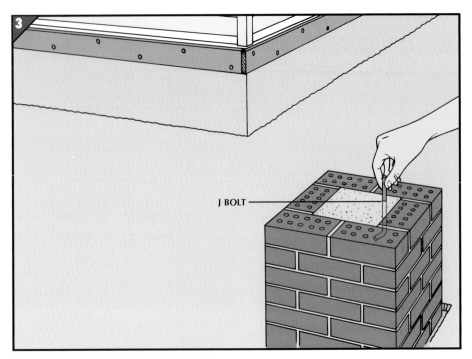

3. Installing J-bolt anchors.

◆ Fill the piers to a point 8 inches below the top with rubble such as stones and chipped brick, then with mortar to the top.

◆ Before the mortar dries, insert a $\frac{1}{2}$- by 8-inch J bolt in each pier. For the large corner pier *(left)*, position the J bolt so it will not obstruct the porch's corner joist. Elsewhere, plant the bolt in the center of the pier. In every case, allow $2\frac{1}{2}$ inches of bolt threads to protrude from the mortar.

J BOLT

WEATHERPROOFING THE LEDGER

1. Flashing the top and ends.

◆ Loosen or remove house siding above the ledger to allow for flashing installation.

◆ Follow the instructions on page 97 to install flashing at both ends of the ledger and along the top of both wings to within 3 inches of the house corner.

◆ Cut two pieces of flashing to make a cap for the ledger corner: Make one piece $7\frac{1}{2}$ inches by 6 inches, and the other $7\frac{1}{2}$ inches by 10 inches.

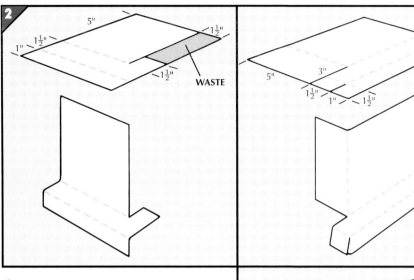

2. Fabricating corner pieces.

◆ Measure and mark the smaller piece of flashing as shown above, top. Cut along the solid lines with a utility knife, then using the edge of a table or a level, bend the flashing along the dotted lines to form the shape shown above, bottom.

◆ Follow the same procedure to mark, cut, and fold the larger piece of flashing into the shape in the illustration above right.

◆ The illustration at right shows how the two pieces overlap to protect the ledger corner.

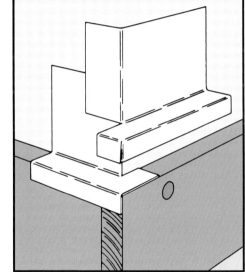

3. Installing corner flashing

◆ Slip the upper edge of the smaller piece under the house siding at the ledger corner. Nail the flashing to the face of the ledger.

◆ Lay a bead of caulk where the seam between the two corner pieces will lie.

◆ Install the larger corner flashing piece. Fit it snugly over the smaller piece of flashing and the corner of the ledger. Nail it to the ledger face.

◆ Caulk all flashing seams.

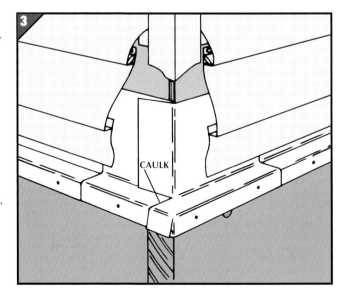

ASSEMBLING THE SUBSTRUCTURE

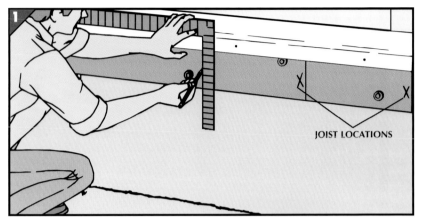

JOIST LOCATIONS

1. Establishing joist positions.

Align the body of a framing square with the top edge of the ledger at the end of one wing. Mark the sides of joist positions every 16 inches from the end of the ledger. To allow room for the installation of the doubled corner joist, adjust the position of the last full-length joist, if necessary, so it is no closer than 5 inches to the ledger corner.

CUT MARK

3"

2. Installing the first joists.

◆ On the top and the side of each pier, scribe a line 3 inches from the outer face of the pier and parallel to the house to mark the thickness of the double band beam.
◆ Select a piece of lumber for an end joist, crown it *(page 34)*, and position it as shown at left. Make a cut mark where the board crosses the line scribed on the pier.
◆ Cut the joist to length. Attach a multipurpose framing anchor to the end with joist-hanger nails, then nail the hanger to the ledger. Repeat the procedure for the joist at the end of the other wing.
◆ Install a joist at each of the remaining 12- by 16-inch piers, attaching them to the ledger with joist hangers. Pier joists may pass no closer than 2 inches from J bolts; shift the joists slightly along the ledger as needed to satisfy this requirement.

INNER BAND BEAM

3. Starting the inner band beam.

◆ Cut a piece of joist lumber to extend from an end joist to a point 3 inches beyond the joist resting on the adjacent pier, then nail it to the ends of both joists with three $3\frac{1}{2}$-inch nails *(left)*.
◆ Trim another beam section to reach 3 inches past the next joist and nail it in place. Work along both wings of the porch toward the corner pier. Where the band beams meet, nail through the face of one into the end of the other. *(Loose joints between band-beam sections will be secured in the next step when the band beam is doubled.)*
◆ Measure and cut joists to fit between the ledger board and the band beam *(above right)*. Attach one end of each joist to the ledger with a joist hanger and nail the band beam to the other end.

END JOIST

STRING

Compensating for an Uneven House Wall

A band beam will mimic undulations in a house wall unless you cut joists to compensate. To find the length for each joist, tie a string above the ledger to nails tapped into the narrow space between the ledger and the joists resting on the first and last small pier of each wing. Sight past the string to a tape measure at each joist location. Note how far the ledger bows in or out and add the distance to—or subtract it from—the length of either end joist, then cut a joist to that measure.

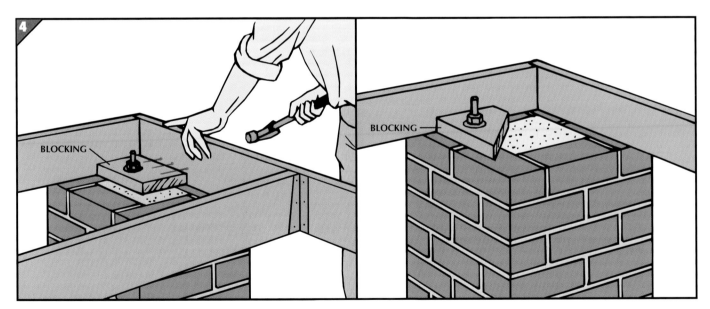

BLOCKING

BLOCKING

4. Securing the frame.

◆ To anchor the porch, select a scrap of joist lumber to serve as blocking. At the small piers (above, left), set the piece on top of the J bolt and against the band beam. Tap the blocking with a hammer and drill a $\frac{3}{4}$-inch hole at the resulting mark. Fasten the board to the bolt with a nut and a washer, then drive three nails through the band beam into the blocking.

◆ At the corner pier (above, right), fit blocking against one arm of the band beam, trimming as necessary to fit the blocking between the beam and the space to be occupied by the corner joist. Bolt the blocking in place, then nail the beam to it.

◆ Finish the band beam by installing a second, outer set of boards alongside those that are already nailed to the blocking. Cut the outer boards to offset the joints between them from the joints between the inner set. Nail the inner and outer beam boards to each other every 8 inches from alternate sides with three $2\frac{1}{2}$-inch nails. Drive additional nails on both sides of every joint.

5. Making a doubled corner joist.

◆ Measure the distance between the ledger corner and inside corner of the band beam. Mark this distance, plus $1\frac{1}{2}$ inches, on two pieces of joist lumber.

◆ Lay the boards edge to edge, crowns outward. Without turning the boards over, cut parallel 45° miters at the ends of each board, then set the boards face to face so that the miters form a point at one end and a V at the other. Nail the boards together from both sides at 16-inch intervals, staggering the rows of nails *(right)*.

◆ Nail a multipurpose framing anchor to each side of the joist at the V-shaped end *(inset)*.

◆ Install the joist, bending the hangers to fit the ledger. Use joist-hanger nails at the ledger, and drive 4-inch nails through the band beam into the pointed end of the joist.

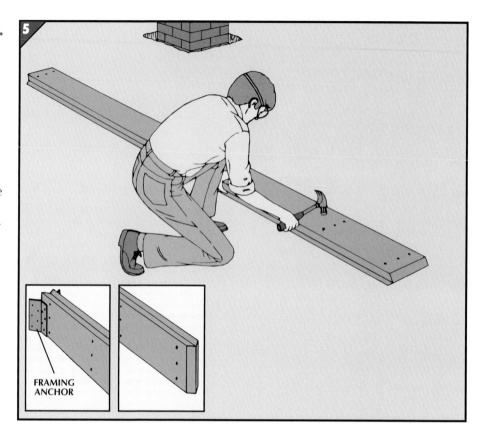

FRAMING ANCHOR

6. Installing jack joists.

◆ Starting at the corner, mark jack-joist positions 16 inches apart on the band beams.

◆ Measure from each mark to the corner joist and cut jack joists with one end mitered to a 45° angle.

◆ Tap a U-shaped joist hanger onto the outer end of each jack joist. While a helper holds the joist in place, nail the mitered end to the corner joist. Then nail the joist hanger to the beam and the joist.

◆ Install the rest of the jack joists, alternating sides as you work.

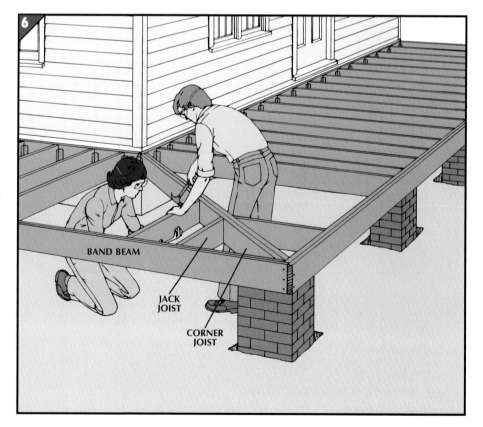

BAND BEAM

JACK JOIST

CORNER JOIST

LAYING FLOORBOARDS

1. Installing the outer rows.
◆ Cut the grooved edge from boards for the first row on one of the porch wings. Paint the cut edges with wood preservative.
◆ Starting where the wings meet, nail the first row of boards to the band beam, tongued edges toward the house, with $2\frac{1}{2}$-inch galvinized finishing nails every 16 inches. Position the boards so that their cut edges overhang the band beam by $1\frac{1}{2}$ inches, and allow the two end boards to overhang the corners about 3 inches.
◆ Trim the next few rows of boards so that their ends meet over joists, randomizing the joints. Before nailing a row of boards in place, measure their distance from the house wall at several points. Adjust the tongue-and-groove joint to make the boards parallel to the wall. Then tongue-nail each board in the row to every joist *(page 215, inset).*

MALLET

NAILER

2. Using a power nailer.
When you have installed at least four rows of boards, speed up the installation by using a power floor nailer. Continue to measure the distance between the boards and the house wall every few rows to be sure they are still parallel. Do not install the last three rows against the house.

3. Mitering floorboards at the corner.
◆ Tack a straight board to the floor parallel to the corner joist to serve as a saw guide. Position the guide so that the saw cuts the boards at the seam in the two-piece joist.
◆ Install flooring for the second wing, precutting 45° angles on board ends that abut the first wing.
◆ Precut and install the last three rows of boards on both wings. Nail through the face of each board into the joists below, taking care not to pierce the ledger flashing. If necessary, trim the last row of boards lengthwise to fit under the siding.
◆ Trim the boards at the end of each wing, leaving a $1\frac{3}{4}$-inch overhang.
◆ Sink exposed nailheads; fill the holes with wood putty.

The All-Important Stairway

To do a large porch justice, a stairway should be wide enough to span the distance between the centers of two piers. For solidity underfoot, plan to install the carriages that support the steps no more than 30 inches apart. Although dimensions can vary, a stairway with carriages cut for steps 7 to 8 inches high and 10 inches deep are the safest and most comfortable to climb.

Getting Ready: Have on hand all the materials you need before beginning the job. In all likelihood, you will have to not only crosscut tread stock—$1\frac{1}{4}$-by-12 lumber with one edge rounded—and risers to length but also rip them to width. Coat with wood preservative any lumber that is not pressure treated. Plan to install the carriages and blocking within 48 hours of pouring the concrete base for the stairs.

MATERIALS

2-by-2s	1-inch fascia and riser
2-by-12s	stock
$1\frac{1}{4}$-inch tread	$1\frac{5}{8}$-inch lath
stock	Wood lattice

1. Positioning the base.
◆ Mark the total run of the stairway on top of a mason's level with tape.
◆ Butt the level against the band beam under the flooring, and hold a folding ruler perpendicular to the level at the tape. Set the level aside and chalk an X where the ruler touches the ground. Connect this mark and two others made the same way with a line the width of the stairway, then outline a trench 2 inches in front of the line, 12 inches behind it, and 6 inches beyond each end.
◆ Dig the trench 4 inches deep and fill it with concrete to grade (page 61).
◆ Recalculate the total rise from the concrete surface and make any necessary adjustments in riser height.

BAND BEAM

MASKING TAPE

2. Making the carriages.
◆ Mark a 2-by-12 with the unit rise and unit run —7 inches and 10 inches in this case—as shown on page 62, making the bottom riser shorter than the others by the thickness of the tread stock. Draw the carriage-back line as shown at right.
◆ Cut out the carriage and check the fit. Remake the piece if the distance between the top tread and the surface of the porch floor is not exactly equal to the thickness of the tread stock.
◆ Use the carriage as a template for the others.

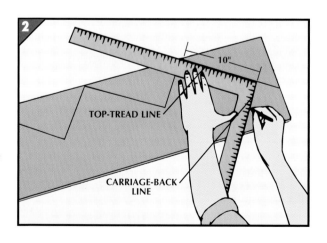

10"

TOP-TREAD LINE

CARRIAGE-BACK LINE

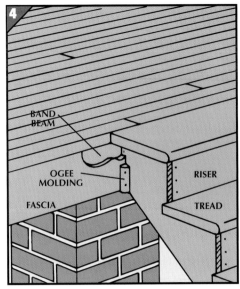

3. Attaching the carriages.

◆ Cut eight pieces of blocking from joist stock to fit between carriages when they are evenly spaced across the width of the stairway.

◆ Rest the center carriage against the band beam. Nail a piece of blocking to the band beam so that the blocking touches the carriage, then nail through the carriage into the blocking. Fasten another length of blocking to the band beam to sandwich the center carriage.

◆ Working from the center outward, anchor the tops of the remaining carriages to blocking.

◆ At the bottom of the stairway, set blocking between an end carriage and an adjacent one. Nail the blocking to the concrete base with $2\frac{1}{2}$-inch masonry nails, then fasten the carriages to the blocking. Install the remaining three pieces of blocking.

4. Adding risers and treads.

◆ From 1-inch stock, cut risers to fit as shown above, and fasten them with $3\frac{1}{2}$-inch galvanized finishing nails.

◆ Trim tread stock for a 1-inch overhang at the front and sides of each step; nail the treads to the carriages.

◆ Make fascia boards from 1-inch lumber, mitering the ends at porch corners for a finished appearance. Attach the fascia to the band beam with galvanized finishing nails.

◆ Cover the seam between the fascia and carriages with ogee molding.

◆ Countersink all nailheads and fill the holes with wood putty.

SKIRTS TO HIDE A CRAWLSPACE

Constructing lattice screens.

◆ Build a 2-by-2 frame to fit between adjacent piers. Nail a section of prefabricated lattice to the frame, then trim the lattice flush. Cover lattice edges with strips of $1\frac{5}{8}$-inch lath.

◆ Attach 2-by-4 furring strips to the sides of the brick piers with masonry nails driven into mortar joints. Position the furring strips so the screen fits snugly against the inner face of the overhanging fascia.

◆ Nail the lattice frame to the furring strips and the fascia.

◆ Countersink all exposed nailheads and fill the holes with wood putty.

◆ Adapt this procedure to make triangular-shaped lattice screens for the sides of the stairway.

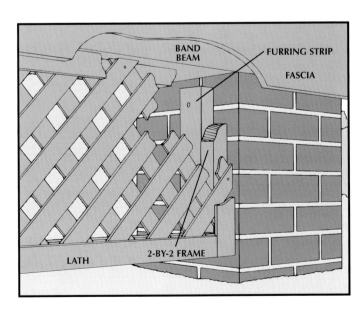

A Hip Roof for a Wraparound Porch

The real trick to roof framing is cutting rafters—common and jack rafters for the wings and a hip rafter at the corner. There is more to these angled boards than meets the eye. The main challenge is to cut a notch called a bird's mouth where the outer end of the rafter rests on a header that supports the roof at the eaves.

The Ideal Pitch: For a porch of a given width, the location and depth of the bird's mouth depend primarily on the pitch of the roof. Most porch roofs have the same slope as the roof of the house they are attached to. To measure the slope of an existing roof, adapt the technique on page 120, Step 1, to measure the number of inches rise per foot of run, a figure called the unit rise.

Because a porch roof may approach second-story window sills no closer than 3 inches, you may have to settle for a gentler slope. The box opposite explains how to predict this outcome, once you know the dimensions of the rafter stock you need. For a porch up to 8 feet wide, use 2-by-6s. Porches between 8 feet and 11 feet wide demand 2-by-8s.

Adjusting Pitch: Decrease the slope if the ideal pitch brings the roof too close to second-story windows. Roofing materials impose limits on this reduction. With a unit rise of 4 or more you may use any material you like—tile, slate, cedar shakes, or asphalt shingles. But a unit rise of 3 disqualifies all but asphalt shingles. Shallower slopes require a built-up roof. Consider lowering the porch-ceiling height—8 feet is standard— slightly to meet the 3-inch limit—or consult a roofer.

Lumber Sizes: Use common-rafter stock for the header, joists, ledger boards, and jack rafters. The hip rafter at the corner and rafter plates attached to the house require boards 2 inches wider.

Porch posts are generally 4-by-4s, but if piers are more than 9 feet apart, use 6-by-6s.

TOOLS

Framing square
Plumb bob
Circular saw
Carpenter's level
Handsaw or saber
    saw

MATERIALS

2-by-4s
2-by-6s, 2-by-8s, or
    2-by-10s

1-by-6s or 1-by-8s
Plywood ($\frac{1}{2}$-inch)
Lag screws ($\frac{1}{2}$- by
    $3\frac{1}{2}$-inch and $\frac{3}{8}$- by
    5-inch)
Joist hangers
Framing, post, and

rafter anchors
15-pound roofing
    felt and nails
Aluminum drip edge
Asphalt shingles
Ridge venting
Aluminum flashing

Self-sealing roofing
    nails
Galvanized common
    nails ($1\frac{1}{2}$-, $2\frac{1}{2}$-,
    and 3-inch)
Gutters and down-
    spouts

Anatomy of a wraparound porch roof.

Joists and sloping boards called common rafters form the skeleton of a porch roof. The corner is shaped by a hip rafter and shorter jack rafters, elements mimicked by a corner joist and jack joists below them. Joists and rafters are anchored at one end to plates fastened to the house wall, and at the other to a header supported by posts centered over brick piers. Asphalt shingles laid over roofing felt and $\frac{1}{2}$-inch plywood sheathing keep out the weather. At the rafter plate, a strip of venting material covered by aluminum flashing promotes air circulation between rafters and joists. A tongue-and-groove ceiling hides the joists. Horizontal boards called lookouts give a nailing surface for the ceiling along the eaves and for the fascia.

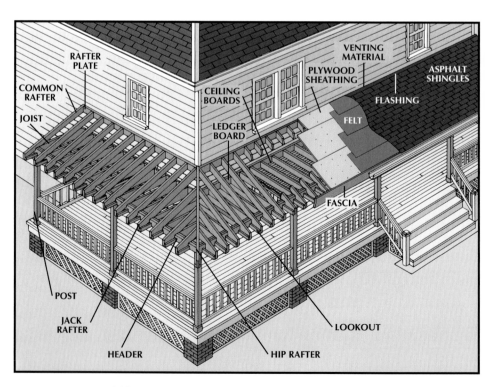

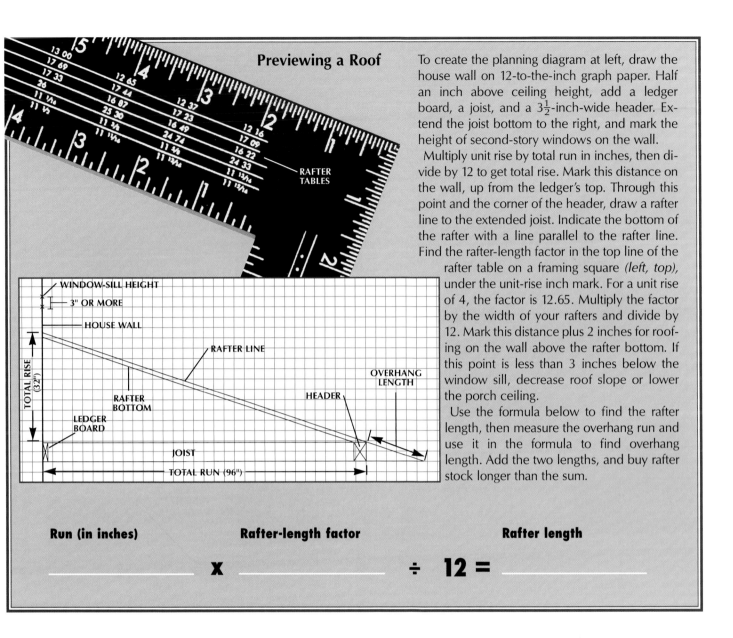

Previewing a Roof

RAFTER TABLES

WINDOW-SILL HEIGHT
3" OR MORE
HOUSE WALL
RAFTER LINE
TOTAL RISE (32")
OVERHANG LENGTH
RAFTER BOTTOM
HEADER
LEDGER BOARD
JOIST
TOTAL RUN (96")

To create the planning diagram at left, draw the house wall on 12-to-the-inch graph paper. Half an inch above ceiling height, add a ledger board, a joist, and a $3\frac{1}{2}$-inch-wide header. Extend the joist bottom to the right, and mark the height of second-story windows on the wall.

Multiply unit rise by total run in inches, then divide by 12 to get total rise. Mark this distance on the wall, up from the ledger's top. Through this point and the corner of the header, draw a rafter line to the extended joist. Indicate the bottom of the rafter with a line parallel to the rafter line. Find the rafter-length factor in the top line of the rafter table on a framing square *(left, top)*, under the unit-rise inch mark. For a unit rise of 4, the factor is 12.65. Multiply the factor by the width of your rafters and divide by 12. Mark this distance plus 2 inches for roofing on the wall above the rafter bottom. If this point is less than 3 inches below the window sill, decrease roof slope or lower the porch ceiling.

Use the formula below to find the rafter length, then measure the overhang run and use it in the formula to find overhang length. Add the two lengths, and buy rafter stock longer than the sum.

Run (in inches)   **Rafter-length factor**   **Rafter length**

$$ \text{_____} \times \text{_____} \div 12 = \text{_____} $$

THE CORRECT HEIGHT FOR A RAFTER PLATE

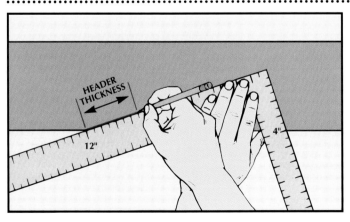

HEADER THICKNESS
12"
4"

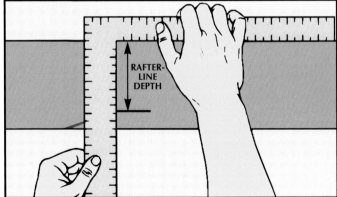

RAFTER-LINE DEPTH

Positioning a rafter line.
Before erecting the rafter plate, determine how much of the width of a rafter will lie above the theoretical roof rise.

◆ Set a framing square on a board of common-rafter stock and align the unit run on the outside of the body—12—and the unit rise—in this case, 4—on the outer edge of the

tongue with the edge of the board as shown *(above, left)*. Starting at the 12, draw a line of a length equal to the thickness of the header—$3\frac{1}{2}$ inches in this example.

◆ Place the square as shown above, and measure the vertical distance from the top edge of the board to the end of the slanted line. This is the rafter-line depth.

SUPPORTS FOR THE ROOF

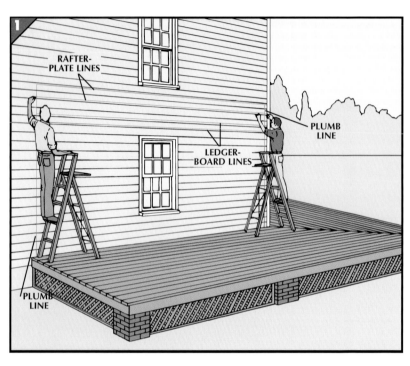

RAFTER-PLATE LINES

PLUMB LINE

LEDGER-BOARD LINES

PLUMB LINE

1. Snapping chalk lines for plates.

◆ For each wing of the porch, snap two plumb chalk lines on the house wall—one 3 inches in from the end of the wing, the other near the house corner. Snap a horizontal chalk line 8 feet, $\frac{1}{2}$ inch above the porch floor to mark the bottom of the ledger board, then add a line to mark the top of the ledger board.

◆ Measure up from this line a distance equal to the sum of the total rise and the rafter-line depth *(page 123)*—plus 2 inches to allow for roofing materials. Snap a horizontal chalk line at this height. Two inches plus the width of the rafter plate lower on the wall, snap another.

◆ Remove the siding at the ledger-board and rafter-plate positions *(page 96)*.

◆ Cut ledgers and rafter plates to overlap at the corner, and attach them to floor framing *(page 97)* or fasten them to studs in the wall with lag screws. Set the bottom edge of the rafter plate against the bottom of the opening in the siding.

POST SUPPORT

WASHER

BAND BEAM

2. Installing post anchors.

◆ On each wing, snap a chalk line along the floor, directly above the outer face of the band beam. Set post anchors at the lines *(inset)*: 3 inches in from the end of each wing, one at the intersection of chalk lines above the large corner pier, and one above the center of each noncorner pier.

◆ Place an offset washer in the base of each anchor, and mark the washer hole on the floor. Drill a $\frac{5}{16}$-inch hole 5 inches deep through the floor into the band beam.

◆ Fasten each anchor to the porch with a 5- by $\frac{3}{8}$-inch lag screw. Set a post support in each anchor.

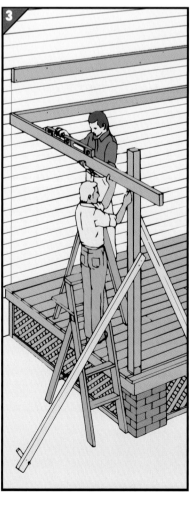

3. Erecting posts.

◆ Set a post, slightly taller than porch-ceiling height, in the anchor at the end of one wing; brace it plumb with scrap 2-by-4s.

◆ Tack a joist to the end of the ledger board. While a helper holds the board level, mark the position of its bottom edge on the post. Take down the post and the joist. Similarly, mark a post for the outer end of the other porch wing. Cut and compare the two posts. If they are the same length, cut all of the posts to that length. Otherwise, custom measure and cut each post.

◆ Nail a post-and-beam connector to the top of each post except the one at the corner, then set each post in its anchor and drive nails partway through the anchor and into the wood. Brace the posts plumb with 2-by-4s.

4. Installing headers.

◆ Cut a pair of joist-stock boards to fit between the outside edge of one wing's end post and the middle of the adjacent post. Put a piece of $\frac{1}{2}$-inch plywood between the boards, and nail the assembly every 8 inches on alternate sides with three 3-inch nails. Make other headers to fit between the centers of adjacent posts, ending at the last post before the corner.

◆ Set the headers atop the posts, and nail them to the post connectors; toenail the abutting ends of adjacent headers together. Install headers on the other wing.

◆ For the corner, build header sections long enough to extend across the top of the corner post, then miter the ends of the headers at a 45° angle (inset); nail the headers to each other and toenail them to the post.

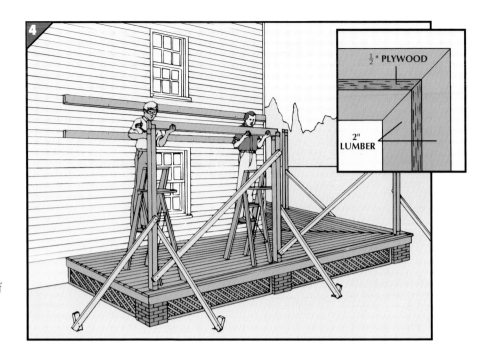

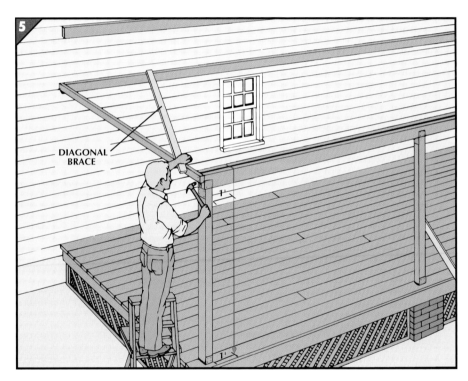

DIAGONAL BRACE

5. Squaring the frame.

◆ Tack a 2-by-4 to the ledger board and the header (above). Lay a second 2-by-4 on the first and tack one end 4 feet along the ledger board to make a diagonal brace for the header. Remove the braces installed at the end post in Step 3 (left).

◆ Mark the header and the floor 1 foot from the end post, then use a plumb line to align the marks. Nail the diagonal brace to the 2-by-4 linking the ledger board and header. Add a second brace at the midpoint of the wing. Steady the other wing in the same way, then finish the nailing begun in Step 3 to secure the posts to the anchors.

◆ Beginning 4 inches from the corner of the house, install ceiling joists every 16 inches along each wing, attaching them with joist hangers. Remove header braces as you approach them. Toenail end joists to the ledger and header. Install corner joists and jack joists as for a floor (page 118, Steps 4 and 5). When all joists are in place, remove the remaining post braces.

CUTTING AND INSTALLING COMMON RAFTERS

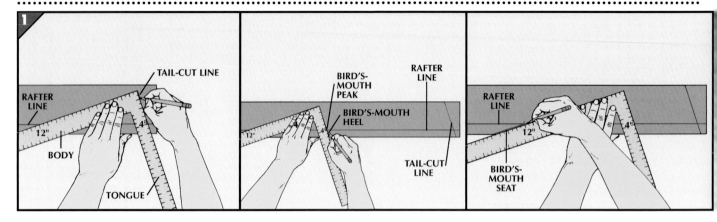

TAIL-CUT LINE

RAFTER LINE

12"

BODY

TONGUE

4"

BIRD'S-MOUTH PEAK

RAFTER LINE

BIRD'S-MOUTH HEEL

TAIL-CUT LINE

12" 4" 4"

RAFTER LINE

12" 4"

BIRD'S-MOUTH SEAT

1. Marking tail and bird's-mouth cuts.

◆ With a chalk line, snap a rafter line along a rafter board at the depth established on page 123.
◆ Place a framing square near one end of the board, with the 12 on the body and the unit rise on the tongue touch-

ing the rafter line. Draw a line along the tongue, then extend it across the board to establish the tail-cut line (*above, left*).
◆ Measuring from the tail-cut line, mark the overhang length on the rafter line to establish the peak of the bird's mouth. Set the unit-rise number at the

peak and the 12 on the rafter line, and draw the heel of the bird's mouth —a line from the peak to the bottom edge of the rafter (*above, center*). Next, set the 12 at the peak and the unit-rise number on the rafter line, and draw the seat of the bird's mouth (*above, right*).

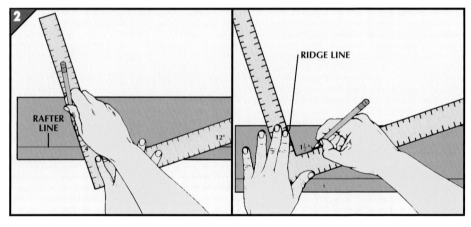

RAFTER LINE

12"

RIDGE LINE

12" 1½"

2. Establishing the ridge cut.

◆ Mark the rafter length, measured from the bird's-mouth peak, on the rafter line. Place the unit-rise number on the framing square at the rafter-length mark and the 12 on the rafter line, then draw a ridge line along the tongue (*far left*).
◆ To adjust rafter length for rafter-plate thickness, lay the tongue's inner edge along the ridge line as shown at left and mark two points $1\frac{1}{2}$ inches from the ridge line. Draw the ridge-cut line through the points.

3. Testing the rafter for fit.

◆ Make the ridge cut and the tail cut on the rafter with a circular saw. Use a saber saw or a handsaw to cut the bird's mouth.
◆ With a helper holding the rafter flush with the face and the end of the rafter plate, set the bird's mouth on the header. Recut the rafter if you find any gaps greater than $\frac{1}{8}$ inch at the rafter plate or bird's mouth (*the tip of the rafter may be higher than the top edge of the rafter plate*). When you have a rafter that fits properly, use it as a template for the remaining common rafters (*inset*).

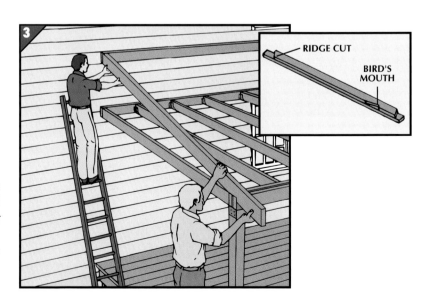

RIDGE CUT

BIRD'S MOUTH

4. Installing common rafters.

◆ Use a plumb bob to help mark the rafter plate directly above the side of each joist facing the porch corner, except for the two joists nearest the corner. For them, mark the plates $1\frac{1}{2}$ inches from the corner.

◆ At each rafter position, nail a multipurpose framing anchor to the rafter plate so that it will not intrude between plate and rafter. Fasten wing-shaped rafter anchors to the header to meet the opposite face of each rafter.

◆ Attach each rafter to the plate and the header, nailing into the rafter face through the framing anchor and through the wing-shaped rafter anchor at the header *(inset)*.

ADDING HIP AND JACK RAFTERS

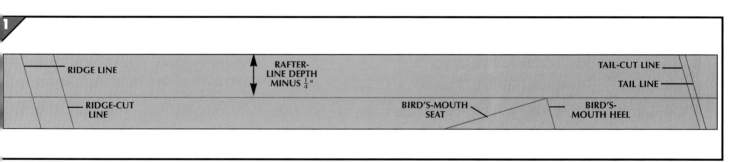

RIDGE LINE

RAFTER-LINE DEPTH MINUS $\frac{1}{4}$"

TAIL-CUT LINE

TAIL LINE

RIDGE-CUT LINE

BIRD'S-MOUTH SEAT

BIRD'S-MOUTH HEEL

1. Making a hip rafter.

◆ Find the length of the hip rafter and its overhang with the formula on page 123. Use common-rafter total run and overhang run in the calculation, but consult the second line of the framing square's rafter table for the reference number.

◆ With a chalk line, snap a rafter line along the rafter board at the depth from the rafter's top edge established on page 123, less $\frac{1}{4}$ inch to compensate

for roof sheathing. Using the number 17 on the body of the square, draw the tail line, the bird's mouth, and the ridge line on the rafter *(page 126, Step 1)*.

◆ For the ridge cut, adjust the ridge line *(page 126, Step 2)* by $3\frac{5}{8}$ inches instead of $1\frac{1}{2}$ inches to compensate for the thickness of the rafter-plate corner. Apply the same procedure to draw a tail-cut line $\frac{3}{4}$ inch closer to the bird's mouth than the tail line. Extend the tail- and ridge-cut lines across the top

and bottom edges of the rafter board with a try square, then connect these lines on the other face of the board.

◆ Cut out the bird's mouth with a saber saw. Set a circular saw at 45° and trim the rafter board along the ridge- and tail-cut lines on both faces to form V-shaped ends on the rafter.

◆ Install the hip rafter by nailing through the common rafters into the ridge end of the hip rafter, then toe-nailing it to the header.

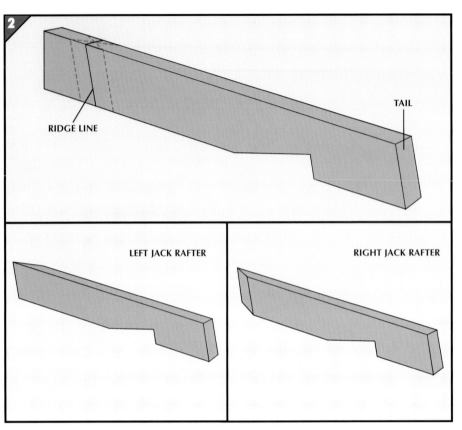

RIDGE LINE

TAIL

LEFT JACK RAFTER

RIGHT JACK RAFTER

2. Cutting the first jack rafters.

◆ Find the length in inches of the two shortest jack rafters under the unit-rise number in the third line of the rafter table, and add to it the overhang length of a common rafter. On boards slightly longer than this sum, mark rafter-line depth, then cut a bird's mouth and the rafter tail cut—all as for a common rafter *(pages 123 and 126)*. Locate and draw the ridge line *(left, top)* at rafter length minus $1\frac{1}{8}$ inches— half the diagonal thickness of the hip rafter—from the peak of the bird's mouth.

◆ On the rafter destined for the left side of the hip rafter, adjust the ridge line away from the tail $\frac{3}{4}$ inch *(blue dotted line)* as shown on page 126, Step 2. On the right-side joist, move the ridge line $\frac{3}{4}$ inch toward the tail *(red dotted line)*.

◆ Set a circular saw at 45° and make the ridge cuts for each side of the hip rafter as shown at left, bottom.

3. Installing the jack rafters.

◆ Cut the remaining jack rafters using one of the short jacks as a template for the tail and bird's-mouth cuts. Mark and cut the ridge bevels as in Step 2, increasing the length of each successive rafter by the number under the unit rise on the third line of the rafter table on the framing square.

◆ Starting with the shortest jack rafters, install each pair in succession, taking care not to bow the hip rafter. Face-nail the jacks to the hip rafter and attach them to the header with rafter anchors.

SHEATHING AND SHINGLES

1. A foundation for shingles.

◆ Lay sheets of Type C-D $\frac{1}{2}$-inch plywood horizontally, C side up, overhanging the rafter tails by $\frac{3}{4}$ inch and the end rafters by 3 inches. Leave $\frac{1}{16}$-inch—$\frac{1}{8}$-inch in very humid climates—expansion gaps between courses. Trim sheets so the ends rest on rafters and the joints of successive courses are staggered. Nail the plywood to the rafters with $1\frac{1}{2}$-inch nails, spacing the nails 6 inches apart at joints and 1 foot apart elsewhere. At the porch corner, trim the sheets for a $\frac{1}{8}$-inch gap at the center of the hip rafter. Leave a 1-inch ventilation opening between the top edge of the sheathing and the rafter plate.

◆ Unroll 15-pound roofing felt even with bottom edge of the plywood and tack the felt to the sheathing every few feet with wide-headed paper nails, ending 1 foot past the hip. Lay succeeding courses of felt to overlap earlier ones by 2 inches.

◆ Along the eave line, install an aluminum drip edge *(inset)*. Secure it with roofing nails driven every foot.

⚠ **CAUTION** *Install temporary 2-by-4 footholds for added security when working on the roof.*

ROOFING FELT

DRIP EDGE

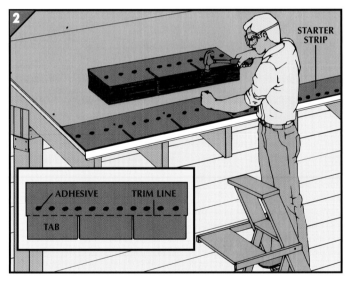

STARTER STRIP

ADHESIVE   TRIM LINE

TAB

2. Laying the first row of shingles.

◆ Trim the tabs from a section of roofing to make a starter strip *(inset)*, then cut 6 inches from one end. Lay the strip in the corner formed by the drip edge and the end of a wing, then fasten it with three roofing nails along the center. Cut and lay full-length starter strips end to end along the eaves.

◆ Lay the first row of shingles on top of the starter course, overhanging porch-wing ends by $\frac{1}{2}$ inch. Fasten each section with $1\frac{1}{4}$-inch roofing nails driven $\frac{5}{8}$ inch above the slots that divide the strip into tabs. Place a nail above each slot and 1 inch from each end. At the corner, trim the shingles along the hip rafter.

3. Working up the roof.

◆ Shorten by 6 inches—half a tab—the first section of shingles in each successive course. Align the cut end with the end of the first shingle in the previous course, adjusting overlap to match the house roof. If the tab at the hip will be shorter than 6 inches, cut half a tab from the preceding section of shingles before laying the last section next to it.

◆ Adjust shingle overlap on the last few courses, if necessary, so that the top row will be at least 6 inches wide. Trim the shingles along the top edge of the sheathing.

WASTE

ADHESIVE

HIP SHINGLES

4. Adding hip shingles.

◆ Make hip shingles by cutting shingle sections into three pieces at the slots, then rounding the upper ends *(inset)*. Fold one shingle down the center and set it at the eave line, then place another folded shingle at the house wall. With the aid of a helper, snap chalk lines down both sides of the hip to mark the edges of the hip shingles.

◆ Beginning at the eave, lay folded shingle tabs between the chalk lines, matching the overlap on the hip of the house roof. Fasten the shingles with a nail on each side, 2 inches above the spots of adhesive on each tab and 1 inch in from the edge.

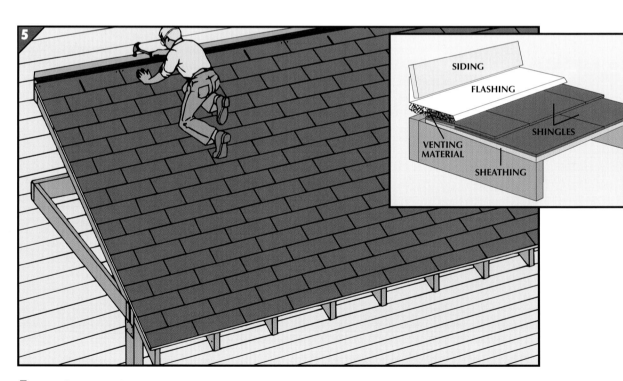

SIDING

FLASHING

SHINGLES

VENTING
MATERIAL

SHEATHING

5. Venting and flashing.

◆ Nail a strip of venting material along the top edge of the roof as shown above, following the manufacturer's instructions.

◆ Install aluminum flashing over the venting material *(inset)*. Buy flashing wide enough to extend 4 inches under the house siding and 1 inch beyond the venting material.

◆ Nail the flashing through the venting material and shingles, and into the roof sheathing at 1-foot intervals. Use self-sealing roofing nails, which are fitted with silicone or neoprene washers.

 CAUTION *Overhammering the nails will crush the venting material.*

SIDE ENCLOSURES AND SOFFIT SUPPORTS

1. Installing lookouts.

◆ Use a level to mark the tail of each rafter flush with the bottom edge of the header, then saw the rafter along the line. Cut 2-by-4 lookouts to fit against the header and even with each rafter tail.

◆ Set the lower edge of the lookout flush with the bottom of the header and the newly cut edge at the rafter overhang. Face-nail the lookout to the rafter, then toenail it to the header (top inset).

◆ Cut a lookout for each side of the hip rafter (bottom inset), making parallel 45° bevels on both ends. Fit the lookouts to the header and hip rafter as in the bottom inset.

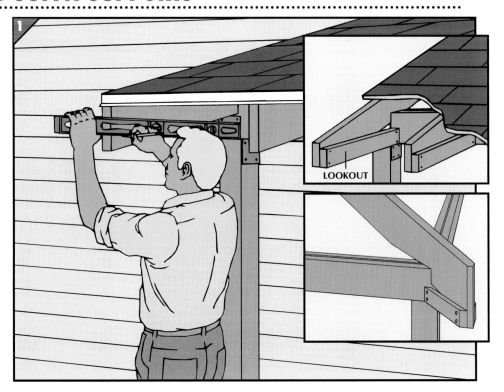

2. Enclosing the ends of the roof.

◆ Cut a piece of $\frac{1}{2}$-inch exterior-grade plywood to cover the triangular space created by the rafter and the joist at the end of each wing. Extend the plywood $\frac{1}{2}$ inch below the bottom of the joist to cover the ends of ceiling boards (page 133). Nail the plywood cover to the rafter and the joist.

◆ From a 1-inch board the same width as a rafter, cut a rake board that matches the common rafters both in length and in the angle of the ridge and tail cuts. Butt the rake against the underside of the plywood sheathing and nail it to the plywood cover. If the plywood sheathing on the roof extends past the outer face of the rake, trim the corner with a strip of quarter-round molding.

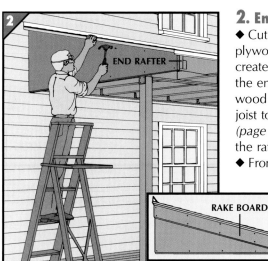

3. Adding a fascia and gutters.

◆ Make fascia boards from 1-inch lumber about 2 inches wider than the depth of rafter tails. Cut the boards so that joints fall at the centers of the tails.

◆ Slip the fascia into the space between the tails and the drip edge, lining up the outer end of the fascia with the outer face of the rake board. Nail the fascia to the rafter tails. At the corner where the two wings meet, miter the ends of the fascia board at a 45° angle.

◆ Attach gutters to the fascia and downspouts to the corner post and end posts according to the manufacturer's instructions (inset).

Ceilings and railings, the finishing touches to a porch, are made of specially milled lumber called porch stock. For ceilings, it consists of tongue-and-groove boards $\frac{1}{2}$ inch thick and 3 inches wide with a bead down the center. These are generally installed from the house wall to the eaves, forming one continuous surface *(below)*.

To allow air to circulate within the enclosed space above the ceiling, screened vents are installed in the ceiling boards of the overhang. The vents are available in several shapes and sizes at hardware stores; your local building code will specify the correct size and spacing for your area.

Wood for Railings: Cap-rail stock for the upper railing is milled with a 1-inch-wide groove on the underside to accept the tops of 1-by-1 pickets. The picket bottoms fit against the angled face of bottom-rail stock as shown on the facing page. All three elements can be purchased specially milled for decorative effect, but they also come in the standard stock shown here, available in 16-foot lengths that can be cut to fit any porch.

MATERIALS

Ceiling boards
4-by-4s
Parting bead
Vents
Cap-rail stock
Bottom-rail stock
Pickets
Post caps
Ogee molding

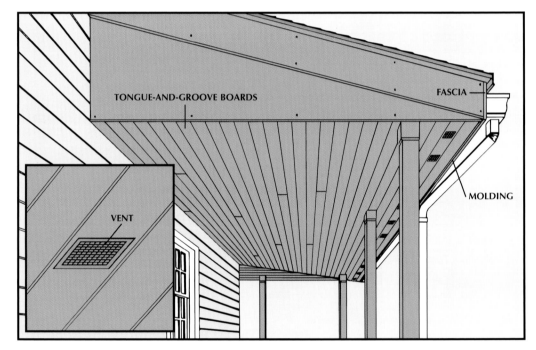

A tongue-and-groove porch ceiling.

◆ Starting at the wall of the house, face-nail tongue-and-groove boards to the ceiling joists with 2-inch finishing nails. Where the two wings meet, miter the ceiling boards to join at a 45° angle. At the ends of the porch, butt the ceiling boards against the inside of the plywood triangle that encloses the roof. Notch the ceiling boards to fit around porch posts.
◆ Finish the ceiling by nailing flat molding such as parting bead around the perimeter of the ceiling to conceal ceiling board joints with the plywood triangles and fascia boards.
◆ Cut holes in the ceiling at the center of the overhang for placement of screened vents *(inset)*.
◆ Before painting, set all nails and fill the holes with putty.

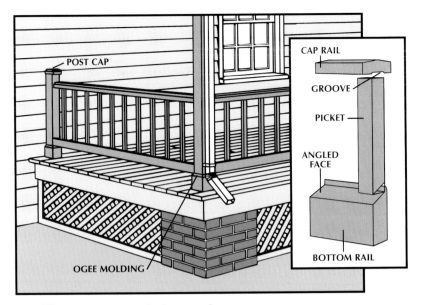

POST CAP

CAP RAIL

GROOVE

PICKET

ANGLED FACE

BOTTOM RAIL

OGEE MOLDING

A railing to surround the porch.

◆ Between porch posts, install 4-by-4 railing posts cut 2 inches longer than the height of the railing as specified by building codes. Mount the uprights on post anchors, placing one post flush against the house at the end of each wing. Install others between porch posts as required by code. Cover the post anchors with 1-by-4 lumber finished with $\frac{1}{2}$-inch ogee molding, and top each post with a post cap.

◆ Toenail the bottom rails to the posts above the molding and with the angled face toward the house, then toenail cap rails to the posts.

◆ Cut a 1-by-1 picket to fit between the rails, mitering one end to the angle of the bottom rail *(inset)*. Use the first picket as a template for marking others. Drill pilot holes to prevent splitting, then toenail the pickets to the rails so that the gaps between pickets are less than 4 inches wide.

A railing for the porch stairs.

◆ Cut posts for the bottom of the stairs to the same height as the other railing posts *(left)*, and fasten them with post anchors to the concrete footing directly against each side of the bottom step, notching the bottom tread as needed. Cover the anchor with trim.

◆ Miter the bottom and cap rails to fit snugly between the posts at the top and bottom of the stairs.

◆ Cut pickets as for the porch railing, then miter the tops and bottoms to match the slope of the railing *(inset)*. Toenail the pickets into place.

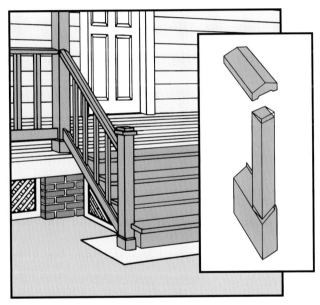

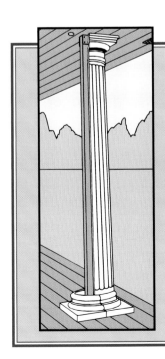

Classical Columns for Purists

A porch on a large house can benefit from posts that are more substantial in appearance than the basic 4-by-4 supports. The simplest to add are the hollow variety that enclose existing posts *(left)*. Available from most large lumberyards in lengths from 8 to 20 feet, they can be ordered made of wood or aluminum, with plain or fluted columns, and topped with a choice of capitals, including some styled after ancient Greek architecture *(right)*. All such columns come split in half for ease of installation.

Columns require weatherproofing whether made of aluminum or wood. Coat the inside with roofing compound to a height of 2 feet. Ventilate the column with two holes in the porch ceiling, one inside the column, the other within 1 foot of the exterior. If the capital protrudes past the fascia, install a strip of aluminum flashing to deflect rain.

IONIC

CORINTHIAN

5

Benches, Planters, Screens, and Skirts

Although a bare deck may be perfectly serviceable, a few additional details will make it feel really homey. Built-in benches provide convenient seating, planters allow you to brighten the deck with flowers and shrubs, and overheads and screens provide shade and privacy. Skirting the outside of a high deck turns unused space into convenient storage.

Built-In Seating   **136**

A Backless Bench
Creating a Storage Area
A Bench with a Back
Benches for the Perimeter

Planters   **146**

Building a Planter

A Screen for Privacy   **150**

Putting Up Boards and Lattice

Skirting the Deck   **154**

Hanging the Boards
Adding a Door

Shade for a Summer's Day   **160**

Erecting a Structural Support
Shade from Slanted Louvers
Sun Shields of Woven Reeds or Snow Fencing
The Versatility of Ordinary Lumber

Adding Screens to Bugproof a Porch   **166**

Framing Alternatives
Studs and Knee Rails
Attaching Screening Directly to the Porch
Securing the Mesh with Spline Molding
Hanging a Wood-framed Storm Door

Benches provide permanent seating on a deck and can be supplemented by outdoor furniture. Built-in units can define areas for eating or conversation, guide traffic flow, or break up long expanses of railing.

Styles: On a low deck, you can build a simple backless bench around the perimeter *(below)*. For a higher level, position such a bench against the railing or build a sloping back that is attached to the railing posts *(pages 140-143)*.

You can also close in the structure to create a storage area *(pages 138-139)*. With either style, make the seat slats of lumber that complements other deck features, such as the decking and stair treads.

Designing for Comfort: Build benches from 15 to 18 inches high, and make seats 12 to 15 inches deep. Slope bench backs at about 15°, with the back slat 12 inches above the seat.

 TOOLS

Combination square
Carpenter's square

Circular saw
Electric drill
Screwdriver
Hand plane

 MATERIALS

Pressure-treated
  2 x 2s, 2 x 4s,
  2 x 6s

Plywood ($\frac{1}{8}$")
Pressure-treated
  5/4 x 4 stock
Deck screws ($2\frac{1}{2}$")
Butt hinges (3" x 3")

 SAFETY TIPS

Put on goggles when using a power tool. Add a dust mask to cut pressure-treated wood, and wash your hands thoroughly after handling the wood.

A BACKLESS BENCH

Anatomy of the bench.

The bench at right has a frame made of 2-by-6s beveled at the corners. The frame is sized to accommodate seven 2-by-2 seat slats with $\frac{1}{8}$-inch gaps between them, but you can use any combination of 2-by-2s, 2-by-4s, or 2-by-6s that adds up to a comfortable seat depth. The slats are held up by 2-by-4 seat supports set $1\frac{1}{2}$ inches below the top of the frame every 16 inches. This bench, which can be built up to 6 feet long, has end legs made of two 2-by-4s with a 2-by-2 cleat between them that secures the structure to the decking. To make a longer bench, add more leg assemblies to provide adequate support.

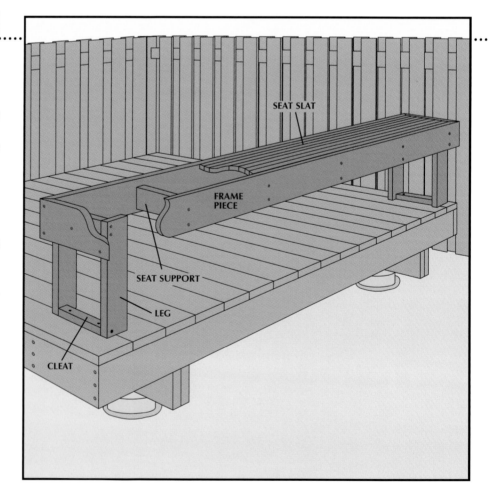

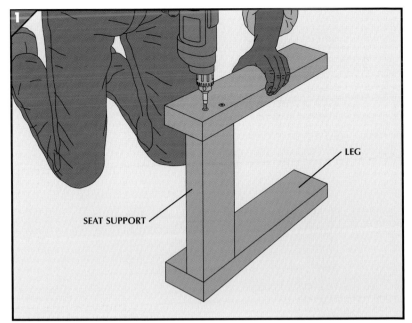

1. Building the leg assemblies.

◆ For each end of the bench, cut two 2-by-4 legs to the desired height of the bench less $1\frac{1}{2}$ inches.

◆ Cut a seat support to the planned inside width of the frame less 3 inches—9 inches for a seat 12 inches wide.

◆ Attach the legs to the seat support so the top edge of the support is flush with the tops of the legs and one side aligns with the legs' outer edges *(left)*; drive two $2\frac{1}{2}$-inch coated deck screws through each leg into the end of the seat support.

2. Attaching the frame.

◆ Cut four 2-by-6s, beveling the ends at 45°, to form a frame with the desired inside width—here, 9 inches—and length.

◆ Fasten each joint with two deck screws.

◆ Fit a leg assembly into each end of the frame and, working with a helper, set the bench upright.

◆ While the helper holds the end in place, set a 2-by-2 scrap on one leg assembly and position the frame so the top edge of the 2-by-2 is flush with the top of the frame.

◆ Fasten the frame to each leg with two deck screws *(right)*.

◆ Attach the other leg assembly in the same way.

◆ Round the beveled corners of the frame slightly with a hand plane.

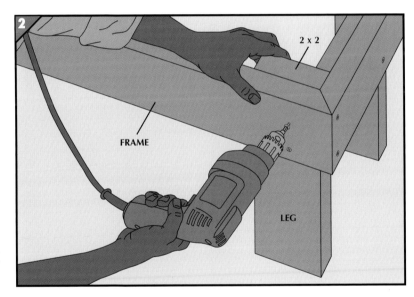

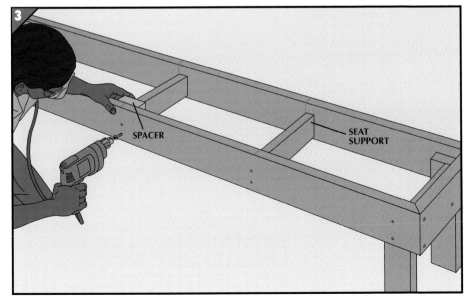

3. Adding seat supports.

◆ On each side of the frame, make a mark every 16 inches. With a combination square, transfer the marks to the inner face of the frame.

◆ For each marked location, cut a 2-by-4 seat support to fit across the inside of the frame.

◆ Place a seat support in the frame, aligning it with its mark.

◆ Holding a short 2-by-2 spacer with its bottom edge on the support and its top edge flush with the top of the frame, drive two deck screws through the frame into each end of the support.

◆ Install the remaining seat supports in the same way *(left)*.

4. Fastening the seat slats.

◆ Cut the seat slats to length, then set them in place astride their supports.
◆ Cut a $\frac{1}{8}$-inch plywood spacer, slip it between the frame and the first slat over an end seat support, and drill a pilot hole for a deck screw through the slat into the support; drill two holes if you are laying 2-by-4 or 2-by-6 slats. Make an additional hole where the slat and each remaining one crosses a support *(right)*, moving the spacer along as you go.
◆ Drive the screws.

SPACER

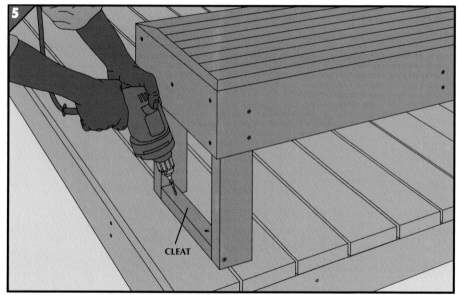

CLEAT

5. Anchoring the bench.

◆ Position the bench on the deck, then cut a 2-by-2 cleat to fit between each set of legs.
◆ Position a cleat between one set of bench legs, flush with their outside edge, and attach each leg to the end of it with one deck screw.
◆ Fasten the cleat to the decking with three deck screws.
◆ Install the other cleat in the same way *(left)*.

CREATING A STORAGE AREA

1. Marking the lid.

◆ Construct a backless bench following Steps 1 to 3 on page 137, making it $16\frac{3}{4}$ inches high and sizing it to hold 2-by-4 or 2-by-6 seat slats.
◆ Cut the slats to length and set them in place.
◆ With a carpenter's square, mark a line across the boards to indicate the sides of a hinged lid, locating each line over a seat support *(right)*. Make the lid no longer than 32 inches.
◆ Label the slats so you can put them back in the same locations after cutting them.

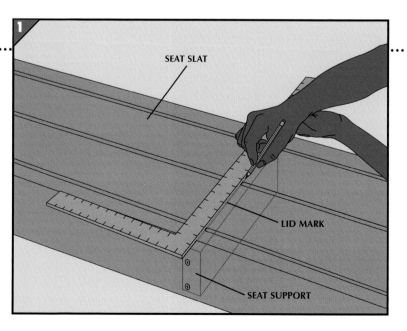

SEAT SLAT

LID MARK

SEAT SUPPORT

2. Making and hinging the lid.

◆ Remove the slats and cut them along the lines.

◆ Place the pieces that will form the lid face down, spacing them $\frac{1}{8}$ inch apart, and draw a line across their middle.

◆ Cut two 2-by-6 and two 2-by-2 cleats as long as the combined width of the slats and set them across the slats, positioning the 2-by-6s $1\frac{1}{2}$ inches from each end and the 2-by-2s 1 inch on each side of the center line.

◆ Fasten the cleats as shown in the inset.

◆ Install the fixed slats at each end of the bench (opposite, Step 4).

◆ Put the lid in place and attach it with three 3- by 3-inch galvanized butt hinges (page 59), placing a hinge 6 inches from each end (right) and a third hinge in between.

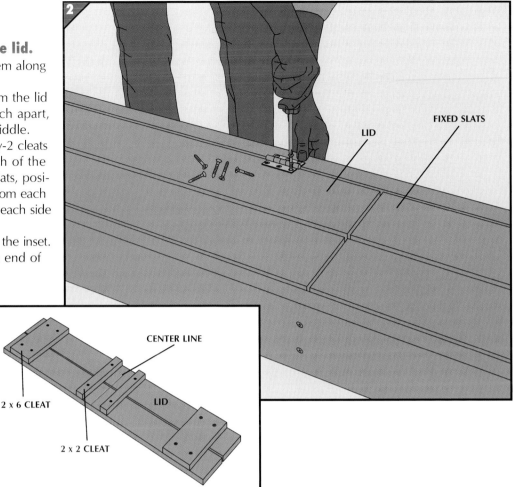

LID

FIXED SLATS

CENTER LINE

2 x 6 CLEAT

2 x 2 CLEAT

LID

FRAME

END PIECE

SIDE PIECE

GAPS

3. Closing in the sides.

◆ Anchor the bench to the deck (opposite, Step 5).

◆ Cut two 2-by-6s to the same length as the side pieces of the frame (page 137, Step 2), beveling the ends.

◆ Set one piece on the deck against the legs and fasten it to each leg with two deck screws.

◆ Attach the second piece in the same way.

◆ Cut two end pieces to fit between the sides, beveling the ends. Fasten each one with two deck screws driven into each side piece.

◆ Add another tier of 2-by-6s, leaving the same gap above and below the boards (left).

◆ Round the beveled corners of the frame slightly with a hand plane.

A BENCH WITH A BACK

Anatomy of the bench.

This bench at right is attached to the railing posts, which can be no more than 5 feet apart. At each post, the bench is supported by a leg assembly consisting of a back support, a seat support, and a leg. The supports at the two ends are the mirror image of each other—in each case, the seat support is fastened to the inside faces of the back support and leg. The top and bottom of the back supports are cut at 15° angles, which tilts the back slightly. The design shown consists of two 2-by-6 seat slats, but any combination of 2-by-4s and 2-by-6s that add up to a comfortable seat depth can be used; simply adjust the length of the seat support to accommodate the combined width of the slats with a $\frac{1}{8}$-inch gap between each. The seat is capped with 5/4-by-4 stock for a finished look. The back slat is a single 2-by-6, but a 2-by-8 or two 2-by-4s could be used for a broader back.

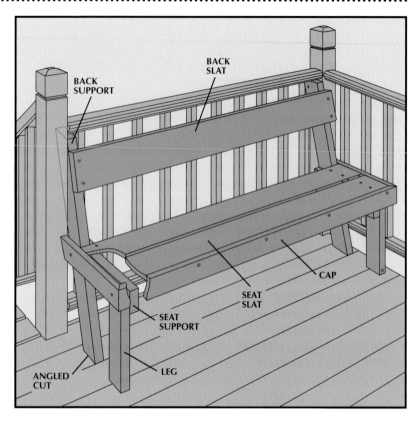

1. Cutting the back support.

◆ Cut a 2-by-4 back support about 4 feet long, mitering one end at 15°.
◆ Set the angled end of the 2-by-4 on the deck and slip the other end through the deck railing and hold it against the outside of the handrail.
◆ Draw a line across the front edge of the 2-by-4 along the underside of the handrail (above), then miter the board along the line at 15°.

2. Cutting the seat support and leg.

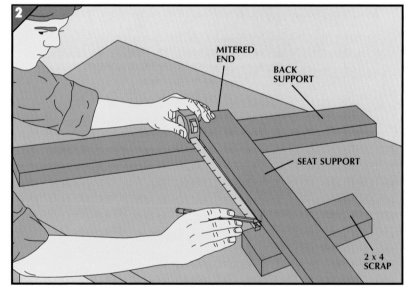

◆ Cut a 2-by-4 seat support about 2 feet long, mitering one end at 15°.
◆ Set the seat support on the back support, aligning the mitered end with the rear edge of the back support and resting the other end on a 2-by-4 scrap.
◆ Measuring from the front edge of the back support, mark the top edge of the seat support at the desired depth of the seat (above)—$11\frac{1}{8}$ inches in this example.
◆ Saw the seat support square at the mark.
◆ Cut a 2-by-4 leg $1\frac{1}{2}$ inches shorter than the desired height of the seat.

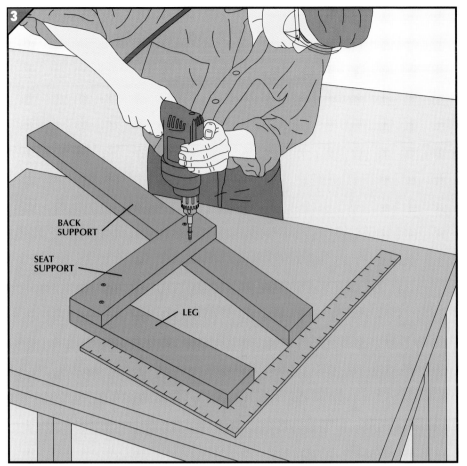

3. Putting the assembly together.

◆ Set the back support and leg flat on a work surface and place the seat support on top so the bottoms of the leg and back support are aligned, the square end of the seat support is flush with the front edge of the leg, and the mitered end is flush with the rear edge of the back support.

◆ Fasten the seat support to the back support and the leg with two deck screws at each joint *(left)*.

◆ Construct a second leg assembly for the other end of the bench, assembling the pieces as the mirror image of the first.

BACK
SUPPORT

SEAT
SUPPORT

LEG

POST

BACK
SUPPORT

LEG

LOCATION
LINE

4. Mounting the leg assemblies.

◆ Position each leg assembly against the inside of the railing post and fasten it to the post with two deck screws through the back support *(above, left)*.

◆ Square the leg assembly on the decking with a carpenter's square, then mark the leg's position.

◆ Keeping the leg on the mark, drive a deck screw at an angle through the leg's front edge into the decking *(above, right)*.

◆ Fasten the other leg in the same manner.

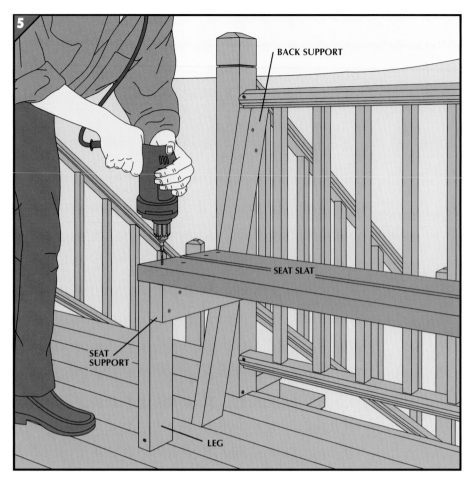

BACK SUPPORT

SEAT SLAT

SEAT
SUPPORT

LEG

5. Fastening the seat slats.

◆ Cut two seat slats to length.

◆ Position one slat at the back of the bench and attach it to each seat support with two deck screws.

◆ Fasten the second slat in the same way, lining up its outer edge with the front ends of the seat supports *(left)*.

If the seat design calls for more than two slats, space the additional ones evenly between the front and back slats.

6. Adding the back slat.

◆ Cut a 2-by-6 to the same length as the seat slats.

◆ Draw a line on each back support 12 inches above the seat.

◆ Align the bottom of the back slat with the marks, then fasten the slat to each back support with two deck screws *(right)*.

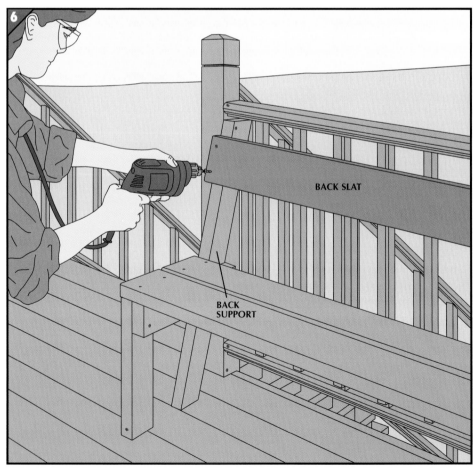

BACK SLAT

BACK
SUPPORT

END CAP

FRONT CAP

BACK SUPPORT

END CAP

MITER CUT

BEVEL CUT

7. Capping the seat.

◆ Miter one end of a 5/4-by-4 board at 15° as an end cap, then position it against the outer faces of a leg and back support so the mitered end lines up with the rear edge of the back support. Mark the other end of the cap where it meets the outer edge of the seat slats.

◆ Make a 45° bevel cut at this mark that will accommodate a beveled cap at the front of the seat *(inset)*.

◆ Reposition the end cap flush with the top of the seat slats and fasten it to the back support and the leg with two deck screws.

◆ Mount an end cap at the other end of the bench.

◆ Cut a front-cap piece to fit between the end caps, beveling both ends at 45°, and fasten it to the front seat slat with a deck screw driven every 8 inches *(right)*.

◆ Lock the corners with two screws driven through the front cap into each end cap.

◆ Round the beveled corners of the frame slightly with a hand plane.

BENCHES FOR THE PERIMETER

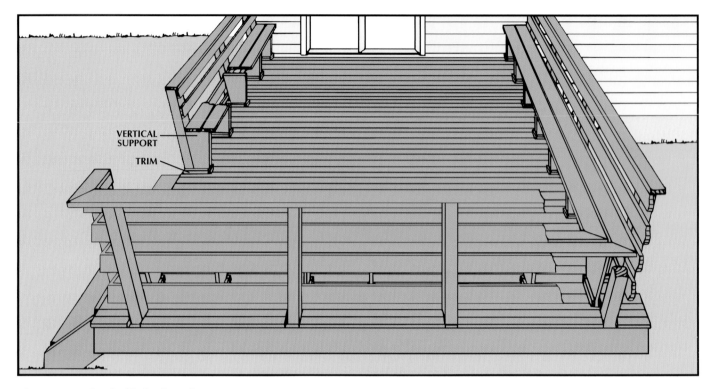

VERTICAL SUPPORT

TRIM

Elements of a built-in bench.
This wraparound bench uses an angled railing *(pages 106-107)* for a backrest. The lower rails on each side of the stair opening are cut away to accommodate vertical supports cut from 2-by-12s to match the angles of the railing posts and trimmed in 1-by-2 lumber at the base. Seat planks made of 2-by-6s rest on the supports, which are set at 30-inch intervals and nailed to the railings and decking.

1. Making bench supports.
◆ Cut 17-inch-long pieces of 2-by-12, one for each support required.
◆ Set the handle of a T bevel on the decking and align the blade with the bottom rail. Draw a line at this angle passing through a corner and across the face of a 2-by-12 support blank. Clamp the blank to a work surface and cut along the line.
◆ Use this support as a template for the others. Make one of them the same shape as the first; cut the others $1\frac{1}{2}$ inches narrower to account for railing thickness *(inset)*.

$1\frac{1}{2}''$

2. Installing the supports.

◆ With a circular saw, trim $1\frac{1}{2}$ inches from the two bottom rails at the stair opening. Position an end support against the post and the rail ends, and drive two $3\frac{1}{4}$-inch nails through the support into the end of each rail. Toenail the support to the decking with three nails angled through each side.

◆ Install intermediate supports at intervals of 30 inches or less. If a support falls at a post, move it far enough to one side to allow nailing through railings. Toenail support bottoms to the decking (inset).

◆ Hide the toenails with strips of 1-by-2 lumber fastened to the supports with 2-inch finishing nails.

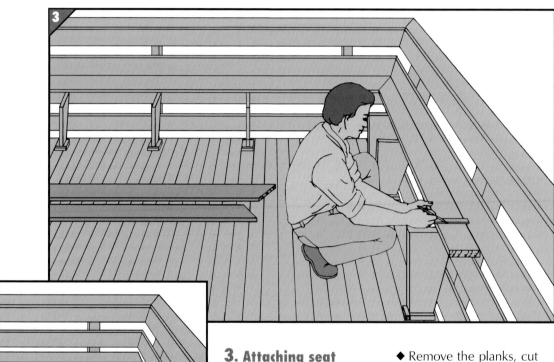

3. Attaching seat planks.

◆ Miter one end of four 2-by-6s at a 45° angle to fit together at a corner. Tack the planks to the supports leaving $\frac{1}{8}$ inch between the boards. Over the midpoint of each support, pencil a mark on the unmitered end, staggering the marks to fall at different supports.

◆ Remove the planks, cut them, and nail them in place with three $3\frac{1}{4}$-inch nails at each support.

◆ Plank the other corners in the same way, then measure, cut, and install intermediate planks.

◆ To make a herringbone corner (inset), leave the plank ends square and butt them end to edge.

Planters

Besides providing plants and flowers with a place to grow, deck planters can serve several other functions. They can be positioned to accentuate a change in levels *(box, below),* to soften the transition between the deck and the yard, or to create a border for a low-level deck. They can also divide areas of activity on a single level. Pairs of planters can frame a doorway or the top of a stairway, or flank the ends of a bench. They are a practical alternative to flower pots, and can be built in a variety of shapes and sizes to fulfill different purposes.

Design Considerations: To build a unit to hold small plantings, you can add a sturdy false bottom to reduce the amount of soil it requires. You may want to fasten a planter to the deck in a permanent location, or place it on casters so it can be moved. Build the units from rot-resistant wood, but avoid stock that has been treated with creosote, which is harmful to plants.

 TOOLS

Carpenter's square
Circular saw
Electric drill

 **MATERIALS**

Pressure-treated
 2 x 2s, 2 x 4s, 1 x 6s
Pressure-treated
 5/4 x 4 stock
Deck screws (2", $2\frac{1}{2}$")

 SAFETY TIPS

Protect your eyes with goggles when using power tools. Put on a dust mask when cutting pressure-treated wood, and wash your hands thoroughly after handling the wood.

ACCENTUATING A LEVEL CHANGE

In this design, a set of broad steps makes the transition between two levels. A double-decker planter rests on the lower level and rises high enough to frame the end of the entire flight of steps. It also blends naturally into the adjacent yard plantings.

BUILDING A PLANTER

Anatomy of a planter.

The planter at right has four side panels of 1-by-6s held together with 2-by-2 cleats at the bottom and 2-by-4 cleats at the top. The side panels can also be made of 1-by-4s or 1-by-8s, depending on the overall dimensions of the planter. Two more cleats on opposite sides support a false bottom made of boards that are set on the cleats with gaps between them for drainage. On a rectangular planter, locate the cleats on the long sides. In this example, the false bottom is halfway up the sides, but it can be set at any height. A cap and strips of outer banding are added around the top. The planter can be fastened to the deck through the bottom cleats.

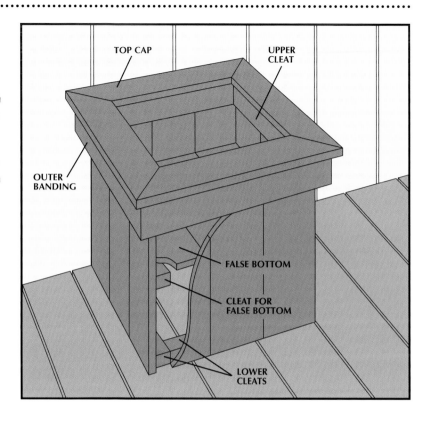

TOP CAP

UPPER CLEAT

OUTER BANDING

FALSE BOTTOM

CLEAT FOR FALSE BOTTOM

LOWER CLEATS

1. Making the side panels.

◆ Cut the boards to length for all four side panels, then lay out the boards for one panel, aligning the ends.

◆ Saw two 2-by-2 cleats 5 inches shorter than the panel width, center a cleat on the panel between the edges and flush with one end, and fasten the cleat to each board with two 2-inch coated deck screws *(inset, left)*.

◆ Assemble a second panel in the same way.

◆ Put the remaining two side panels together with cleats only 1 inch shorter than the panel width and flush with one edge rather than centered between the edges *(inset, right)*.

◆ With a carpenter's square, draw a line across the inner side of each of these last two panels at the appropriate height for the false bottom *(left)*.

◆ Cut two cleats 2 inches shorter than the panel width, center each one along the marked line, then fasten it in place.

BOTTOM CLEAT

PANEL

CLEAT FOR FALSE BOTTOM

CLEATS

PANEL WITH CENTERED CLEAT

PANEL WITH OFFSET CLEAT

2. Assembling the panels.

◆ Assemble the panel as shown in the inset. Hold a panel with an offset cleat against one with a centered cleat so the cleat and panel butt against the inner face of the side and the sides form a 90° angle, then fasten them together with three deck screws.

◆ Add the remaining panel with an offset cleat so its inner face butts against the edge of the centered-cleat side (right), then fasten the last centered-cleat panel.

◆ Position the planter on the deck and, if desired, anchor it to the decking with two $2\frac{1}{2}$-inch coated deck screws driven through each bottom cleat.

◆ Cut the required number of 1-by boards for the false bottom to length, sawing them to width to maintain $\frac{1}{8}$-inch gaps between them, then place them on their cleats.

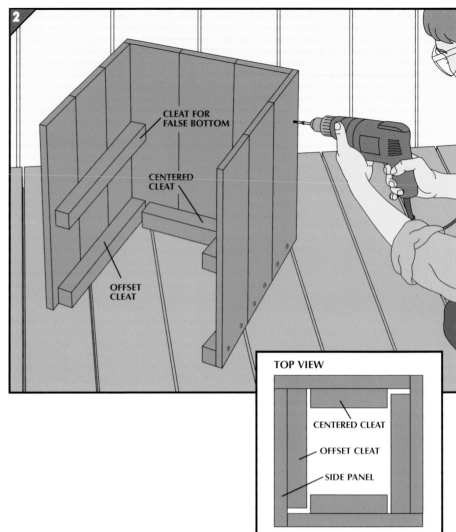

CLEAT FOR
FALSE BOTTOM

CENTERED
CLEAT

OFFSET
CLEAT

TOP VIEW

CENTERED CLEAT

OFFSET CLEAT

SIDE PANEL

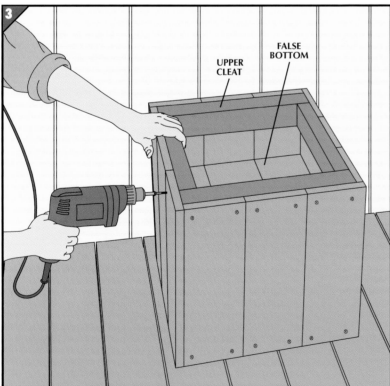

UPPER
CLEAT

FALSE
BOTTOM

3. Fastening the upper cleats.

◆ Cut two 2-by-4 cleats to the inside width of the planter, position one of them across a side panel with its upper edge flush with the top, and fasten it in place with two 2-inch coated deck screws driven through each board.

◆ Attach the second cleat to the opposite panel in the same way.

◆ Cut two more cleats to fit between the first pair and fasten them in place (left).

148

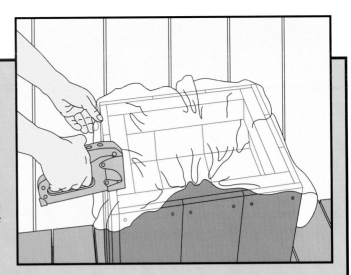

TRICKS OF THE TRADE

Containing Soil

The gaps in the false bottom of a planter are designed to let water escape easily, since good drainage is necessary for plants to thrive; however, soil may leak out as well. To keep soil contained in a planter, place plastic sheeting on the false bottom and sides before you add the top cap *(Step 4)*. Staple the sheeting to the upper cleats *(right)*, then trim off the excess with scissors. Punch a few small holes in the plastic to allow adequate drainage.

4. Anchoring the top cap.

◆ Cut four pieces of 5/4-by-4 stock to cap the top of the planter, mitering the corners so the joints will align with the corners of the planter.
◆ Fasten one piece to an upper cleat with $2\frac{1}{2}$-inch coated deck screws spaced about every 6 inches so the mitered ends are in line with the corners and the inner edge is flush with the inner face of the cleat *(right)*.
◆ Add the remaining three pieces, pulling each corner joint tight.
◆ Pin each corner with a screw driven through one side of the joint.

TOP CAP

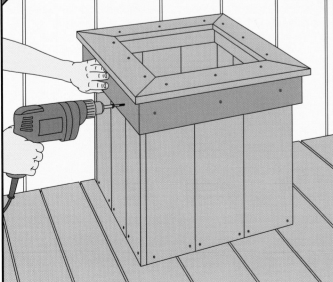

5. Adding the outer banding.

◆ Cut four pieces of 5/4-by-4 stock to fit as banding around the planter under the top cap, beveling the ends.
◆ Fasten the banding pieces in place, driving deck screws spaced about every 6 inches through the sides and into the upper cleats *(left)*.
◆ Pin the corners with two screws driven through one side of each joint.

A Screen for Privacy

Closing in a section of a deck with a high screen instead of a railing offers privacy, shade, and shelter from the wind. It can also serve as a trellis for vines.

Design: A screen's basic structure is similar to that of a railing *(pages 69-79)*. Horizontal rails run between 4-by-4 posts notched and fastened to the deck. The space between the rails can be filled in with a variety of materials, including vertical boards or lattice, or a combination of both *(below)*. A screen can be virtually any height, but about 6 feet is typical.

Buying Lattice: Lattice for outdoor use comes in cedar, pressure-treated wood, or vinyl and is generally available in 4- by 8- or 2- by 8-foot sheets. The size of the openings in the sheets varies from $1\frac{3}{4}$ inches to $3\frac{5}{8}$ inches—screens with smaller holes provide more privacy. Although you can cut lattice *(page 153, box)* or have it trimmed at the lumberyard, your job will be easier if you can design the screen to incorporate full sheets.

 TOOLS

Circular saw
Electric drill

 **MATERIALS**

Pressure-treated
  1 x 2s, 1 x 6s,
  2 x 2s, 2 x 4s,
  4 x 4s

Lattice ($\frac{1}{2}$")
Deck screws
  (2", $2\frac{1}{2}$")

 SAFETY TIPS

Wear goggles when using a power tool. Put on a dust mask to cut pressure-treated wood, and wash your hands thoroughly after handling the lumber.

Anatomy of a screen.

In the design at right, three rails made of 2-by-4s are attached between 4-by-4 posts, forming upper and lower sections. Posts are set at the ends of the screen and every 8 feet in between. In the bottom section, 2-by-2 cleats run down the middle of the lower and middle rails, and vertical 1-by-6 boards are fastened to the cleats. In this example, successive boards are staggered on each side of the cleats to form a solid barrier when viewed straight on, but they let light through at an angle. The width and spacing of the boards can be varied to achieve the desired effect. The upper section is sized to accommodate a 2- by 8-foot sheet of $\frac{1}{2}$-inch-thick lattice. Vertical 1-by cleats fastened to the posts between the middle and upper rails and horizontal cleats running along the rails hold the lattice in place.

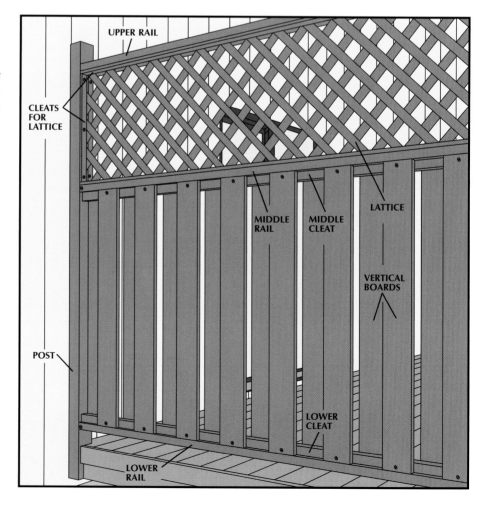

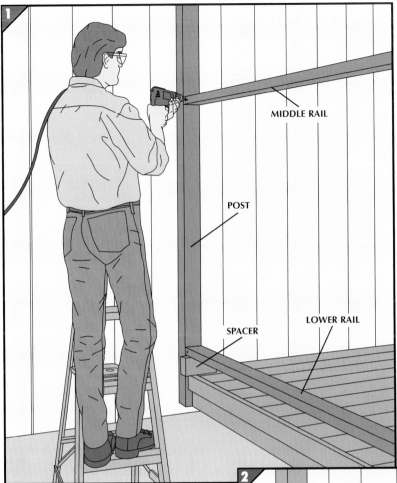

MIDDLE RAIL

POST

SPACER

LOWER RAIL

1. Installing posts and rails.

◆ Cut 4-by-4 posts to extend from the bottom of the rim or end joist to the desired height of the screen above the deck. Notch and install a post (pages 70-72) at each end of the screen and at least every 8 feet in between.

◆ Cut three 2-by-4s to fit as rails between each pair of adjacent posts.

◆ Set a 2-by-4 spacer on the deck next to each post and place a rail on the spacers.

◆ Fasten the rail to each post, driving a $2\frac{1}{2}$-inch coated deck screw at an angle through the edge of the rail into the post—alternatively, use a galvanized framing anchor.

◆ Mark the height of the middle rail on the posts and, working with a helper, install it in the same way (left).

◆ Mount the upper rail at the desired height.

2. Adding the horizontal cleats.

◆ Cut two 2-by-2 cleats to the same length as the rails.

◆ Center one cleat on the bottom rail and fasten it with $2\frac{1}{2}$-inch coated deck screws driven every 8 inches (right).

◆ Working with a helper, fasten the second cleat to the underside of the middle rail.

CLEAT

LOWER
RAIL

3. Fastening the vertical boards.

◆ Cut 1-by-6 boards to fit between the top and bottom rails, and cut a short spacer from the same stock or from wood that is the width you have chosen for the gaps between boards.

◆ Starting at one end of the screen, butt a 1-by-6 against the post and one side of the upper and lower cleats, then fasten it to the cleats with two 2-inch coated deck screws.

◆ Hold the edge of the spacer against this first board, butt the second board against the spacer, and fasten it to the cleats. Continue to install boards until you reach the opposite post, cutting the last board to width if necessary.

◆ Starting at the same post, install boards on the opposite side of the cleats *(right)*, but use the spacer to off-set the first board from the first one on the other side by the width of a board.

4. Installing the lattice cleats.

◆ Cut two 1-by-2s to fit between the posts as cleats to support the lattice.

◆ Set a cleat along the middle rail, flush with the outside edge of the screen, and fasten it in place with a deck screw driven every 8 inches.

◆ Attach a cleat to the underside of the upper rail in the same way.

◆ Cut two more cleats to fit vertically between the horizontal cleats. Fasten one to each post flush with the outer edge *(left)*.

CLEAT

5. Installing the lattice.

◆ Place the lattice against the cleats and tack it in place.

◆ Install a second set of cleats on the inside of the lattice, butting them tight against the lattice so their edges are flush with the inner edges of the rails and posts *(left)*.

Cutting Lattice

Lattice can be tricky to cut because it tends to flex and bind in the saw. For best results, make the cutting mark on the lattice with a chalk line and set the piece on a 2-by-4 on the ground with the cutting mark a few inches past the edge of the board. Check that the lattice is square to the 2-by-4, then tack the lattice to the board in three or four places. Make a cutting jig by attaching a 4-inch strip of particleboard to a 12-inch strip so the factory-cut edge of the narrower piece divides the wider one; then clamp the jig to a work surface. Cut the wider strip with a circular saw, guiding the tool's base plate along the narrow-

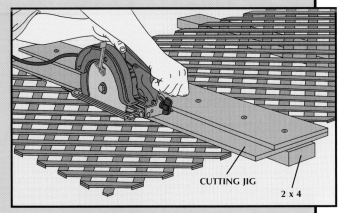

CUTTING JIG

2 x 4

er strip. Set the jig on top of the lattice with the edge aligned with the cutting mark and screw it to the 2-by-4. Install a plywood-cutting blade on the circular saw and cut the lattice, guiding the saw base along the jig *(above)*.

The area under a raised deck can be enclosed with skirting to hide the framing lumber and give the structure a more finished appearance. Skirting also inhibits the growth of weeds beneath the deck because it blocks light. To leave the area accessible for storage, include a door in the design.

Materials: Deck skirts are most often made from lattice panels or vertical boards. Vertical boards are the sturdier choice and provide a more solid support for a door; the style shown below is appropriate for decks up to 4 feet high.

Installation: Board skirting is ideal for a deck with a colonial railing *(pages 74-77)* and either overhanging decking or cap boards between the posts; in this design, the tops of the skirt boards are hidden. A slightly different installation technique is needed for a deck with a traditional railing *(page 156, box)*.

 TOOLS

Carpenter's square
Carpenter's level (4')
Chalk line
Circular saw
Electric drill
Screwdriver

 MATERIALS

Pressure-treated
  1 x 6s, 2 x 2s, 2 x 4s
Masonry screws ($2\frac{1}{2}$")
Deck screws (2")
Butt hinges (3" x 3")
Gate latch

 SAFETY TIPS

Put on goggles when working with power tools. Add a dust mask when cutting pressure-treated wood; wash thoroughly after handling the lumber.

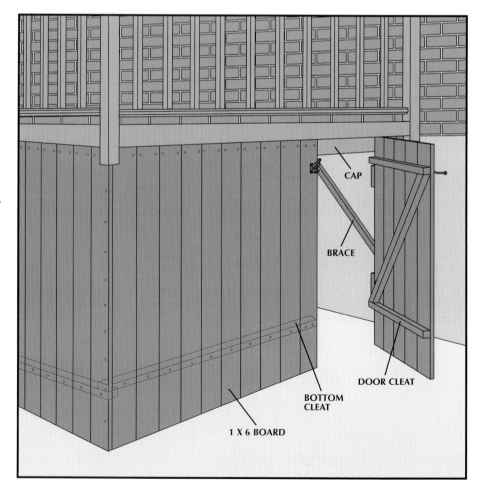

Anatomy of a board skirt.
In the design shown at right, 1-by-6 boards are fastened to the rim joist under the deck cap *(page 73, box)* or under the decking if it overhangs. Cleats run along the inside of the boards near the bottom, and both the boards and the cleats are pinned together at the corners. Constructed from 1-by-6s with cleats in a Z pattern on the back, the door is hinged to the boards on one side of the opening. A brace attached to the deck framing on each side of the door opening adds stability. For a deck more than 3 feet high, additional braces are installed every 8 feet.

CAP

BRACE

DOOR CLEAT

BOTTOM CLEAT

1 X 6 BOARD

HANGING THE BOARDS

END JOIST

CLEAT

1. Attaching the wall cleat.

◆ With a carpenter's level, mark a plumb line on the house wall in line with the outside face of the end joist.

◆ Cut a 2-by-2 cleat long enough to extend from the bottom of the rim joist to the ground.

◆ While a helper holds the cleat against the house wall flush with the plumb line, drill a pilot hole for a $2\frac{1}{2}$-inch masonry screw through the cleat and into the wall every 8 inches *(left)*, then drive the screws.

2. Fastening the boards.

◆ Measure the distance from the bottom of the cap or overhanging decking to the ground and cut 1-by-6 boards to this length—if the ground is uneven, vary the length of the boards to follow the terrain.

◆ Hold the first board against the wall cleat and outline the bottom of the post on its inner face. Notch the board to fit the post, then fasten it to the end joist with two 2-inch coated deck screws and to the wall cleat with screws driven about every 8 inches.

◆ Set the second board against the first and fasten it to the end joist.

◆ Continue fastening the boards *(right)* until you reach the proposed door opening. Leave a gap $\frac{1}{2}$ inch larger than the combined width of five boards, then resume hanging the boards.

◆ When you are within about 3 feet of the next post, measure the remaining distance and cut the remaining boards to width to fit the space; notch the last board to fit around the post.

POST

NOTCHED BOARD

A deck with a traditional railing *(pages 77-79)* has no cap or overhanging decking to hide the top of the skirt boards. To hang skirting from this structure, fasten 2-by-6 cleats horizontally along the back of the end and rim joists so about half of each cleat extends past the bottom edge of the joists. You can then attach the skirt boards to the cleats.

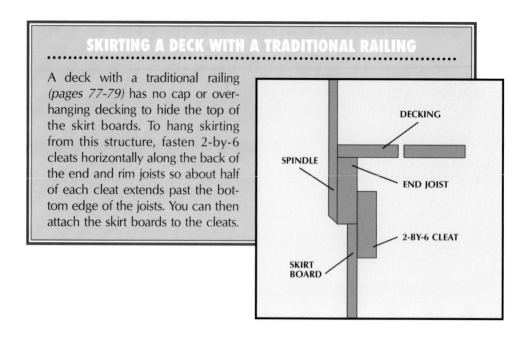

DECKING

SPINDLE

END JOIST

2-BY-6 CLEAT

SKIRT BOARD

BOTTOM CLEAT

3. Cleating the boards.
◆ Cut a 2-by-4 cleat to the length of the completed section of skirting. Where there is a door opening, make a cleat for each side of the opening.
◆ On the inside of the skirt, measure down from the top of the end joist and make a mark at each end of the section of skirting about 8 inches above the ground. Measure down the same distance on the outside of the skirt and snap a chalk line along the outer faces of the boards.
◆ Have a helper hold the cleat with its edge against the inside of the skirt, centering it over the mark at each end. Aligning the drill with the chalk line, drive a screw through a skirt board to fasten each end of the cleat *(left)*.
◆ Using the chalk line as a guide, drive a screw through each skirt board into the cleat.

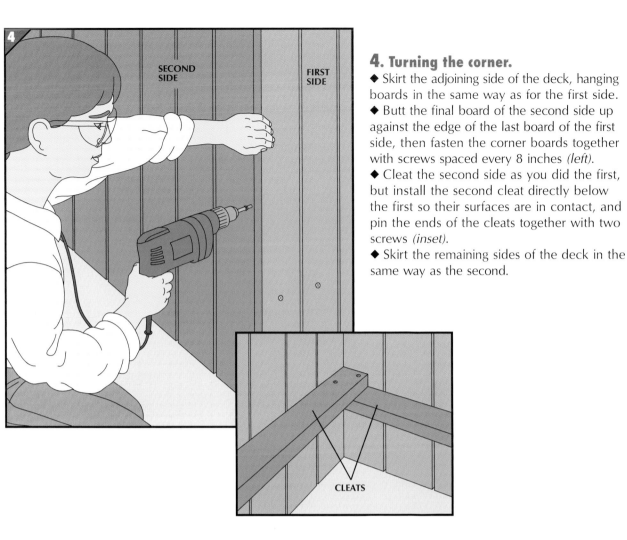

4. Turning the corner.

◆ Skirt the adjoining side of the deck, hanging boards in the same way as for the first side.
◆ Butt the final board of the second side up against the edge of the last board of the first side, then fasten the corner boards together with screws spaced every 8 inches *(left)*.
◆ Cleat the second side as you did the first, but install the second cleat directly below the first so their surfaces are in contact, and pin the ends of the cleats together with two screws *(inset)*.
◆ Skirt the remaining sides of the deck in the same way as the second.

5. Bracing the skirt.

◆ Cut a 2-by-2 6 feet long, mitering one end at 45°.
◆ Rest the mitered end of the brace against a deck joist and the other end against an edge of the door opening.
◆ While a helper plumbs the skirt, mark the brace along the inner face of the skirt board at the opening *(right)*. Miter the brace at the mark.
◆ Use the brace as a template to cut another for the other side of the opening and any additional braces that are required to keep the skirt plumb.
◆ Reposition the first brace between the deck joist and the inside face of the skirting, then fasten it at each end with a deck screw driven at an angle.
◆ Install the remaining braces in the same way.

ADDING A DOOR

CLEAT

1. Assembling the door.
◆ Cut five boards $\frac{1}{4}$ inch shorter than the skirt boards adjoining the door opening and lay them flat, edge-to-edge and ends aligned.
◆ Make two 2-by-2 cleats to span the width of the boards, place them across the pieces 1 foot from each end, and

attach them to each board with a 2-inch screw *(above, left)*.
◆ Turn the door over and, with a carpenter's square, mark a line across the surface in line with the middle of each cleat *(above, right)*.
◆ Using the line as a guide, drive two screws through each board into the cleat.

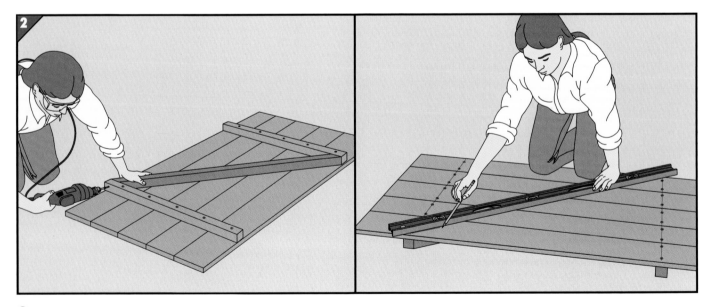

2. Adding a diagonal brace.
◆ Cut a cleat to fit diagonally between the first two as described on page 58, Step 2.
◆ Drive a screw through each horizontal cleat into the end of the diagonal one *(above, left)*.

◆ Turn the door over and, with a straightedge, mark a line across the door in line with the middle of the diagonal cleat *(above, right)*.
◆ Following the line, drive a screw through each board into the diagonal brace.

3. Positioning the door.

◆ Fit the door into its opening $\frac{1}{4}$ inch below the cap or overhanging decking.

◆ While a helper holds the door in position, tack it to the end joist with three screws *(left)*.

4. Hinging the door.

◆ Position a 3- by 3-inch butt hinge about one-quarter of the way down from the top of the door so the pin loops are centered on the seam between the door and the skirt, then mark the screw holes on the door and the adjoining skirt board.

◆ Remove the hinge, drill a pilot hole for a screw at each mark, then fasten the hinge in place *(right)*.

◆ Add a second hinge about one-quarter of the way up from the bottom of the door. For a door more than 3 feet high, add a third hinge between the first two. Remove the three screws installed in Step 3.

◆ Install a gate latch as described on page 81, Step 4.

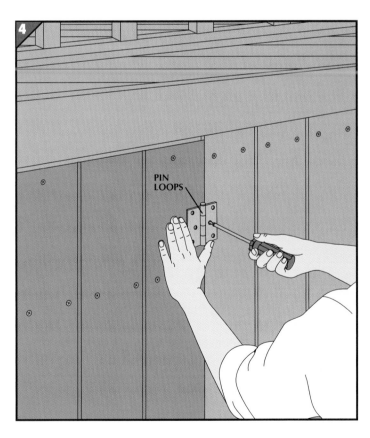

PIN LOOPS

Shade for a Hot Summer's Day

Adding an overhead covering to a deck serves two purposes: It shields the outdoor living space from the sun, and it helps to integrate the deck with the architecture of the house. The covering can be a leafy bower, a simple arrangement of snow fencing unrolled on top of cleats, or a permanent structure of sun-filtering wooden louvers.

Building the Frame: The 8- by 10-foot frame illustrated on the following pages can be used to support these coverings and others. It will bear a moderate snow load of 20 pounds per square foot; if you live in an area of heavy snow, you should consult your local building department or a structural engineer for appropriate modifications.

Although the frame here is shown attached to a deck, you can adapt it for a concrete patio by securing the posts to the slab with post anchors and expansion shields. You can also build a covering if there is no underlying structure; in that case, the posts rest on concrete footings *(page 25)*.

In preparing to build the frame, buy posts somewhat longer than needed, so they can be cut to the right length once they are in place. You may also want to cut simple decorative ends on the beam and rafters, as shown on pages 161 and 162, before beginning construction.

Covering Options: The choice of covering depends largely on orientation and ventilation. If the deck or patio faces south and is heated by daylong sun, you may prefer a very dense covering for maximum shade. On the other hand, ventilation may be a concern; a solid cover attached to two or more house walls, for example, can trap hot air. In such a case, a more open covering would be a better choice. A deck or patio facing north is usually shaded by the house, so the covering can be chosen for its looks alone.

For decks with an eastern or western exposure, a covering that offers partial shade should be sufficient. A 24-inch eggcrate grid *(page 164)* gives moderate shade, especially in the midmorning and midafternoon. For more shade, install a checkerboard of 2-by-2 slats over the grid. Other choices for deep shade include snow fencing and fixed louvers.

In winter, a dense covering can keep warming sunlight from reaching the house. One solution to this problem is a covering that can be removed and stored. Another option is a deciduous vine *(page 165)*, which will lose its leaves in winter.

 TOOLS

 MATERIALS

Water level
Protractor or T bevel
Circular saw
Chalk line
Staple gun
Saber saw
Combination square
Nail set

Flashing
4-by-4 posts
2-by-6 or larger
   framing lumber
1-by-6 lumber
   for spacers
2-by-2 slats
Snow-fencing or
   woven-reed panels
Post-and-beam
   connectors

Joist hangers
Carriage bolts
   ($\frac{1}{2}$- by 6-inch)
Galvanized nails
   (2-inch and 3-inch)
Galvanized
   finishing nails
   (2$\frac{1}{2}$-inch and
   3-inch)
Copper staples
   ($\frac{1}{2}$-inch)

SAFETY TIPS

Protect your eyes when hammering nails and when using a circular saw. Earplugs reduce the noise of this tool to a safe level, and a dust mask is advisable when sawing pressure-treated lumber, which contains arsenic compounds as a preservative. Wash any exposed skin thoroughly after handling pressure-treated lumber.

Choosing Lumber of the Right Size

When building a framework over a deck, the standard post size is 4-by-4. Lumber for the beam and rafters varies in dimension, depending on the distances they span. Use the chart below to determine the correct lumber for your needs.

BEAM

Distance between posts	Beam size
6 feet	two 2 x 6s
8 feet	two 2 x 8s

RAFTERS

Distance between ledger and beam	Rafter size
10 feet	2 x 6
12 feet	2 x 8
16 feet	2 x 10

ERECTING A STRUCTURAL SUPPORT

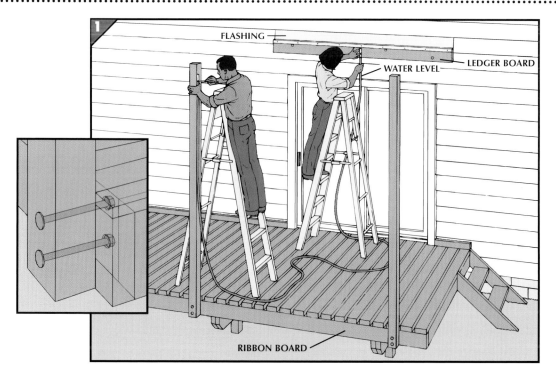

FLASHING

WATER LEVEL

LEDGER BOARD

RIBBON BOARD

1. Securing the posts.

◆ Bolt a ledger board on the side of the house and add flashing *(page 97)*.
◆ On the outside edge of the deck, position two 4-by-4 posts flush with the bottom of the ribbon board,

aligning the outer edges of the posts so that they are 2 inches in from the ends of the ledger; this leaves room to nail the outermost joist hangers to the ledger. Attach the posts to the ribbon board with 6-inch-long

$\frac{1}{2}$-inch carriage bolts *(inset)*.
◆ With a helper, use a water level to mark each post at the height of the ledger's bottom edge. Then subtract the width of the beam lumber and cut the posts to that height.

2. Attaching the beam.

◆ Cut 2 boards for the beam, each 2 feet longer than the distance between posts to allow for an overhang on both sides.
◆ Nail the boards together at 16-inch intervals, using 3-inch galvanized nails and working from alternate sides of the assembly.
◆ Attach post-and-beam connectors to the top of each post and, with a helper, lift the assembled beam into them. Center the beam and nail it to the brackets.

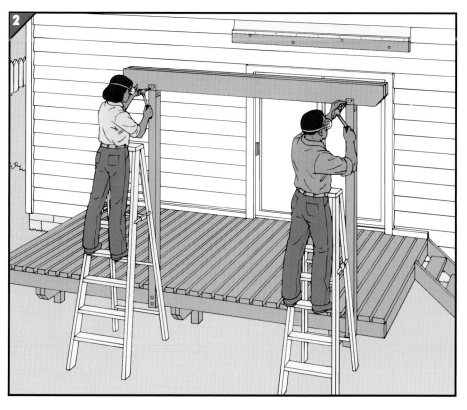

3. Installing the rafters.

◆ Draw a vertical pencil line $2\frac{3}{4}$ inches in from each end of the ledger board to mark where the end rafters will be centered; this measure includes 2 inches for the joist hangers, plus half the thickness of the rafter.

◆ Subdivide the distance between the lines so that the interior rafters will be evenly spaced and no more than 2 feet apart. Center and nail a joist hanger over each mark.

◆ Mark corresponding lines on top of the beam, beginning $\frac{3}{4}$ inch in from the outer face of each post.

◆ Cut the rafters to length, allowing for a decorative overhang beyond the beam. Slip one end of each rafter into a joist hanger, and center the rafter over the corresponding line on the beam. Nail the rafter end to the joist hanger, then toenail the rafter to the beam using two 3-inch nails on each side.

◆ From the same size lumber you used for the rafters, cut blocking boards that will fit on top of the beam between the rafters to prevent them from twisting. Stagger the boards so you can end-nail them through the sides of the rafters.

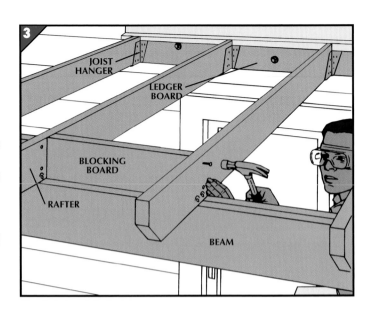

SHADE FROM SLANTED LOUVERS

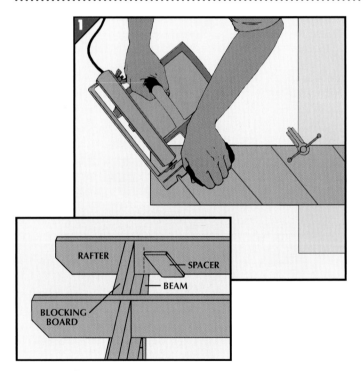

1. Cutting the spacers.

◆ With a protractor or a T bevel, mark a length of 1-by-4 lumber with parallel lines spaced 4 inches apart and angled to the desired slant of the louvers (box, right). Then cut along the lines with a circular saw.

◆ Nail spacers to the beam ends of a pair of rafters with 2-inch galvanized finishing nails. The spacers should extend only as far as the inner edge of the beam (inset).

Planning for Louvers

Shade provided by louvers depends mainly on two factors. One is the direction of the louvers. For decks with a southern exposure, louvers that slope down toward the house admit more sunlight, while louvers that slope up toward the house provide more shade. For an eastern exposure, downward-slanted louvers give the most sunlight in the morning; reversing the tilt offers more sun in the afternoon. The opposite holds for decks facing west.

The other consideration is louver angle. Although louvers are commonly angled between 40° and 50°, you may wish to calculate a louver angle that will capture maximum winter sun for your house. Find your latitude in an atlas. Round it to the nearest degree, and subtract it from 66° (the latitude of the Arctic Circle). Installing your louvers at the resulting angle will give you the greatest warmth in winter. This setting also blocks about 75 percent of solar radiation on the longest day of summer. To let in more summer sun, increase the louver angle; for less, decrease it.

2. Installing the louvers.

◆ Cut a 1-by-6 louver to fit between the two rafters, and nail it to the spacers with 3-inch nails. Place a second pair of spacers snugly against the louver and face-nail them to the rafters with 2-inch galvanized finishing nails. Attach a second louver to the spacers.

◆ Continue adding spacers and louvers until the entire row has been filled.

◆ Cut two filler-spacers shaped to fit between the last louver and the vertical face of the ledger, then nail them to the rafters.

◆ Add spacers and louvers between each pair of rafters in the same way *(inset)*.

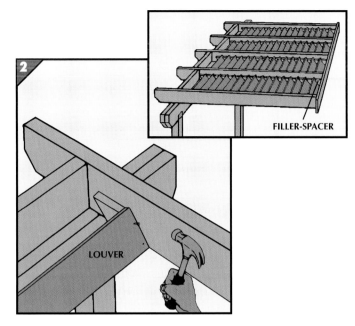

FILLER-SPACER

LOUVER

SUN SHIELDS OF WOVEN REEDS OR SNOW FENCING

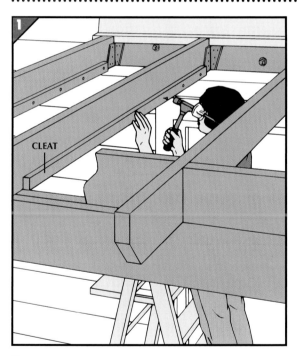

CLEAT

1. Installing cleats.

◆ To support frames for woven-reed panels, nail 1-by-2 cleats along the lower edge of each rafter with 2-inch nails. Make the cleats long enough to extend from the inner face of the beam to the joist hanger.

◆ Build rectangular frames of 2-by-2s to rest securely on the cleats, but fit them loosely enough to be removed in winter. The frame pieces can simply be butt-nailed to each other at the corners with 3-inch nails.

FRAME

2. Attaching the reed.

◆ Lay a roll of woven-reed fencing over a frame and fasten it in place *(above)* with $\frac{1}{2}$-inch copper-plated staples spaced 2 inches apart. Trim away all of the excess fencing with a saber saw. Repeat this procedure for each frame.

◆ Lower the frames into place on top of the cleats *(inset)*.

◆ In windy areas, secure the frames with screw eyes set into the underside of the frames and screw hooks fastened into the cleats.

163

Shading with snow fencing.

◆ Install cleats in the same manner as for woven-reed panels *(page 163)*.

◆ Cut the fencing to fit between the rafters, leaving intact one of the two binding wires that hold the fence pickets together. Lay the trimmed fencing directly on top of the cleats.

◆ Nail a second set of 1-by-2 cleats on top of the fencing to hold it in place.

CLEATS

SNOW FENCING

THE VERSATILITY OF ORDINARY LUMBER

Constructing an airy eggcrate.

◆ Beginning 2 feet from the ledger board, mark the bottoms of the end rafters at 2-foot intervals. Snap a chalk line between the pairs of marks to transfer the measurements to interior rafters. Then use a combination square to extend these marks to the vertical faces of each rafter.

◆ Cut crosspieces of rafter lumber to fit between the rafters.

◆ Nail the crosspieces between rafters at the marks with 3-inch galvanized finishing nails. Butt-nail the crosspieces through the sides of the rafters wherever possible, and use a nail set to sink nail heads into the rafter so they will not interfere with the installation of other crosspieces. Where butt-nailing is not possible, toenail the crosspieces to the rafters.

Adding a checkerboard grid.

For deeper shade, top each square of an eggcrate covering with eight 2-by-2 slats, each cut 24 inches long.

◆ Starting with a corner square at the ledger, place the first slat across two rafters so that its ends overlap half of each rafter and its inner edge overlaps half the ledger. Nail each end to a rafter with $2\frac{1}{2}$-inch galvanized finishing nails; make sure the nails do not angle back toward the ledger and pierce the flashing.

◆ Center the second slat between the rafters at the opposite end of the square, aligning its outer edge with the midpoint of the crosspiece. Nail its ends to the rafters.

◆ Fill the intervening area with six more slats, evenly spaced and nailed in the same manner. For less shade, use fewer, more widely spaced boards.

◆ On the adjacent squares, reverse the direction of the slats. To protect the top of the ledger flashing, face-nail a 2-by-2 nailing board to the ledger between the rafters. Nail the slats to the nailing board and the crosspiece.

◆ Continue in this fashion, alternating the direction of the slats on adjacent squares, to create a checkerboard pattern (inset).

A LEAFY BOWER

Chosen and placed with care, a vine trained over an eggcrate covering, as shown at left, will control not only how much shade you get but when you get it.

There are many varieties to choose from. Some survive for years but may develop slowly; others, such as morning glory or moonflower, grow as much as 25 feet in their single season of life, providing nearly instant cover.

Wisteria, grape, and other deciduous vines will cool a patio in summer; in the fall they will drop their leaves to let the winter sun reach the house. Evergreens, such as jasmine and Cape honeysuckle, will shelter decks and patios in southern climates all year long.

How much shade a vine will provide depends both on its growth habits and on its leaves. Vines that cling by means of hooks, thorns, or tendrils do not offer as much shade as those that twist densely around themselves and their supports. Vines with small, translucent leaves like those of the silver-lace simply filter the sunshine, while the large, opaque leaves of the English ivy or hop vine can overlap one another to blot out the sun.

Many vines have decorative fruits and flowers—but these can be a mixed blessing. Keep in mind that flowers, fruits, and berries tend to litter a deck or patio. They also attract bees and birds, a nuisance to some. And beware of some intriguing flowers, such as those of the Dutchman's pipe, which have an objectionable smell.

Enclosing a porch with screens requires a suitable framework for attaching the mesh. If your porch has a knee wall—a partition approximately 3 feet high around the perimeter of the porch—and square posts no more than 5 feet apart, you may need to add only a doorframe and studs against the house wall at the ends of the porch. To keep flying insects out, notch the studs to match the siding *(opposite)*. Build the doorframe to fit the width of the door, but buy a door slightly taller than you need so it can be trimmed to fit.

Porches without knee walls vary in the amount of construction needed for screening. In addition to a doorframe, some may lack only a few uprights. Others may need a complete set of vertical and horizontal supports. Pick the elements that are appropriate for

your porch from the ones shown on the following pages.

Attaching the Mesh: No matter what type of screening you choose *(page 210)*, there are a number of ways to attach it to the porch. The simplest is to staple the screen directly to the supporting structure and cover the seams with molding.

Or you can install screen-spline channels that fasten to the porch. The channels anchor the mesh with a flexible spline identical to that used in aluminum screens *(page 210)*. A decorative cover hides the spline and the screen edges.

A third option is wood-framed screens *(page 212)*. Although more expensive and time-consuming than the preceding methods, framed screens complement a large, elegant porch better than the others.

TOOLS

Crosscut or circular saw	Staple gun
Saber saw	Hammer
Compass	Utility knife
Chalk line	Belt sander
Miter box and backsaw	Drill
	Screwdriver
	Screen-spline roller

MATERIALS

2-by-4s	Galvanized common nails (3-inch)
Doorstop molding	
Screen bead	Galvanized finishing nails (2-inch)
Screen door	
Door hinges and latch	Screws
	Copper-coated staples ($\frac{1}{4}$-inch)
Screening	
Screen spline and molding	Brads ($\frac{3}{4}$-inch)
	Turn buttons

FRAMING ALTERNATIVES

A screened porch that stands alone.

The framework for enclosing a porch consists of 2-by-4 studs toenailed to the floor and ceiling. If you wish to attach screening to this supporting structure, space the studs no more than 5 feet apart, 3 feet if you plan wood-framed screens. Blocking between the studs at the floor and ceiling helps to keep the uprights from warping, while knee rails 3 feet above the floor help anchor the mesh.

A porch with decorative columns or posts *(right)* demands that the framework be recessed from the edges of the porch to accommodate doubled corner studs. If the porch has posts with flat surfaces *(inset)*, they can serve as the corner studs.

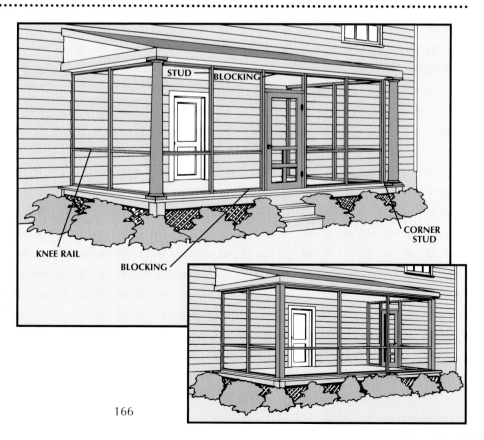

STUDS AND KNEE RAILS

1. Notching an end stud.
◆ To notch a stud for siding, place the face of the board against the house wall. Open a compass to the thickness of the siding, then move the metal point of the compass vertically down the siding so that the pencil transfers the siding profile to the stud *(below)*. Cut out the profile with a saber saw.

◆ Snap a chalk line along the edges of the porch as a guide to installing studs, allowing for corner studs if you must add them.

◆ Nail the notched stud to the house with 3-inch galvanized nails set at 8-inch intervals, then install additional studs along the chalk lines, toenailing them to floor and ceiling.

2. The remaining studs and doorframe.
◆ Cut two jack studs the height of the doorway and nail them to full-length studs, called king studs *(above)*. For a door at the front of the porch, the studs on both sides of the frame are equal in length. For a side door, they are different lengths to compensate for the drainage slope of the porch floor.

◆ Toenail the two stud assemblies, jack studs facing each other, to the floor and ceiling so that the distance between them is $\frac{1}{4}$ inch greater than the width of the door you plan to install.

◆ Measure and cut a 2-by-4 header to fit atop the jack studs. Fasten it with nails driven through each king stud into the header's ends.

3. Adding blocking and a knee rail.

Cut 2-by-4s to fit between the studs at the ceiling, at a height of about 3 feet, and at the floor. Between each pair of studs, nail one blocking board to the floor and another to the ceiling. End-nail the knee-rail pieces through the studs where possible; otherwise toe-nail them to the studs.

BLOCKING

KNEE RAIL

BLOCKING

GUIDELINE

TURN BUTTON

SCREEN

FRAME

4. Installing stops for framed screens.

Molding nailed to all four sides of each porch opening prevents the frame from falling inward and positions the frame flush with the exterior face of the supporting structure.

◆ Rule a line around each opening as a guide to recessing the molding a distance equal to the thickness of the frame you will build.

◆ Cut pieces of doorstop molding—mitered ends result in the most craftsmanlike appearance—to fit along the sides, top, and bottom of each porch opening, then fasten the molding with a 2-inch galvanized finishing nail every 8 inches.

◆ Fasten a pair of turn buttons *(inset)* to both sides of each opening to hold the frame against the stops.

ATTACHING SCREENING DIRECTLY TO THE PORCH

STAPLES

1. Stapling the screening.

◆ Cut a length of screening larger than the opening, and fasten the top of the piece to the porch with $\frac{1}{4}$-inch staples driven $\frac{1}{4}$ inch from the opening. Staple one top corner and then the other, restapling as needed to make sure that the top edge is taut and straight. Next, staple the rest of the upper edge at 2-inch intervals.

◆ Pull the screen down evenly over the opening and staple along the bottom at 2-inch intervals, beginning with the corners; then staple from the top to the bottom of the studs and across the knee rail.

◆ Cut away the excess screening $\frac{1}{4}$ inch outside the lines of staples.

2. Trimming with screen bead.

◆ Miter-cut four lengths of $\frac{5}{8}$-inch screen bead to cover the staples and to frame the opening flush with its edges. Nail the screen bead around the opening with $\frac{3}{4}$-inch brads every 6 inches. To prevent the bead from warping, alternate the brads from one edge of the bead to the other.

◆ Square-cut a length of bead to fit the knee rail and nail it in place.

SECURING THE MESH WITH SPLINE MOLDING

Unusual cuts at intersections.

◆ To install dual-channel screen-spline molding so that neither channel is blocked *(right)*, miter corners of the molding and its cover as shown for a wood frame on page 212.

◆ Where a stud crosses the knee rail, cut a 45° point on each piece of molding. The four points meet at the center of the intersection.

◆ At T intersections, cut a point on the molding piece that represents the up-right of the T and use it to mark a notch on the crosspiece *(inset)*.

◆ After screwing the molding to the frame, secure the mesh with a screen-spline roller *(page 210)* one opening at a time, first across the top, then at the bottom, and finally along the sides.

◆ Trim away the excess screening, and snap the spline cover into place *(far right)*.

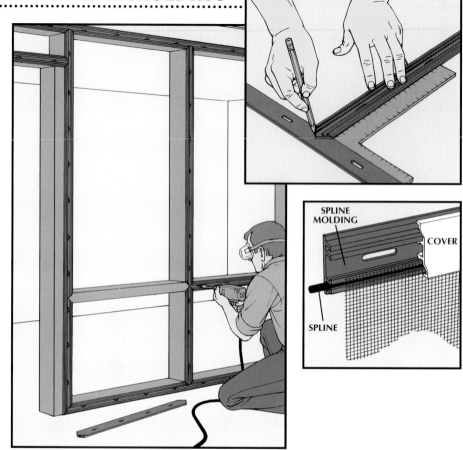

HANGING A WOOD-FRAMED SCREEN DOOR

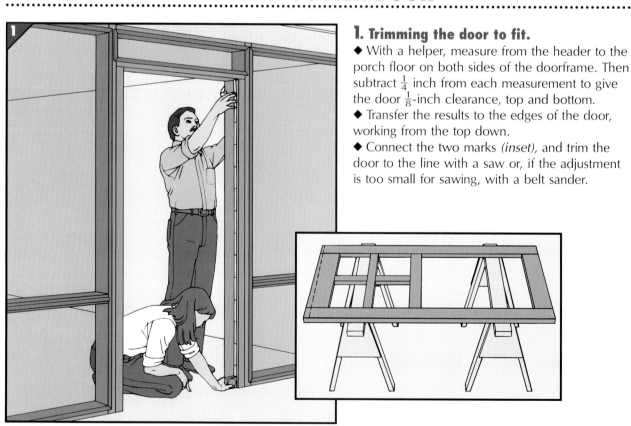

1. Trimming the door to fit.

◆ With a helper, measure from the header to the porch floor on both sides of the doorframe. Then subtract $\frac{1}{4}$ inch from each measurement to give the door $\frac{1}{8}$-inch clearance, top and bottom.

◆ Transfer the results to the edges of the door, working from the top down.

◆ Connect the two marks *(inset)*, and trim the door to the line with a saw or, if the adjustment is too small for sawing, with a belt sander.

SPACERS

FOOT LEVER

2. Hanging the door.

◆ Screw two hinges to the outer face of the door—1 foot from the top and 1 foot from the bottom. To ensure clearance between door and frame, tape $\frac{1}{8}$-inch-thick spacers above both hinges on the door's edge and on top of the door. Nickels, strips of corrugated cardboard, or $2\frac{1}{2}$-inch-long common nails work well as spacers.

◆ Have a helper hold the door in the frame so that the spacers touch the top and side of the frame. Shim the door to support it or use a block of wood and a pry bar as a foot lever *(left)*. On the doorframe, mark the holes for hinge screws.

◆ Set the door aside and drill pilot holes at the marks, then position the door in the opening and screw the hinges to the frame.

◆ Untape the spacers, and check the door's operation. Shave any edges that bind with a block plane or a wood rasp.

3. Installing a doorstop and latch.

To keep the door from closing too far, nail a band of molding to the doorframe.

◆ While a helper holds the door flush with the outside of the doorframe, mark a line on the frame along the top and sides of the door.

◆ Cut three strips of doorstop molding to fit along the top and sides of the frame. Miter the top molding and the upper ends of the side moldings; then cut the bottom ends of the side moldings square.

◆ With the door swung open, place the pieces along the guidelines drawn earlier, and nail them to the doorframe with 2-inch finishing nails set 8 inches apart *(inset)*.

◆ Finally, install a latch according to the manufacturer's directions.

DOORSTOP MOLDING

6

Patios of Brick and Concrete

Masonry surfaces actually float on the surface of the ground, rising and subsiding with spring thaws and winter frosts. In the case of concrete, the slab floats on a layer of gravel, while bricks and stone embedded in sand shift individually to adapt to changing contours. Either structure requires considerable excavation, heavy work lightened by a rotary tiller used to loosen soil for easier removal.

Patterns to Set in Sand or Mortar   174

Pavers for Patios
Options with Brick

Bricks without Mortar   176

Two Methods for Cutting Bricks
Excavating for a Patio
Laying Bricks in Sand
A Circular Patio to Surround a Tree
Setting Bricks in Overlapping Scallops

Groundwork for a Concrete Slab   182

Calculations for Slope and Volume
Tilting a Slab for Drainage
Curved Forms for a Rounded Slab

Pouring and Finishing Concrete   190

Filling the Forms
Finishing the Surface
Combining Redwood with Concrete
Pebbles for a Topcoat

A Curved Bench beside a Free-Form Patio   195

Brick or Flagstone Set in Mortar   196

Brick Veneer for a Concrete Slab
Random Shapes from Flagstones

The Many Possibilities of Tile   200

Composing Patterns with Shaped Tiles
Starting the Tile Sequence
Three Techniques for Cutting Tiles
Laying Tiles on Mortar
Filling Joints with Grout

Patterns to Set in Sand or Mortar

A patio with a surface of bricks or concrete paving blocks is weather-resistant and enduring. Because the brick or concrete pavers are small and uniform in size, such a patio is also easy to install and maintain.

The Spectrum of Materials: Standing water and changing temperatures are tough on brick patios; buy paving bricks, which are stronger than those used to build vertical structures. As shown opposite, you can combine them in a number of patterns. Molded concrete paving blocks, on the other hand, are designed to interlock.

Choosing Sand or Concrete: Both brick and concrete pavers may be set on a tightly compacted bed of sand *(pages 176-181)* or on a concrete slab with mortar *(page 197)*. Sand is self-draining and lets the pavers move independently as the earth shifts, and pavers set on sand can be leveled or replaced individually. Patios of mortared bricks or blocks, however, last longer, need less upkeep, and rarely have weeds.

Maintaining the Patio: Whether the pavers are on sand or concrete, moss may be a problem. Although it can be attractive, moss can also be a slippery hazard. To eliminate it, apply moss killer, sold at garden-supply stores. If your patio develops mildew stains, scrub it with household bleach. Finally, weeds can grow between pavers laid on sand, even when a weed-control barrier has been placed underneath. If that happens, you may need to spray all gaps with herbicide, taking care not to spray near trees and other desirable plants.

SAFETY TIPS

Wear hard-toed shoes when you are transporting brick or concrete pavers. If you are working with mortar, leather-palmed work gloves will protect your hands from irritants.

PAVERS FOR PATIOS

Brick pavers.
The paving brick at near right measures about $3\frac{5}{8}$ inches wide by $7\frac{5}{8}$ inches long; these dimensions allow for ample mortar joints between bricks. You can also purchase paving bricks like the one above it, which is exactly twice as long as it is wide. For use on a sand bed, these bricks fit together without gaps to help keep weeds from poking through. In climates where the ground freezes, use paving bricks that are rated SX, which means they can withstand severe weather.

Concrete pavers.
Molded concrete paving blocks come in numerous shapes; the three shown at right are among the more common. Because the blocks are laid down in interlocking patterns, they are less likely to shift position during or after installation.

4″ x 8″

$3\frac{5}{8}″$ x $7\frac{5}{8}″$

OPTIONS WITH BRICK

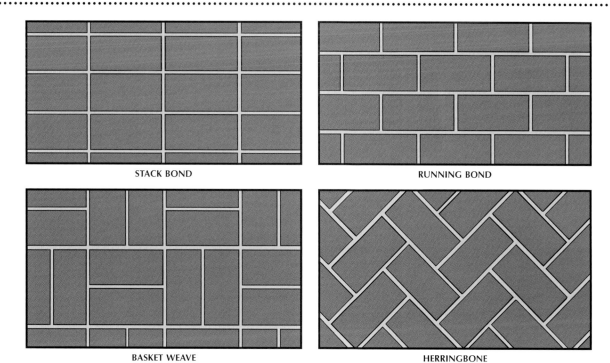

STACK BOND

RUNNING BOND

BASKET WEAVE

HERRINGBONE

An emphasis on regularity.
You can set rectangular bricks in any of the four classic patterns shown above, or combine the patterns to give varied surface designs. Avoid the stack-bond arrangement for large patios, since it is difficult to align; instead, frame other patterns with a stack-bond border. A running-bond pattern, in which the bricks are staggered, is easier to lay uniformly over a broad area.

Interlocking patterns like basket weave and herringbone, in which brick orientation varies, increase the durability of a sand-bed patio, since each brick is held in place by its neighbors. The basket weave above has brick faces exposed; another version has the bricks set on their sides, three to a square. Herringbone, with its directional nature, is useful for directing a viewer's eye to a particular spot.

Layouts based on circles.
To accommodate a tree, a fountain, or other fixed object, lay a circular pattern *(far left)*. Begin at the center with two rings of half bricks, then add rings of full-size bricks to fill an area of any size *(page 180)*.

A scalloped effect like that used on European boulevards *(near left)* is achieved with overlapping arcs of brick as shown on page 181. Loosely fill the scallops with whole and half bricks.

Bricks without Mortar

By far the easiest patio to build is one made of bricks set into a bed of sand. A sand base allows rainwater to seep down to tree or shrub roots, and sand lets bricks accommodate the earth below as it settles or shifts with freezing and thawing.

When planning a patio, consider the stability of the ground. Recent landfill more than 3 feet deep or water found within 1 foot of the surface may cause settling problems. If such conditions exist—or if you live in an earthquake zone—consult a landscape architect.

Laying Out a Sand Bed: To minimize brick cutting, lay a dry run around the patio perimeter before excavating, adjusting the patio dimensions to incorporate as many whole bricks as possible. Be sure to plan for a permanent edging *(page 178)*, required to keep sand-laid bricks from shifting. Chop out tree roots near the surface that would prevent bricks from lying flat. Before digging, check with a building inspector to see if you must erect a silt fence to keep eroded soil on your property.

Drainage: Usually, 2 inches of sand on well-tamped earth offers adequate drainage. Dense clay soils or heavy rainfall, however, often require the added drainage of a 4-inch layer of gravel under the sand. Use the estimator on page 182 to figure the amounts you need. To prevent sand from sifting down into the gravel, cover it with 15-pound roofing felt or 6-mil polyethylene sheeting punctured to let rainwater through. If drainage is a

particular problem, slope the sand bed away from the house about 1 inch every 4 to 6 feet. Perforated drain tile or plastic tubing laid in the gravel layer helps drain water away from wet spots.

Choosing the Right Bricks: Untextured, exterior-grade bricks are best; rough or grooved surfaces collect water that can crack bricks when it freezes. But avoid glazed bricks, which become slippery when wet. "Bricks" of molded concrete, which come in a wide array of colors and shapes, offer an alternative to traditional clay brick.

With Gaps or Without: Patterns of bricks laid tight against one another control weeds better than bricks laid with gaps between them. For a gapless patio, buy special paving bricks exactly half as wide as they are long.

Other paving bricks are sized for mortar joints between them. The gap both accentuates the pattern and channels rainwater down the long side of the brick— away from the house, if you align the long edges with any slope the site may have. Plastic sheeting laid on the sand bed before the bricks are laid helps keep weeds from growing in the gaps, and sand swept into the gaps keeps the bricks from moving.

⚠️ **CAUTION** *Before excavating, establish the locations of underground obstacles such as electric, water, and sewer lines, and dry wells, septic tanks, and cesspools.*

 TOOLS

Brickset
4-pound maul
Mason's hammer
Rubber mallet
Level
Framing square
Circular saw with a carbide
　　masonry blade

 **MATERIALS**

Bricks
Washed gravel ($\frac{3}{4}$-inch)
Polyethylene sheeting
Sand
2-by-2 stakes
String

 **SAFETY TIPS**

Wear eye protection when cutting bricks. A dust mask is recommended when trimming brick with a circular saw. Gloves help prevent blisters and abrasions.

TWO METHODS FOR CUTTING BRICKS

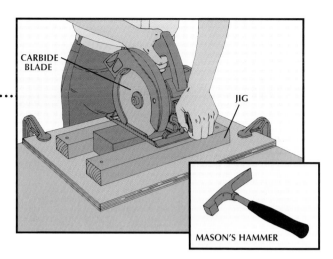

Using a brickset.
To cut a small number of bricks, use a wide chisel—called a brickset—and a 4-pound maul. Draw a cutting line on the brick, then cushion the brick on sand or a board. Hold the brickset vertically with the beveled edge facing away from you and strike the tool sharply. Then tilt the brickset slightly toward you and strike again, thus splitting the brick. Practice on a few broken bricks before you cut the bricks you will use.

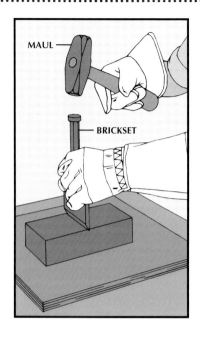

Scoring bricks with a circular saw.
Large numbers of bricks are more easily cut with the help of a circular saw fitted with a carbide masonry blade. Hold the brick in a simple jig made of 2-by-4 scraps, spaced a brick's width apart and nailed to a piece of plywood. Set the saw for a $\frac{1}{4}$-inch cut, then slowly guide the blade along the cutting line, grooving the brick. Make a matching groove on the other side, then hold the brick in your hand and break off the unwanted portion with the blunt end of a mason's hammer *(inset)*.

EXCAVATING FOR A PATIO

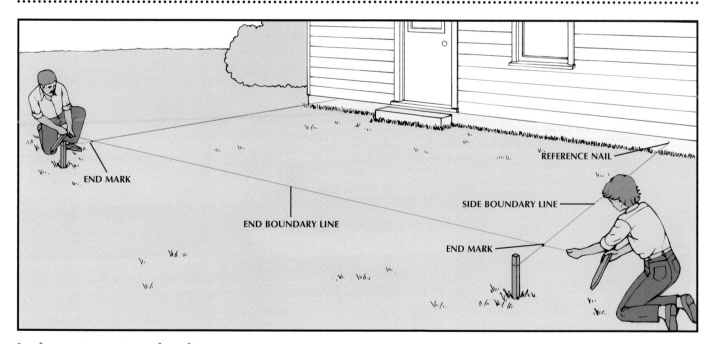

Laying out a rectangular site.
◆ Drive reference nails into the wall of the house to mark both sides of the patio.
◆ Use the method shown on page 21 to establish positions for 2-by-2 stakes opposite the nails and 2 feet beyond the end of the future patio.
◆ Tie string between the nails and stakes to establish side boundary lines for the patio and mark each string where the patio will end.
◆ With a helper stake a third string so that it crosses the marks you made on the side boundary lines *(above)*.
◆ To excavate the area, first dig a trench along the boundary lines. Make the trench deep enough to accommodate the bricks, sand, and gravel if any. Work in parallel rows, back and forth between the perimeter trenches.

Laying out an irregular shape.

◆ Draw the patio on graph paper, with each square representing 1 square foot. To estimate the area of the patio, assign a rough fractional value to parts of squares inside the outline. Then add up the full squares and the fractions. Use this figure when buying brick, sand, and gravel.

◆ Lay out a garden hose in the shape of the patio, then outline the perimeter on the ground with a dispenser of powdered chalk *(page 188)*. Trench around the perimeter, then excavate.

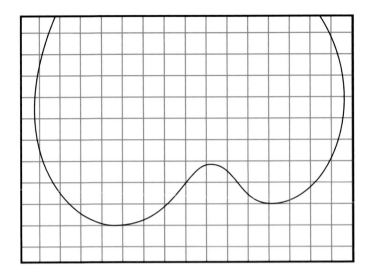

LAYING BRICKS IN SAND

1. Edging the perimeter.

◆ First, compact the earth inside the excavation with a tamper *(page 183)*.

◆ Around the perimeter, dig a narrow trench such that the top of a brick stood on end in the trench will be even with the patio surface. *(If a side of the patio will border a flower bed, let the edging extend 2 inches higher.)*

◆ Tamp the bottom of the trench with the end of a 2-by-4, then stretch reference strings as guides for aligning the tops of the edging bricks with one another. Next, stand bricks upright around the perimeter *(above)*, with their top edges touching the strings. Press earth against the bricks to hold them up.

◆ Add washed gravel as necessary, distributing it evenly over the surface with a rake. Cover the gravel with roofing felt, or polyethylene sheeting that has been punctured with drainage holes at 4- to 6-inch intervals.

◆ Spread a 2-inch layer of sand over the bed. Dampen the sand, then tamp the surface again.

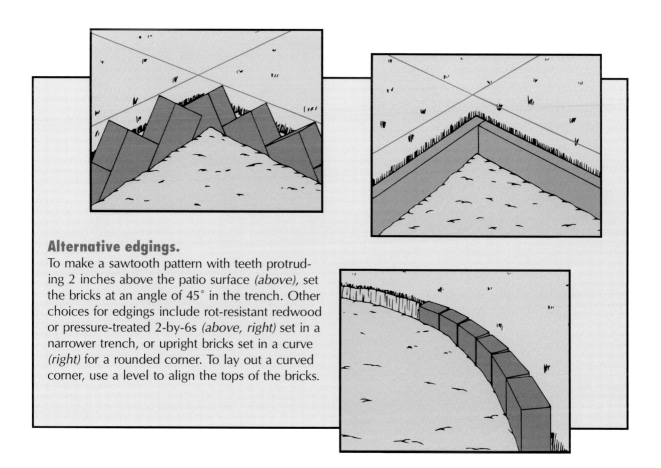

Alternative edgings.

To make a sawtooth pattern with teeth protruding 2 inches above the patio surface *(above)*, set the bricks at an angle of 45° in the trench. Other choices for edgings include rot-resistant redwood or pressure-treated 2-by-6s *(above, right)* set in a narrower trench, or upright bricks set in a curve *(right)* for a rounded corner. To lay out a curved corner, use a level to align the tops of the bricks.

2. Laying the bricks.

◆ Use a reference string to help align bricks in the pattern you choose for your patio. Begin a herringbone pattern, for example, with a brick set at a 45° angle to the edging in each of two adjacent patio corners. Tap the bricks into the sand with a rubber mallet to make them flush with the edging bricks.

◆ Stretch a string between two spare bricks, set just outside the edging, so that the string passes over the corners of the two corner bricks. As you set bricks in the first row, align corners with the string. Use the mallet or adjust the sand bed to keep the bricks even with one another.

◆ To begin a new row, lay a brick at each end as a guide for positioning the reference string. Fill in the row, smoothing any sand you may have disturbed. Repeat for each row.

◆ Fill triangular spaces along the patio edges with brick that you have cut to fit, then gently sweep sand into any gaps that remain. Add more sand if necessary after it rains.

A CIRCULAR PATIO TO SURROUND A TREE

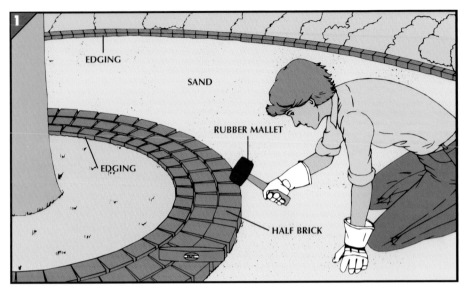

EDGING
SAND
RUBBER MALLET
EDGING
HALF BRICK

1. Starting with half bricks.
◆ Loop a garden hose around the tree to mark inner and outer perimeters for the patio. Make the inner circle at least 3 feet in diameter to avoid wide gaps between the half bricks used in the first two courses.
◆ Excavate and edge the area to be paved, then prepare the sand bed.
◆ Cut half bricks for the first course and tap them into place with a rubber mallet, wedging the inner corners of the bricks tight against each other *(left).* Use a level to align the tops of the bricks. Trim the last half brick in each course as needed for a snug fit.
◆ Lay a second course of half bricks against the first.

2. Setting the whole bricks.
◆ Place concentric circles of whole bricks in the sand bed so that their inner edges touch at the corners and butt against the preceding course. Tap each brick into place with a rubber mallet. Use a 4-foot mason's level to align the brick, adding or removing sand as necessary.
◆ Continue laying whole bricks in concentric circles out to the edging.

3. Filling gaps at the edge.
◆ Mark a brick to fit each oddly shaped nook along the patio's outer perimeter. Cut the brick with a brickset as shown on page 177, then trim as needed by chipping it with the sharp end of a mason's hammer. Set the brick into place with a rubber mallet.
◆ Gently brush sand into the gaps between bricks, repeating the process as necessary to refill the cracks after a rain.

BRICKSET
MAUL

SETTING BRICKS IN OVERLAPPING SCALLOPS

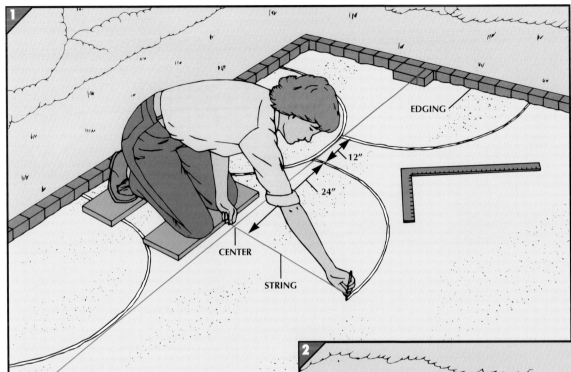

EDGING

12"

24"

CENTER

STRING

1. Scribing scallop arcs.

◆ Use the edging of a sand bed to establish a base line for drawing semicircles in the sand. Arcs that have a radius of 24 inches and are spaced with their centers 60 inches apart make an attractive pattern. Scribe arcs across one end of the sand bed, with partial arcs at the sides if necessary.

◆ Stretch a string between two bricks so that it crosses the tops of the arcs in the first row *(above)*. Kneeling on boards to avoid disturbing arcs already drawn, scribe another row of arcs with centers midway between those in the first row. A framing square helps in marking these centers and those in subsequent rows. Use partial arcs in the last row if necessary.

2. Paving the scallops.

◆ Arrange whole bricks along each arc *(right)*, then with a partial brick, start filling each scallop at the narrow space between arcs. Half a brick, followed by three-quarters of a brick in the next course, works well with 24-inch arcs.

◆ Pave the rest of each scallop with whole bricks laid in slightly curving rows *(inset)*. Fill partial scallops with whole bricks and any cavities with cut bricks or sand.

◆ Sweep sand into any gaps that remain.

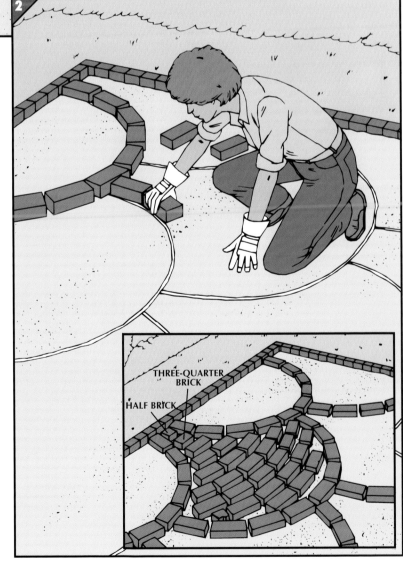

THREE-QUARTER BRICK

HALF BRICK

Groundwork for a Concrete Slab

A concrete slab consists of a layer of concrete, usually reinforced with wire mesh, that rests on a drainage bed of gravel. Although the 4-inch reinforced slab on 4 inches of gravel described on the following pages satisfies many building codes, always check with local authorities for the correct specifications.

Building codes may also specify the degree of slope required for water runoff and whether a silt fence is needed during construction to limit soil erosion. Local zoning laws may dictate the location, design, and size of a slab.

Getting Started: Selecting a site for a slab requires the same care as choosing one for a brick patio *(page 176)*. When your plan is completed use the estimator below to calculate how much concrete and gravel you'll use, based on the area of the slab and the thickness of the concrete plus the gravel bed.

To prepare the site for a rectangular slab, lay out boundaries with wood stakes and string as shown on page 177, and excavate the site. Dig 2 feet beyond the strings to accommodate form boards and

braces, then proceed as shown here. Site preparation for a free-form slab appears on pages 188-189. Save sod and dirt to fill in at the sides of the finished slab.

Expansion Joints: Many local codes require a strip of asphalt-impregnated expansion-joint filler in the concrete every 8 to 10 feet of a slab's length and between the slab and the house foundation *(page 186, Step 7)*. The purpose of the joints is to prevent damage as concrete expands and contracts with changes in temperature. Try to buy joint filler as wide as the thickness of the slab. If unavailable, somewhat narrower or wider filler is satisfactory.

Forms to Shape Concrete: Unless you plan on a decorative pattern of permanent form boards *(page 187)*, build forms from inexpensive woods such as fir, spruce, or pine. Plywood, made flexible with the technique shown on page 188, is used to mold the curves of a free-form slab. Double-headed nails allow both types of temporary forms to be quickly disassembled.

 TOOLS

Common carpentry tools
Spade
Tamper
Screed
Rake
4-pound maul
Line level
Wire cutters

 **MATERIALS**

1-by-2s
2-by-4s
Plywood ($\frac{3}{4}$-inch)
2-by-2 stakes
Mason's cord
Double-headed nails (2-inch)
Common nails (3-inch)
Spikes (6-inch)
Masonry nails ($1\frac{1}{2}$-inch)
Washed gravel ($\frac{3}{4}$-inch)
Expansion-joint filler
Reinforcing mesh
Binding wire
Concrete blocks
Powdered chalk
Lath

 SAFETY TIPS

Wear goggles when nailing form boards together and joint filler to the house. Gloves protect your hands from blisters, splinters, and especially cuts when handling wire mesh.

CALCULATIONS FOR SLOPE AND VOLUME

Length of a side boundary line in feet

_____ x 0.25 = _____ inches

Area in square feet   **Thickness in inches**

_____ x _____ x 0.0033 = _____ cubic yards

Calculating slope.
For a slope of $\frac{1}{4}$ inch per foot, use the formula above to determine the difference in height between the edge of the slab that abuts the house and the edge parallel to it. Multiply by 0.125 instead of 0.25 for a slope of $\frac{1}{8}$ inch per foot.

Estimating cubic yardage.
Use the estimator above to find the amount of concrete or gravel needed for a slab or drainage bed. The result in cubic yards—the bulk measure in which such materials are sold—includes an 8 percent allowance for waste and spillage.

TILTING A SLAB FOR DRAINAGE

1. Leveling the excavated area.
◆ Using a rake, break up any clods of earth; then, with a helper, pull an 8-foot-long 2-by-4 leveling board across the area to smooth it *(above)*.

◆ Dampen the area with a hose, and compact the surface by pounding it with a tamper. You can rent one or build one from a 2-foot square of $\frac{3}{4}$-inch plywood with a braced handle, 4 feet high, made of 2-by-4s.
◆ After tamping, pull the leveling board across the area again, using it as a straightedge to make sure that the surface is reasonably even.

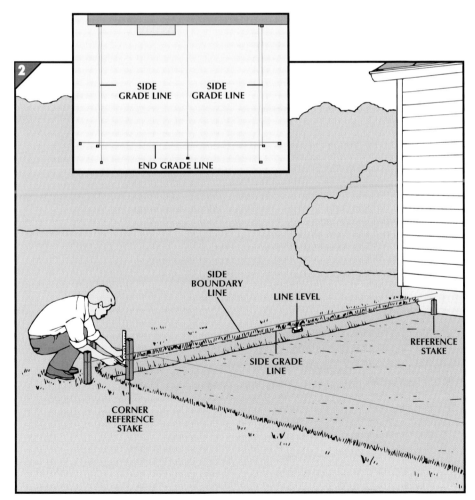

2. Establishing the grade.
◆ Mark the slab height—the sum of the slab and gravel-bed thicknesses—on the house wall, 2 inches outside a side boundary line. Center a 2-by-2 reference stake on the mark and drive it into the ground next to the house wall, bringing the top even with the slab-height mark. Center a nail on top of the stake and hammer it in partway.
◆ Measure along the side boundary line to a point 2 inches beyond the end boundary line, and drive a corner reference stake opposite the first. Loop a string around the second stake and tie it to the nail in the other. Hang a line level at the center of the string and adjust the string at the corner stake to make the string level.
◆ Use the formula on the preceding page to calculate slope, and mark the resulting distance on the corner stake, below the string. Lower the string to the mark, called a grade mark.
◆ Repeat for the other side of the slab.
◆ Connect the grade marks on the corner stakes with a third string to make an end grade line. Use that line and a reference stake near the house to establish a grade line within the slab for each expansion joint required.

3. Adding support stakes.

◆ Mark the grade lines at 2-foot intervals. Directly below each marker, drive a 2-by-2 form-support stake deep enough so you can't pull it out by hand and so the grade line just touches the top of the stake. Place stakes precisely to ensure that corners will be square and the slab sloped correctly.

◆ When all of the support stakes are in place, remove the grade lines and use a handsaw to trim the corner reference stakes to the height marked earlier for the grade lines. Then remove all the boundary-marker strings and stakes; leave only the support stakes and the corner reference stakes.

4. Installing form boards.

◆ Cut a 2-by-4 form board 4 inches longer than the distance from the house to the outer edge of the reference stake. Use more than one if needed, butting the boards.

◆ Set a board against the inside faces of the support stakes, one end against the house. Rest the board on wood blocks so that the top edge is even with the tops of the stakes.

◆ Drive a 2-inch double-headed nail through each end stake into the board, using a maul as an anvil *(above)*. Then nail the board to the intermediate stakes.

◆ Install a form board for the other side of the slab in the same way.

◆ Nail a form board for the end of the slab to its support stakes. Where this board abuts the side boards, toenail the joints with 3-inch common nails.

◆ For each expansion joint, cut a board $\frac{1}{2}$ inch shorter than the distance between the house and the end board. Nail the board to its support stakes on the side of the slab that will be poured first, leaving a $\frac{1}{2}$-inch space at the wall.

◆ Where boards abut *(inset)*, drive a support stake 6 inches to each side of the joint. Nail the boards to the stakes, then nail a strip of $\frac{1}{2}$-inch plywood over the joint.

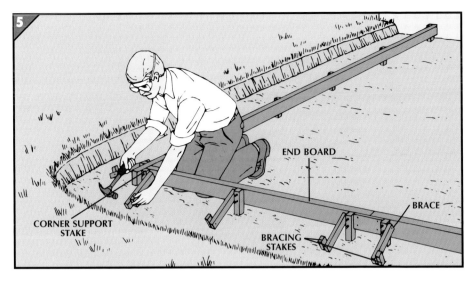

5. Bracing the form boards.

◆ Drive a support stake at the corners where end and side boards meet.
◆ Reinforce each support stake, including those flanking a joint, with a 1-by-2 brace nailed to a stake driven about 1 foot from the form board.
◆ Excavate the slab area along the end board to match the slope of the side form boards, then smooth and tamp.

END BOARD

BRACE

CORNER SUPPORT
STAKE

BRACING
STAKES

6. Screeding the gravel.

Pour a layer of $\frac{3}{4}$-inch gravel into each section of the slab, allowing it to spill out under the form boards. With a helper, smooth the gravel by dragging a screed across its surface.

TRICKS OF THE TRADE

To Make a Screed

The function of a screed is to assure a smooth gravel surface and a uniform slab thickness. To make the screed shown here, which is designed for a slab 4 inches thick, cut a 1-by-8 board 2 inches shorter than the distance between forms, and a 2-by-4 board 10 inches longer than this distance. Center the 1-by-8 on the 2-by-4. Offset the 1-by-8 board $\frac{1}{4}$ inch and nail the boards together. To the face of the 1-by-8, toenail two 2-by-2 handles, each 4 feet long and cut at a 30° angle at one end. Brace the handles with 2-by-2s nailed to the top of the 2-by-4.

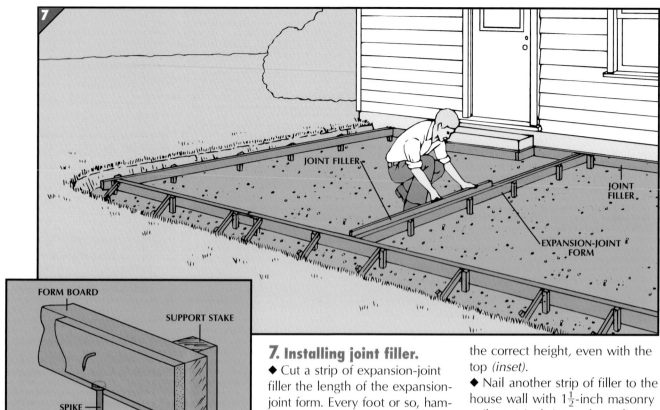

7. Installing joint filler.

◆ Cut a strip of expansion-joint filler the length of the expansion-joint form. Every foot or so, hammer 3-inch nails through one side of the filler and bend the points slightly to anchor it in the slab.

◆ Set the filler against the form *(above)*. Use 6-inch spikes, if necessary, to support the filler at the correct height, even with the top *(inset)*.

◆ Nail another strip of filler to the house wall with $1\frac{1}{2}$-inch masonry nails at 6-inch intervals, outlining any existing stairs. Butt the filler against the side form boards and work it into the $\frac{1}{2}$-inch space between expansion-joint forms and the house.

8. Laying wire mesh.

◆ Wearing gloves, unroll mesh over the gravel. Begin at the outer edge of the slab, and leave 2 inches between the mesh and the form boards. Weigh down the mesh with concrete blocks as you go. When you reach the other side of a section, use wirecutters to trim the mesh 2 inches short of the form board. Then turn the mesh over, and walk on it to flatten it.

◆ Cover the gravel in the section you intend to pour first, allowing panels of mesh to overlap 6 inches. Cut the mesh to fit around steps or other obstacles, then tie panels together with binding wire.

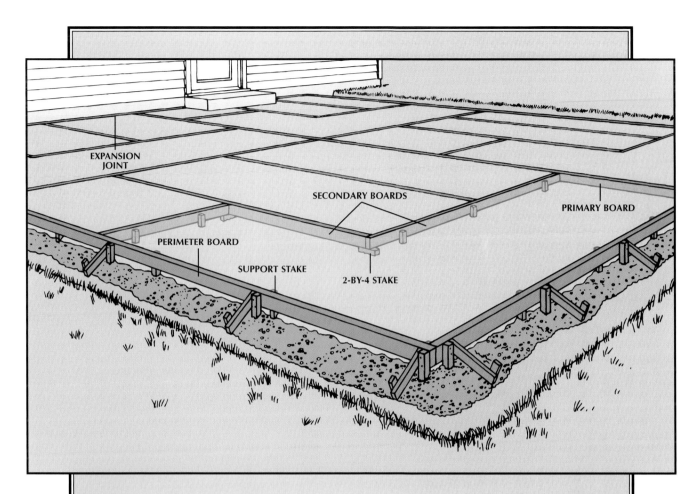

EXPANSION
JOINT

SECONDARY BOARDS

PRIMARY BOARD

PERIMETER BOARD

SUPPORT STAKE

2-BY-4 STAKE

THE APPEAL OF PERMANENT FORM BOARDS

In most instances, form boards become scrap lumber after a slab is poured. A decorative option, however, is to leave them in place as a frame around the slab or, as shown here, to lay out an attractive pattern of interior form boards. For this purpose, pressure-treated or other weather-resistant wood is superior to the pine or spruce used for temporary forms.

Installing permanent form boards follows the same principles used for setting up temporary boards—with a few differences. When laying out the perimeter for such a slab, take into account that the form boards will contribute to its length and width. Set up and brace perimeter form boards as shown on pages 184 to 185, but drive support stakes for interior boards as well as perimeter boards an inch below the planned surface of the slab so that the concrete will conceal them.

Establish the slope of the slab as shown on page 183. Each interior board that will lie perpendicular to the house needs a

grade line. Boards oriented parallel to the house each require a string set up in the same way as an end line *(page 183)*.

Permanent form boards replace expansion joints within the slab but not the one along the house. Boards that cross from one side of the slab to the other are called primary form boards. Next to the house, use stakes to secure the ends of primary form boards; nail through perimeter form boards to secure other ends.

Secondary form boards are shorter than the width or length of the patio. Where secondary form boards meet perimeter or primary form boards, they can be face-nailed. Where two secondary boards meet, nail one to the other and toenail both to a 2-by-4 stake driven into the ground under the joint.

Before pouring the slab, drive 3-inch nails halfway into all the form boards to help anchor them in the concrete, and cover their top edges with heavy-duty tape to prevent concrete stains.

CURVED FORMS FOR A ROUNDED SLAB

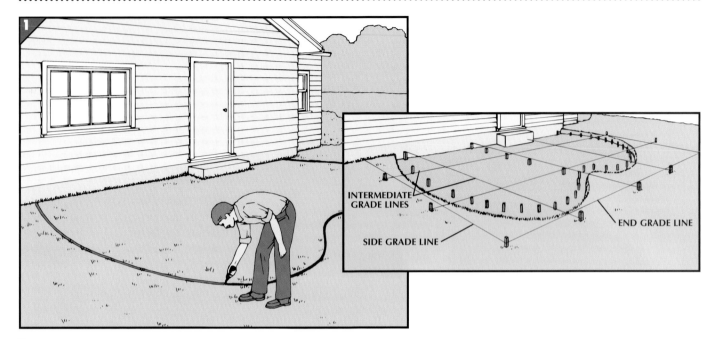

INTERMEDIATE GRADE LINES

SIDE GRADE LINE

END GRADE LINE

1. Excavating the slab area.

◆ Establish the slab shape with a garden hose, then mark the shape on the ground with powdered chalk.

◆ Remove the hose, and excavate the area a distance 2 feet beyond the chalk line. Dig to a depth equal to the thickness of the drainage bed plus the thickness of the slab. Dig back and forth across the area in parallel rows, then smooth and tamp the soil

in the bottom of the excavation.

◆ To establish drainage away from the house, first set up boundary lines and grade lines for a rectangle a foot or two larger in each dimension than the slab's maximum length and width *(inset)*.

◆ Tie intermediate grade lines at 3-foot intervals between the side lines, and between the wall of the house and the end line; at the house, tie

the strings to masonry nails.

◆ Drive 2-by-2 support stakes into the ground around the slab perimeter, 2 feet in from the edge of the excavation. Space the stakes 2 feet apart along gradual curves, 1 foot apart around sharp curves.

◆ Add support stakes for any interior forms required, spacing them at 2-foot intervals. Set the tops of the stakes even with the strings.

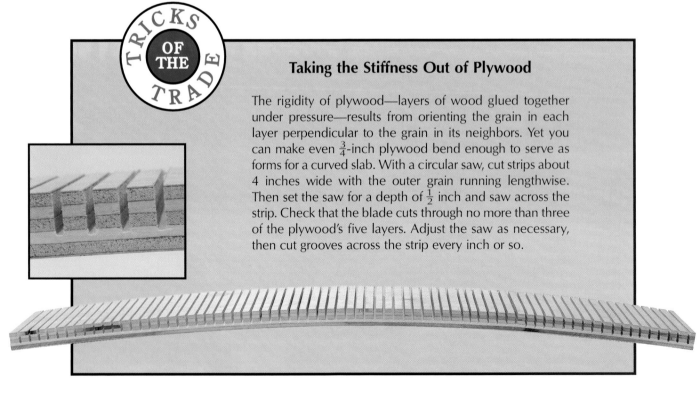

TRICKS OF THE TRADE

Taking the Stiffness Out of Plywood

The rigidity of plywood—layers of wood glued together under pressure—results from orienting the grain in each layer perpendicular to the grain in its neighbors. Yet you can make even $\frac{3}{4}$-inch plywood bend enough to serve as forms for a curved slab. With a circular saw, cut strips about 4 inches wide with the outer grain running lengthwise. Then set the saw for a depth of $\frac{1}{2}$ inch and saw across the strip. Check that the blade cuts through no more than three of the plywood's five layers. Adjust the saw as necessary, then cut grooves across the strip every inch or so.

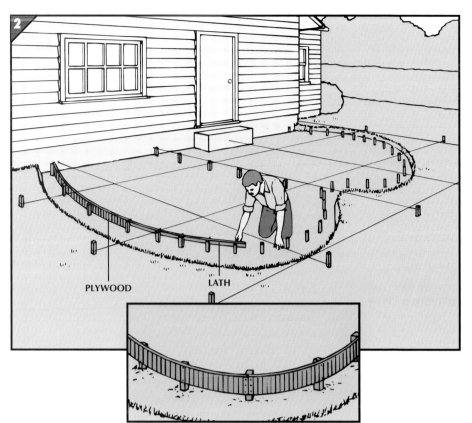

PLYWOOD LATH

2. Installing form boards.

◆ To measure for curved form boards, first cut a strip of lath 4 to 8 feet long. Tack it to support stakes, even with the tops and butted against the house.
◆ Mark the lath at the midpoint of the support stake nearest the end, then pry off the lath and transfer the mark to a strip of $\frac{3}{4}$-inch plywood cut as wide as the slab depth. Trim the plywood at the mark.
◆ Cut slots in the plywood to make it pliable *(opposite),* then nail it to the support stakes.
◆ Proceed around the slab perimeter in this fashion, butting sections of plywood at support stakes *(inset).*
◆ Install expansion-joint forms as necessary *(page 184).*

3. Sloping the forms.

◆ Work around the curved form, lifting or hammering down the boards and stakes until the top edge of the form just grazes the grading lines. Repeat for the straight forms of the expansion joints.
◆ When both the curved and the straight forms are adjusted, secure the support stakes with braces *(page 185).*
◆ Correct the depth of the excavation to match the slope of the grade, then spread a gravel drainage bed 4 inches thick.
◆ Install joint filler as shown on page 186.

4. Cutting mesh to fit the form.

◆ Unroll a length of wire mesh over a section of the form, letting it overlap the curve of the form boards where necessary.
◆ Anchor the mesh temporarily with cinder blocks, then cut the mesh along the curve, 2 inches inside the form.
◆ Flatten the mesh either by bending or by removing it from the form and walking it flat.
◆ Cut additional sections of mesh, allowing each to overlap the previous section by 6 inches. Flatten the sections and tie them together with binding wire.

The key requirement for pouring and finishing a concrete slab is speed. On a dry, windy day, it may take only three hours for freshly poured concrete to become too stiff to work. For a 10-by-12 slab, two people will need about an hour for the heavy work of pouring, leveling, and smoothing the concrete, plus up to three hours to finish the surface. Until you have some experience, it's best to pour concrete in sections no larger than 120 square feet.

Mixing Your Own: A good source of concrete is a ready-mix company specializing in small loads—unless the slab is far from the street. In that case, haul the concrete in a rented trailer and mixer.

When making concrete yourself, test the mixture's consistency frequently *(below)*. Between checks, add water sparingly—1 cup per cubic foot of concrete at a time.

Planning for the Finish: Smooth and textured finishes to concrete *(pages 192-193)* need no advance preparation, but surfacing with oth-er materials requires forethought. For example, if you intend to apply a pebble-aggregate surface *(page 194)*, you will need a stiffer-than-average concrete mix. Furthermore, you must thoroughly wet the pebbles before pouring the concrete. Order $\frac{1}{3}$ cubic yard of gravel for every 100 square feet of slab.

Redwood rounds *(page 193)*, which are suitable only in dry climates, must be in place before concrete is poured. Positioning them requires cutting openings for them in the slab's mesh reinforcement.

The Process of Curing: After a slab is finished, it must be cured—kept moist and warm—for at least a week to allow for the gradual chemical reactions that give concrete its full structural strength. The most common method of curing is to cover the slab with a polyethylene sheet. Colored slabs and pebble-aggregate surfaces are air-cured, however—left uncovered and sprinkled several times a day with water. Wait until the slab has cured to remove the outside forms.

TOOLS

Concrete mixer	Mason's trowel
Shovel	Edger
Rake	Hand float
Spade	Rectangular trowel
2-by-4 screed	Convex jointer
Bull float	Darby
Ladder	

Concrete Checklist

✔ When ordering concrete, tell the ready-mix company the dimensions of your slab and whether you intend to apply a pebble-aggregate surface or wish to have it colored.

✔ If you live in an area subject to freezes and thaws, make sure that an air-entraining agent—a chemical that creates tiny air bubbles in the concrete to prevent cracking—is added to the mix.

✔ Make arrangements for the ready-mix truck to arrive early; concrete sets more slowly in the cool of the morning.

✔ Have the truck park on the street, then lay a path of planks for carrying the concrete to the slab in wheelbarrows.

✔ Transport approximately 1 cubic foot (150 pounds) in a wheelbarrow at a time.

TRICKS OF THE TRADE

Perfect Concrete

Mixing the correct amount of water into concrete is crucial: Too little and a smooth finish on the concrete will be difficult to attain, too much and the material will lack strength and durability. The concrete in the left photograph above, although appearing somewhat dry, is actually just right; light troweling produces a smooth surface. A dash or two more water produces a mudlike mixture that is too wet for use *(above, right)*.

FILLING THE FORMS

1. Adding the concrete.

◆ Support the wire mesh on bricks, and oil the form boards to prevent sticking.

◆ Dump enough concrete into the first form to overfill by $\frac{1}{2}$ inch a 3- to 4-foot-wide section between the form boards, packing each load against the preceding one with a shovel. Use the shovel after each load to push the concrete into form corners and against the joint filler.

◆ Work a flat spade between the forms and the concrete to force the stones in the mix away from the sides. Then jab the spade vertically into the concrete throughout the section to eliminate air pockets.

◆ If the wire reinforcement sags into the gravel base under the concrete's weight, hook it with a rake and lift it to the middle of the concrete.

2. Screeding the concrete.

◆ As each 3- to 4-foot section is filled, set a screed—a straight 2-by-4, cut 2 feet wider than the width of the form—on edge across the form boards. With the aid of a helper, lift and lower the screed in a chopping motion to force the aggregate down into the concrete.

◆ Then, starting at one end of the filled section, pull the screed across the surface of the concrete, simultaneously sliding it from side to side in a sawlike motion. Tilt the screed toward you as you pull it, so that the bottom of the board acts as a cutting edge.

◆ To level any remaining low spots or bumps, pull the screed across the concrete again, tilting it away from you. In areas around obstacles such as steps or window wells, use a short screed, cut to fit the space.

◆ Fill and level the rest of the form in successive 3- to 4-foot sections.

3. Bull-floating the surface.

◆ To compact and smooth the concrete, first push the float forward, tilting the front edge of the blade upward. Then draw it back, keeping the blade flat against the surface.

◆ Shovel fresh concrete into any remaining depressions. To reach areas beyond arm's length, bridge the wet concrete with a ladder supported on concrete blocks.

◆ Bull-float the surface again.

4. Edging the concrete.

◆ When the concrete is firm enough to hold its shape, run a mason's trowel between the form boards and the outside edge of the slab to separate the top inch of concrete from the wood *(right)*.

◆ Push an edger back and forth along the slot *(far right)*, tilting the leading edge of the tool slightly upward to avoid gouging the concrete. Any deep indentations will be difficult to fill during later finishing steps.

◆ Wait for any surface water to evaporate from the slab before applying the finish.

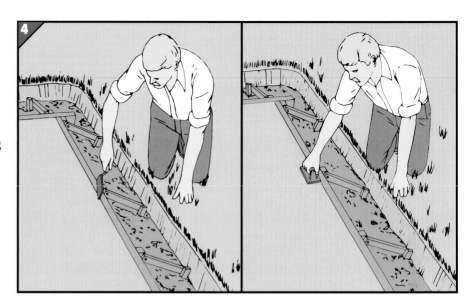

FINISHING THE SURFACE

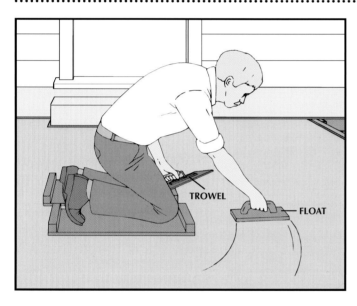

Troweling a smooth finish.

◆ Place a pair of knee boards—1- by 2-foot pieces of $\frac{3}{8}$-inch plywood with 2-by-2 handles nailed at the ends—on the slab. Kneeling on the boards, smooth the concrete with a hand float, holding it flat and sweeping it in overlapping arcs across the surface. Then sweep a rectangular steel trowel, held flat, across the same area. Similarly float and trowel the rest of the slab, moving the knee boards as necessary. *(The concrete will be firm enough to walk on at this stage.)*

◆ After floating and troweling, go over the slab again with the trowel alone, this time tilting the tool slightly. Work the surface until no concrete collects on the trowel and the blade makes a ringing sound indicating that the concrete is too firm to work any further.

◆ Run the edger between the form boards and the edges of the slab *(above)* to restore edging lines.

Brooming a skidproof surface.

Hand-float the concrete and trowel it once *(above)*. Instead of the final troweling, draw a damp, stiff-bristled utility brush across the surface. Either score straight lines at right angles to the forms or move the broom in arcs to produce a curved pattern. If the broom picks up small lumps of concrete, hose down the bristles to clean them; give the slab a few more minutes' drying time before you continue. If you have to press hard to score the concrete, work fast; the concrete will soon be too firm to take a finish.

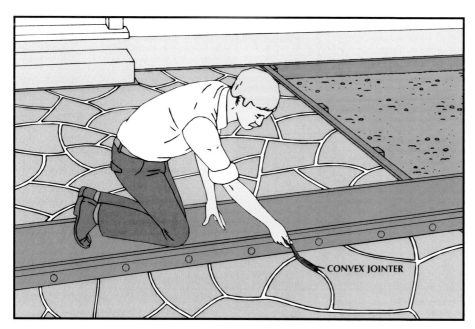

Creating a flagstone effect.
◆ Immediately after bull-floating the concrete *(page 191)*, score the surface with irregularly spaced grooves, $\frac{1}{2}$- to $\frac{3}{4}$-inch deep, using a convex jointer. Place a ladder across forms as a bridge to reach inaccessible spots.
◆ After surface water has evaporated, hand-float and trowel the surface, then retool the grooves to restore the flagstone pattern to its original clarity.
◆ Brush out the grooves with a dry paintbrush to remove any remaining loose bits of concrete.

CONVEX JOINTER

COMBINING REDWOOD WITH CONCRETE

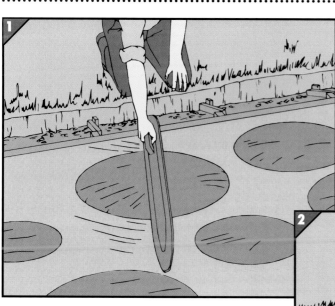

1. Installing redwood rounds.
◆ Arrange 4-inch-thick redwood rounds directly on the gravel bed. Cover the top of each round with a sheet of 4-mil polyethylene, fastened with staples; then pour or shovel concrete carefully around each round.
◆ Level the concrete with a 2-by-4 screed cut short enough to fit between the rounds. Smooth the surface with a darby *(above)* instead of a bull float. Hold the darby flat, and move it sideways in a sawing motion to cut off bumps and fill in holes. Run the darby over the slab a second time, sweeping it over the surface in broad arcs.

2. Finishing the edges.
◆ When the concrete is firm enough to hold its shape, run the pointed end of a mason's trowel around the outside of each round to cut a V-shaped groove, $\frac{1}{4}$ inch deep.
◆ Finish the slab with a hand float and a trowel as on page 192. When the concrete has cured, remove the polyethylene covers.

PEBBLES FOR A TOPCOAT

1. Preparing the surface.
◆ Fill the form with concrete as on page 191, Step 1, but pack it even with the tops of the boards rather than above them.
◆ Level the concrete with a screed notched at each end so that its bottom edge rides $\frac{1}{2}$ inch below the tops of the form boards, then bull-float the surface.
◆ Scatter the damp pebbles evenly over the concrete with a shovel. Cover the surface with a single layer of stones, using a ladder bridge, if necessary, to reach inner areas.

2. Embedding the aggregate.
Tap the stones into the concrete with a bull float, forcing them just below the surface. After you have gone over the entire slab with the bull float, press down any stones that are still visible with a hand float, using a ladder bridge, if needed, to reach the interior of the slab. Then run the hand float across the surface as on page 192, covering the stones with a thin, smooth layer of concrete.

3. Exposing the aggregate.
◆ After surface water has evaporated and the concrete is firm enough to resist indentation, brush the surface lightly with a stiff nylon broom to expose the tops of the stones.
◆ While a helper sprays the slab with water, brush it again, uncovering between a quarter and a half of the stones' circumference. If you dislodge any stones, stop brushing and wait until the concrete is a bit firmer before continuing. If the concrete is difficult to wash off, work quickly to expose the aggregate before the surface becomes too stiff.
◆ After exposing the stones, continue to spray the surface until there is no noticeable cement film left on the aggregate. Scrub individual spots missed in the general wash with a scrub brush and a pail of water.
◆ Two to four hours after exposing the aggregate, wash and lightly brush the surface again to remove any cloudy residue from the stones.

A Curved Bench beside a Free-Form Patio

A wood bench is a handsome addendum to any patio, brick or concrete. The design shown here—for a bench shaped to a curved patio—is easily adapted to a rectangular one.

Choose a wood that is sufficiently resistant to decay and insects to be used outdoors. Pressure-treated pine is the least expensive but has a tendency to warp. Cedar, cypress, and redwood stand up well. Left untreated, they weather to a soft, attractive gray.

1. Anchoring posts.

◆ Use a 3-foot length of lath as a guide for chalking posthole marks on the edge of the patio *(right)*. Dig a hole about 7 inches wide, 11 inches long, and 1 foot deep centered on each mark.

◆ Cut a 3-foot-long 4-by-4 post for each hole, and anchor the posts in concrete. Let the concrete set for 48 hours.

◆ With a water level, mark each post $15\frac{1}{2}$ inches above ground level and trim them to that height.

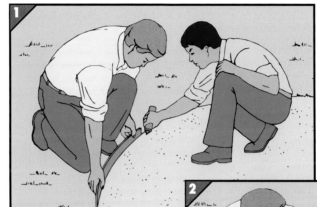

2. Installing crosspieces.

◆ Cut two $3\frac{1}{2}$-inch by 1-inch notches in the top of each post.

◆ For each notch, cut a 2-by-4 crosspiece, $17\frac{3}{4}$ inches long. Center the crosspieces in the notches and nail them in place with $2\frac{1}{2}$-inch galvanized nails.

◆ Drill two $\frac{3}{8}$-inch holes, diagonally spaced, through the braces and posts. Fasten the crosspieces with 5-inch galvanized carriage bolts—or use brass ones from a marine-supply store.

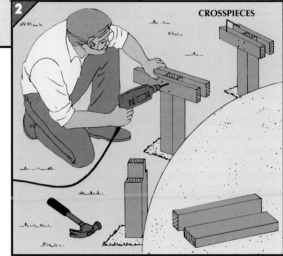

CROSSPIECES

3. Making the seat.

◆ Cut fifteen 1-by-2 slats long enough—at least 7 feet—to overhang the end-most crosspieces. Rip several $\frac{3}{8}$-inch strips from a 2-by-4, and cut them into 5-inch spacers, 42 in all.

◆ Position a slat so that it extends beyond the ends of the crosspieces by about $\frac{1}{4}$ inch *(left)*, and nail it, edge up, to the crosspieces with 3-inch galvanized finishing nails, beginning at the center post. Next, set a spacer on each post, next to the slat. You need not nail the spacers.

◆ Alternate the slats with spacers to cover the crosspieces. Then, using a circular saw, cut off the ends of the slats parallel to the end crosspieces.

◆ Add 1-by-2 caps to the ends of the slats *(inset)*. Fasten the caps to each slat with 2-inch brass or galvanized wood screws.

◆ Reinforce outside slats with a screw driven through them into the spacers behind them.

SPACER

CAP

Brick or flagstone set in mortar can transform a drab concrete slab into an attractive focus for relaxing and entertaining. Unless you have recently poured a new slab, test it for soundness before proceeding *(page 218)*. Regardless of results—and no matter how new the concrete—use a metal straightedge to check the entire surface for high and low spots. Bricks and flagstones may rock on high spots and break loose. Water can collect in low spots and cause mortar to deteriorate.

Flatten high spots with a mason's rubbing brick or with a silicon carbide wheel in an electric drill. Break up low spots covering more than 1 square foot with a cold chisel and fill them as you would a hole *(pages 218-219)*.

Estimating Materials: Find the area of the slab. *(For a free-form slab, use the method shown on page 178.)* You will need $4\frac{1}{2}$ paving bricks to 1 square foot. For materials with nonstandard dimensions and for flagstones, consult a dealer. In either case, add about 5 percent for breakage and repair. Some flagstones are soft enough to be cut with a brickset; others are so hard that they must be scored with a masonry blade in a circular saw.

One cubic foot of mortar mix is enough to lay about 35 bricks or 12 square feet of flagstones. Buy additional mix to grout joints between bricks and flagstones.

Laying a Dry Run: Arranging the bricks or stones in a dry run is an essential first step. With bricks, orient the long sides with the slope of the slab. Doing so channels rainwater away from the house. Use a piece of $\frac{1}{2}$-inch plywood to space a row of bricks along two adjacent sides of the slab, trimming bricks as needed *(page 177)* to fill the rows. *(To lay a dry run on a free form, see the advice for tile on page 202.)* Leave the dry run in place as a guide for a string marker.

In a dry run of flagstones, vary the sizes of adjacent stones to avoid long joint lines. Spaces between stones should range from $\frac{1}{2}$ inch to 2 inches wide. Large gaps can be filled with pieces cut from stones that overlap *(page 198)*.

Expansion Joints: Always leave the expansion joint between the slab and the house uncovered. At the end of the job, after the mortar has set, press polyethylene rope into the joint, then cover the rope with self-leveling polysulfide or silicone caulk. If the slab is divided by expansion joints, matching joints are required when veneering with brick but not with flagstones, which can withstand expansion forces that can crack or loosen brick.

A Frame around the Patio: You may want to install edging around brick or flagstone to protect vulnerable corners and cover the sides of the patio. Set pressure-treated 2-by-8s or 2-by-10s in the ground on edge, even with the veneer surface. Metal edging is available for free-form slabs. An application of masonry sealant helps prevent the growth of moss and mildew, which can be unsightly and slippery.

TOOLS

Mason's rubbing brick	Rubber mallet
2-by-2 stakes	Mortar tub
Mason's cord	Hoe
Cold chisel	Mason's trowel
Brickset	Pointing trowel
Mason's hammer	$\frac{1}{2}$-inch joint filler
4-pound maul	Grout bag
	Wire brush

MATERIALS

Bricks or flagstones
Mortar mix
Chalk
Muriatic acid
Masonry sealant

Mortar and Grout

✔ Buy type M mortar, available premixed from building suppliers.

✔ Mix batches no larger than you can use in 10 to 15 minutes, about half a bag.

✔ Heap the dry ingredients in a wheelbarrow or mortar tub and make a depression in the center. Into the depression, gradually pour cold water as recommended by the manufacturer. Stir with a hoe.

✔ Mortar should be just wet enough to slide easily off the hoe. Grout should have the consistency of a thick milkshake. Both must be completely free of lumps.

✔ Before mixing a new batch, scrape or rinse all dried mortar out of the mortar tub.

✔ Moisten both the slab and the veneering materials before beginning work so they will not absorb water from your mortar and grout.

BRICK VENEER FOR A CONCRETE SLAB

1. Setting brick in mortar.

◆ Use a large mason's trowel to spread a $\frac{1}{2}$-inch layer of mortar on the rough face of the first brick in the dry run. Make a shallow groove in the mortar with the point of the trowel.

◆ Set the brick at the edge of the slab and tamp it firmly with the trowel handle to level it. Working one brick at a time, use the $\frac{1}{2}$-inch plywood spacer to position succeeding bricks. Level the bricks before proceeding.

◆ Stake a guide string to align bricks of the second course with the second brick of the dry run. Where a house wall prevents the use of a stake, tie the string to a brick and set it on a scrap of $\frac{1}{2}$-inch plywood.

◆ Level the bricks in each course, then reposition the guide string for the next.

◆ Wait at least 24 hours before proceeding to the next step.

STRING

PLYWOOD SPACER

 SAFETY TIPS

Use leather-palmed gloves to protect your hands from rough edges of brick or stone. Irritants in mortar and grout call for a dust mask and gloves. Wear goggles when grinding or chipping at a slab, mixing mortar, cutting brick or stone, and when working with muriatic acid.

2. Grouting the joints.

◆ Fill a grout bag with a $\frac{1}{2}$-inch nozzle about two-thirds full and roll the top to squeeze grout into the gaps between bricks. With a $\frac{1}{2}$-inch joint filler, pack the grout into the gaps to a level slightly below the brick surfaces to make a drainage channel. Smooth the grout with the joint filler.

◆ Wait an hour, then remove ragged bits of grout with the trowel. Three hours later, smooth the joints with a wire brush, and hose the patio clean.

◆ Allow the grout to cure for several days. Then remove any grout stains on the bricks with a mild solution of muriatic acid and a wire brush. Hose away the residue.

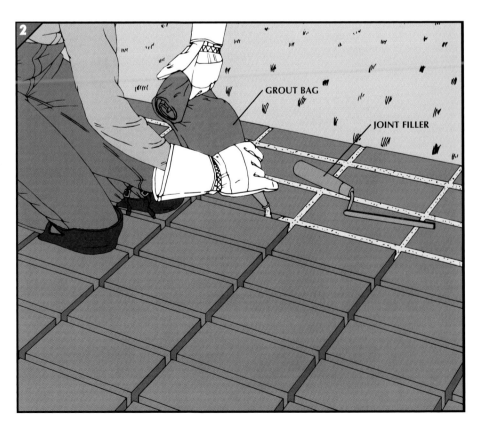

GROUT BAG

JOINT FILLER

RANDOM SHAPES FROM FLAGSTONES

1. Laying out a dry run.
◆ Arrange the flagstones on the slab allowing $\frac{1}{2}$- to 2-inch gaps between adjacent stones. Ignore any expansion joints except the one adjacent to the house wall.

◆ Where a stone hangs over the edge of the slab, mark a cutting line on it with chalk, using the edge of the slab as a guide.

◆ Where stones overlap each other, mark one of the stones, allowing space for the mortar joint between them. Cutting lines should be straight; you can approximate a curve with several short cuts.

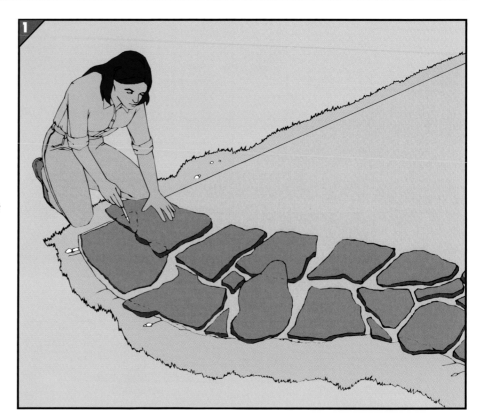

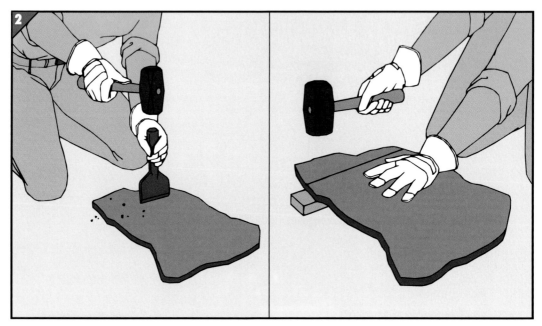

2. Cutting a stone.
◆ Remove marked stones one by one and score each for cutting. To do so, hold a brickset against the chalk line and tap it several times with a maul *(above, left)*; then move the brickset along the line and tap again.

◆ For stones that are more than 1 inch thick, score a corresponding line on the other side by extending the first line down the edges of the stone and marking a connecting line on the back.

◆ Rest the stone on a board, with the scored line no more than $\frac{1}{4}$ inch beyond the edge. Then tap the overhang with the maul to snap it off *(above, right)*. As each stone is cut, return it to its position on the slab.

3. Laying the stones in mortar.
◆ At a corner or along an edge, set a section of stones about 4 by 4 feet in area next to the slab as they were arranged in the dry run.
◆ Moisten the exposed slab with water, then trowel on a 1-inch-thick mortar bed.
◆ Position the stones on the mortar, seating them with a rubber mallet. Fill any large spaces with pieces of cut stone.

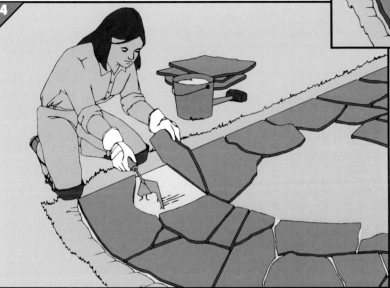

4. Making an even surface.
◆ Examine the flagstones just laid. If a stone sits too high, lift it aside and scoop out some of the mortar with a pointing trowel. If a stone is too low, add mortar and smooth it with the trowel to ensure a good bond.
◆ Finish each section by using a pointing trowel or a tongue depressor to remove any excess mortar that has pushed up between stones. Sponge stray mortar off the stones.

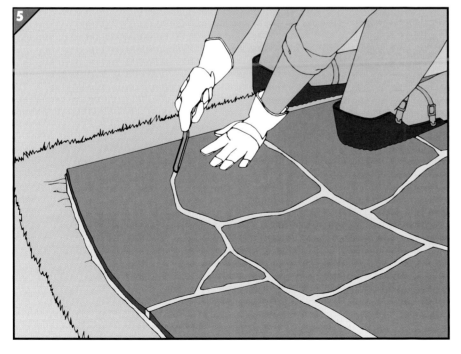

5. Grouting the joints.
◆ After the mortar has cured 24 to 48 hours, trowel grout into the joints. Then use a joint filler to compact the grout to a depth of $\frac{1}{16}$ inch below the stone surface.
◆ Wipe away excess grout with a wet rag within 10 minutes to prevent stains. Do not use muriatic acid; it may discolor flagstone.
◆ To ensure that the wide joints between flagstones cure adequately, mist the stonework with water every four hours for the first day, and allow the grout to cure three more days before walking on the patio.

The Many Possibilities of Tile

Hard-fired ceramic-clay tiles set in mortar on a concrete slab offer attractive, durable choices for outdoor patios or at poolside. Any outdoor tile must be frost-proof; purchase tile with an absorption rate of 6 percent or less.

Types of Tile: Quarry tiles have a smooth surface and come in squares, rectangles, hexagons, and octagons of various sizes. Paver tiles are thicker than quarry tiles and are commonly cast in squares and hexagons with a textured surface and rough or rounded edges.

Mosaic tiles, mounted for correct spacing on a 1- or 2-foot-square mesh backing, make fast work of intricate designs. For outdoor use, choose mosaic tiles with a matte glaze so the surface will not be slippery when it is wet.

Preliminary Steps: First, check the slab you intend to tile for flaws *(page 196)*. To estimate the number of tiles you need, calculate the area of the slab *(page 178)*, and purchase tile accordingly.

Laying a Dry Run: Note the position of expansion joints, if any, between sections of slab, and design your tile pattern around them *(page 202)*. Lay a dry run of tile to ensure accurate placement. Plastic spacers or lugs molded into the edges of tiles help position them precisely.

Cutting Tiles: You can cut quarry tiles with the hand tools shown on pages 203 and 204. Buy the micro-cutter and nippers; rent the more expensive senior cutter.

Tiles more than $\frac{1}{2}$-inch thick require a circular saw with a silicon carbide masonry blade *(page 177)* or an electric tub saw, in which water cools the blade and flushes away ceramic chips and dust. Regardless of the tool you use, always cut ribbed tiles across the ribs.

Latex-Base Mortar: A tiled patio lasts longer and requires less maintenance when the mortar for anchoring the tiles and the grout for filling joints between them are made with a latex tile-setting liquid instead of water. Ceramic-tile grout comes pre-

mixed in a variety of colors; a 10-pound bag is enough for about 10 square feet of paver or quarry tile, or 20 square feet of mosaic tile. You can make your own grout by mixing equal parts of Portland cement and fine masonry sand with enough latex liquid to make a thick paste.

When you are ready to lay tiles, dampen the slab and trowel on a thin bed of mortar. Set the tiles in small sections while the mortar is still soft, planning the work so that you do not disturb freshly laid tiles.

Allow the mortar to cure 24 hours before grouting the joints. Do the grouting within the next 24 hours, however, to ensure a solid bond to the mortar.

Preserving Your Patio: To protect tiles and grout from stains, you can seal the finished paving with commercial masonry sealer or a 5 percent silicone solution. You may prefer to seal only the grout, which usually is lighter and more absorbent than the tile and shows stains more readily.

 TOOLS

Tile cutters
Mortar tub
Mason's trowel
Notched trowel
Grout float
Caulking gun

 MATERIALS

Tile spacers
Mortar/grout mix
Latex tile-setting liquid
Polyethylene-foam rope
Silicone or polysulfide caulk
Masonry sealer

A typical tile.
Outdoor tiles like the textured example above commonly have ribbed backs to improve the bond between mortar and tile. Most tiles are available in a bullnose shape, rounded on one edge or two and used along the perimeter and at the corners of a patio.

 **SAFETY TIPS**

When cutting tile, wear safety goggles and heavy work gloves to protect yourself against chips and sharp edges.

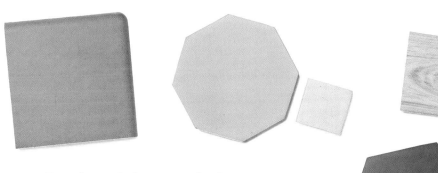

A variety of shapes and colors.
The square tile above, perhaps the most familiar, is just one of many styles available. Six-sided tiles are best used alone *(right)*, but 8-sided tiles can be combined with small squares in an octagon-and-dot pattern *(below, middle row, left)*. Besides traditional terra cotta, tiles come in many colors and patterns, including a wood-grain finish *(above, far right)*.

COMPOSING PATTERNS WITH SHAPED TILES

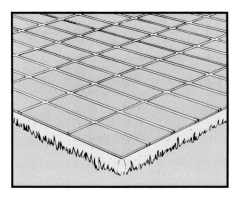

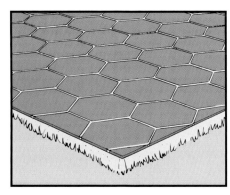

Repeating a single shape.
Some patterns are inherent in the shapes of tiles. At far left is a stacked pattern of rectangular tiles—square ones are also suitable. At left is a honeycomb formed of hexagons; octagons may also be used.

Repeating two shapes.
The octagon-and-dot pattern *(right)* builds automatically with 8-inch octagons and 3-inch squares, or dots. A square-and-picket pattern *(far right)* builds from 8-inch squares surrounded by 3-by 11-inch pickets.

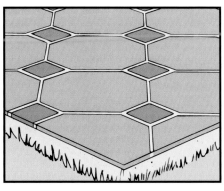

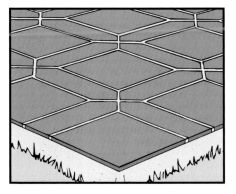

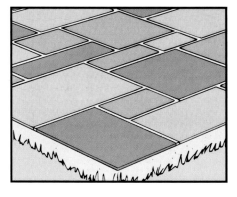

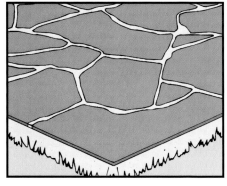

Patterns from many shapes.
Rectangular and square tiles, whose dimensions are multiples of the smallest unit, make a lively pattern with little cutting *(far left)*. The rubble pattern is achieved using broken paver tiles with their edges smoothed.

201

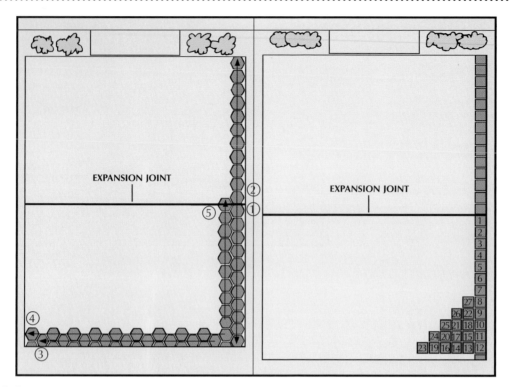

Rectangular slabs.

If there is an expansion joint, begin work there.

◆ For 6- or 8-sided tiles, set the first row to a far corner *(above left, Arrow 1)*, trimming a tile at the end of the row if necessary.

◆ Extend the row toward the house *(Arrow 2)*, leaving a gap at the joint; trim the corner tile as needed.

◆ Using the last full tile nearest the far corner as a guide, set a row of tiles perpendicular to the first, along the edge of the slab *(Arrow 3)*. Alternate tiles may have to be cut.

◆ Set succeeding rows *(Arrows 4 and 5)* in the same manner, letting some tiles bridge the expansion joint, until the entire slab is covered.

◆ Finally, cut tiles to fill in the gaps remaining around the edge.

◆ For square or rectangular tiles in a simple stack pattern, follow the numbers *(above, right)* to set the first row out to a far corner.

◆ There, use the last full tile as the apex of a triangle, and set tiles in diagonal rows until one section of the slab is covered, then proceed with the other section.

◆ Cut tiles to fill any gaps left around the edges.

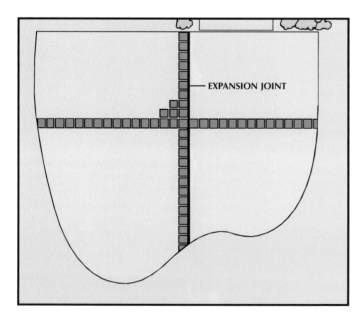

Free-form slabs.

If the shape of the slab is irregular or curved, snap perpendicular chalk lines across its widest dimensions or use expansion joints to divide it into quadrants. Starting at the intersection near the center of the patio, lay tile along each axis toward the edges. Mark tiles for cutting as necessary. Then fill in each quadrant as shown above, right.

Interrupted slabs.

◆ To tile around a tree or pool, first lay a rectangular frame around the obstacle, then fill in the frame as necessary with tiles trimmed to fit. Add an edge of border tiles, if desired.

◆ Divide the slab into quadrants, using a tile at the midpoint of each side of the frame as a reference point.

◆ Lay rows of tiles along the quadrant lines, and fill in each section with parallel rows of tiles. Cut the outermost tile in each row to fit the edge of the slab.

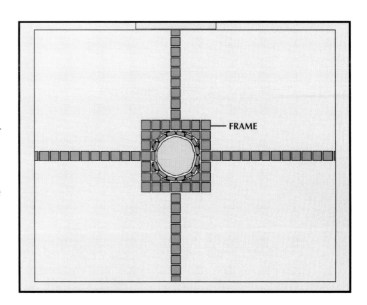

FRAME

THREE TECHNIQUES FOR CUTTING TILES

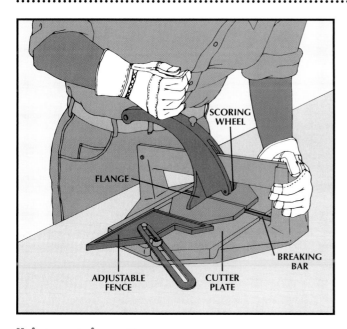

SCORING WHEEL

FLANGE

ADJUSTABLE FENCE

CUTTER PLATE

BREAKING BAR

Using a senior cutter.

◆ Place a marked tile on the cutter plate, with the cutting line directly above the breaking bar. Set and lock the adjustable fence to hold the tile firmly in place.

◆ Slide the cutter handle toward you, then lift the handle until the scoring wheel rests on the line. Push the handle forward in one continuous motion, scoring the tile.

◆ Rest the flanges on the tile at its midpoint, then strike the handle sharply with your fist (above), causing the flanges to snap the tile over the breaking bar.

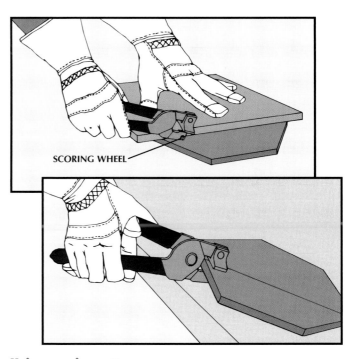

SCORING WHEEL

Using a microcutter.

◆ On the tile, draw a cutting line; it may be straight or gently curved. Set the scoring wheel on the line, hold the tile firm, and run the scoring wheel along the line in one continuous motion. For a straight cut, use a plywood scrap or uncut tile as a guide. Follow curves freehand. In either case, score the tile once; a second pass increases the chance of a ragged break.

◆ Center the jaws of the cutter on the scored line (above) and squeeze the cutter handles. The tile will snap along the scored line.

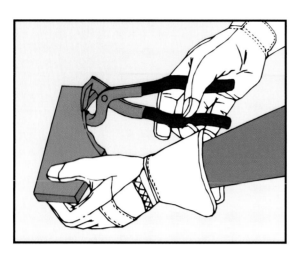

Cutting with tile nippers.

◆ Score a cutting line on the tile followed by a crosshatch pattern in the area to be cut away.

◆ Grasping the tile firmly in one hand, work from the edge toward the cutting line, chipping off small pieces. Hold the nippers with the jaws at an angle to the section of line you are approaching.

◆ When the rough cut is complete, smooth the edges with a piece of brick or a small stone.

LAYING TILES ON MORTAR

1. Applying the mortar bed.

◆ Set dry-run tiles next to the slab, then spray the concrete with water in the area to be tiled first.

◆ Working in sections of 3 square feet or so, spread a thin layer of mortar over the dampened slab with the smooth edge of a rectangular notched-blade trowel. Turn the trowel and draw the notched edge through the mortar, leaving a pattern of uniform ridges. Keep a pointing trowel nearby for removing excess mortar and scraping dripped mortar from the slab. Rinse both trowels often in a bucket of water to remove mortar before it dries.

2. Laying the tiles.

◆ Hold a tile by its edges and lower it onto the mortar bed with as little sideways motion as possible. Tap the tile with a rubber mallet to seat it firmly.

◆ Unless your tiles are molded with spacer lugs, lay plastic spacers on the mortar at the corners of the tile, then place the second tile against the spacers.

◆ Lay all the full tiles, checking the tiled surface every four or five tiles for evenness. When laying interlocking tiles near an expansion joint, stand $\frac{3}{8}$-inch furniture dowels—available in bulk at hardware stores or home-improvement centers —between the tiles next to the joint (inset).

◆ Cut tiles for the edge of the slab as needed and mortar them in place.

◆ Allow the mortar to cure for 24 hours.

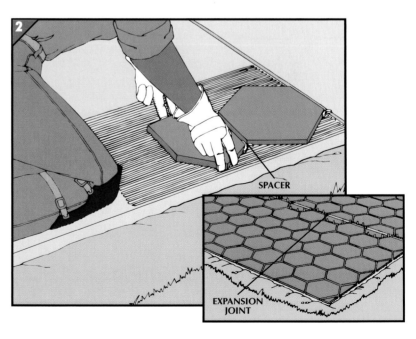

SPACER

EXPANSION JOINT

FILLING JOINTS WITH GROUT

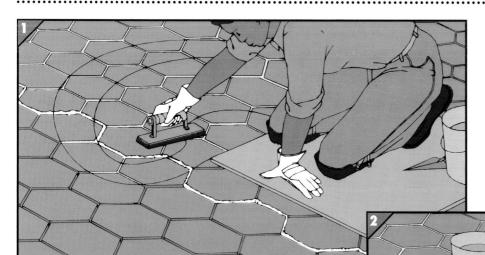

1. Grouting the joints.

◆ If you used plastic spacers between tiles—and if they are less than $\frac{1}{4}$ inch below the tiled surface—remove them.

◆ Extract any dowel spacers near an expansion joint and gently fill the gap with strips of rolled newspaper to keep it free of grout.

◆ Place small mounds of grout at intervals along the mortar joints over an area 3- or 4-feet square. Kneeling on a piece of plywood to distribute your weight and avoid dislodging tiles, force the grout between the tiles with a rubber grout float dampened with water. Dip the float in a bucket of water occasionally to keep it wet.

2. Cleaning the tiles.

◆ Let the grout dry for about 10 minutes, but not longer than specified by the manufacturer.

◆ Wipe away any excess grout with a damp sponge, using a light, circular motion. Rinse the sponge often in clean water, but wring it well to avoid saturating the grout or washing the pigment out of colored grout.

◆ Mist the tiled surface with water every 4 hours for the first day to let the grout cure slowly. After the third day, remove hazy grout residue from the tile surface by buffing with a dry cloth.

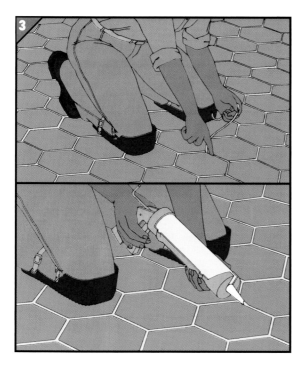

3. Filling the expansion joint.

◆ After the grout has cured, remove the rolled newspaper from the expansion joint and press $\frac{3}{8}$-inch polyethylene-foam rope to the bottom of the gap (left, top).

◆ Fill any space remaining with silicone or poly-sulfide caulk (left, bottom), wiping excess caulk off the tiles immediately with the solvent recommended by the manufacturer. Let the caulk dry before walking on the tiles.

◆ If you intend to seal the tiles, wait a week or more to allow the grout to dry completely, then apply two coats of sealer.

7 Maintenance, Repairs, and Refurbishments

After years of service, even the sturdiest deck, porch, or patio may need a measure of restoration. Screens are damaged with surprising ease. Wooden structures eventually begin to deteriorate even if built of rot-resistant lumber, and concrete may crack, admitting water that can crumble a patio. Timely repairs can prevent irreparable damage and assure continued durability—and even safety—of valued outdoor amenities.

Protecting the Deck with a Finish   208

Fixing Screens   210

    Covering a Hole
    New Screen for an Aluminum Frame
    Rescreening a Wood Frame
    Support for a Sagging Door
    Assembling a Frame for a Screen

Extending the Life of Wood Structures   213

    Patching a Tongue-and-Groove Floor
    Strengthening Joists
    Removing Porch Posts and Columns
    Salvaging a Deck Support

Making Repairs in Concrete   218

    Patching a Large Hole or Crack
    Rebuilding a Crumbling Step Corner

Nature can take a toll on a deck. Water can cause the wood to warp and crack; the ultraviolet (UV) rays of the sun can change its color; mildew can stain it; and fungus and insects may attack it. Although the deck understructure generally does not need to be finished, the decking, railings, and other details may need a protective coating formulated to defend the wood against one or more of these enemies. The ideal finish for a deck depends on local climate, the type of wood, and the desired appearance. Some areas have strict controls on the level of volatile organic compounds (VOCs) in finishes. In the absence of such regulations, select a finish marked "VOC compliant."

Pressure-Treated Wood: Designed to resist fungus and insects, this type of wood lasts longer if it is coated with a water-repellent finish; for best results, choose one that also contains a mildewcide. A clear water repellent with UV protection will preserve the color of the wood; without UV protection, it will weather to gray. To change the color or mask the green tint of some pressure-treated woods, use a tinted water repellent or a semi-transparent stain. Do not paint a deck—paint wears quickly and refinishing is difficult.

Redwood and Cedar: Boards milled from the tree heartwood—the generally darker wood around the middle of the trunk—is naturally resistant to fungus and insects; it requires only a water repellent containing a mildewcide. For lumber that contains some sapwood—the lighter-colored wood surrounding the heartwood—use a finish that also includes preservatives to guard against fungus and insects. A finish with UV protection will maintain the natural color of the boards, whereas one without it will let them weather to gray. Since redwood and cedar are often chosen for their natural beauty, they are not usually stained.

Finishing and Refinishing: In general, wait three or four weeks—but no more than a month, depending on the manufacturer's requirements—after the deck is built before applying a finish. Choose a cool, windless day for the job, and make sure the wood is completely dry.

Regular maintenance *(below)* will increase the life of a deck. To determine if it is time for refinishing, check if water beads on the surface or soaks in. If the latter, refinish the deck.

⚠️ **CAUTION** *To avoid spontaneous combustion of rags or rollers soaked with finish, dry them outside, then store them in a sealed glass or metal container.*

 TOOLS

Broom
Paintbrush
Paint roller and extension pole
Roller tray

 **MATERIALS**

Deck finish

 SAFETY TIPS

Put on gloves when applying a deck finish; add goggles if using a sprayer.

A Maintenance Checklist

✔ Sweep the deck regularly so debris doesn't block drainage between deck boards. With a putty knife, clear out any debris that collects between boards.

✔ Hose the deck down periodically so dirt isn't ground into the finish.

✔ Move furniture and other accessories occasionally to allow the deck surface to dry thoroughly.

✔ Check for popped nails and reset them.

✔ Refinish the deck as required—generally about every two years.

✔ To check for wood rot, drive an awl or a sharp knife into framing members where they meet each other or the ground. If the tool penetrates easily, replace the affected piece.

✔ Inspect the deck for signs of insect damage such as tiny holes or pitted surfaces. If necessary, consult a pest-control expert.

Applying the finish.

◆ Sweep the deck surface clean.

◆ With the type of paintbrush recommended by the finish manufacturer, first apply the product to the deck railing and any other details. Working in small sections, apply a second coat of finish before the first dries. Apply up to three additional coats to end grain. After the finish has dried for about an hour, wipe up or brush in wet spots.

◆ Finish the decking in the same manner, but with a paint roller and an extension pole *(left)*. To speed the application of the finish, you can buy a pressure sprayer *(below)*.

PRESSURE SPRAYING FOR A QUICK FINISH

A pressure sprayer can greatly speed up the job of applying a deck finish, particularly on detailed parts such as railings. Be sure to buy a sprayer that is intended for finishes, not pesticides or other garden chemicals. With its large two-gallon tank, the model shown at right has sufficient capacity to cover 300 to 500 square feet without refilling. The nozzle is designed to give an even, flat spray pattern that resembles a brush stroke.

Although they are tough and durable, screens are often accidentally torn or punctured. Holes up to a few inches across can be patched with the technique shown below, but repairing greater damage—or deterioration from age—requires a new panel of mesh.

Types of Mesh: Replacement screening comes in a variety of widths and mesh sizes in lengths up to 100 feet. Standard widths are 24, 36, 48, 60, and 72 inches. The most common mesh size is 16 by 18. Having 16 horizontal filaments per inch and 18 per inch vertically, this mesh is fine enough to keep out most flies and mosquitoes.

Among screening materials, fiberglass and aluminum are the most popular. Aluminum is the more durable choice, but fiberglass is less expensive, is available in more colors, and comes in a densely woven variety called solar screening. This type of mesh blocks up to two-thirds of the sun's rays, making it a good choice for southern and western exposures.

Wood Frames or Aluminum: To replace screening on a wood frame, you'll need shears to cut the mesh, a stiff putty knife to pry molding off the frame, and a staple gun loaded with $\frac{3}{8}$-inch copper-coated staples. If the frame is rotten or broken, build a new one *(page 212)*. To do so you will need a miter box and backsaw to cut the frame pieces, as well as corner clamps to hold the pieces for nailing. To install mesh in an aluminum frame, buy several feet of vinyl cord called screen spline and a tool called a screen-spline roller.

Covering a hole.
◆ Cut a piece of matching screening about twice as large as the opening.
◆ For aluminum screening, fold opposite sides of the patch to 90° angles, about $\frac{1}{2}$ inch from the edges, as shown at right. Then detach wires to make a fringe *(inset)*.
◆ Pass the wires through the screen mesh around the hole and fold them against the screen to hold the patch in place.
◆ For fiberglass screening, sew the patch around the edges with nylon monofilament thread.

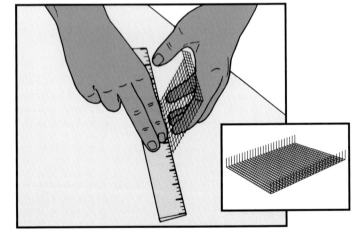

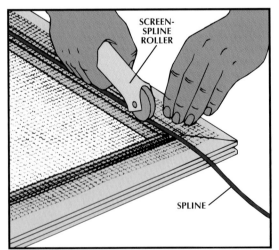

SCREEN-SPLINE ROLLER

SPLINE

New screen for an aluminum frame.
◆ Remove damaged screening by pulling the flexible vinyl spline out of the channel around the edge, and cut a new piece of screening that overlaps the spline channel by 1 inch on each side.
◆ If you are using aluminum screening, crease it into the channel with a screen-spline roller. *(Skip this step with fiberglass screening.)*
◆ Position a length of new spline over the screening at one end of the frame, and roll the spline and screening into the channel. Trim away excess spline at the corners.
◆ Repeat this procedure at the opposite end and then along the sides, pulling the screen tight as you work. When finished, trim the screen along the outer edge of the spline.

Rescreening a wood frame.

◆ Pry off the molding that covers the screen edges and remove the old screening.

◆ Clamp the middle of the frame to boards laid across sawhorses or other supports and push narrow shims under each corner so that the frame is slightly bowed *(right)*.

◆ Unroll the screening over the frame, overlapping the ends of the frame by at least 1 inch. Starting at one corner, staple the screening to one end of the frame at 2-inch intervals, $\frac{1}{2}$ inch

SHIM   SHIM

from the inside edge of the frame.

◆ Pull the screening to remove wrinkles and staple it across the other end. Next, remove the shims and staple the screen to the sides, corner to corner,

then use a utility knife to trim the edges about $\frac{1}{2}$ inch from the staples.

◆ If the molding is sound, reinstall it; otherwise, cut new molding *(page 212, Step 1)*.

WIRE CLAMP

Support for a sagging door.

To stop a screen door from scraping a porch floor or patio as it opens and closes, true the door with a wire-and-turnbuckle stay.

◆ Open a 3-inch turnbuckle to its full extension, and attach a 4-foot length of woven wire to each of its eyes with a wire clamp *(inset)*.

◆ Drive $\frac{1}{2}$-inch screw eyes into the corners of the door as shown above and clamp the free ends of the turnbuckle wires to them. Trim excess wire.

◆ Using pliers if needed, tighten the turnbuckle to restore the door to a rectangular shape.

ASSEMBLING A FRAME FOR A SCREEN

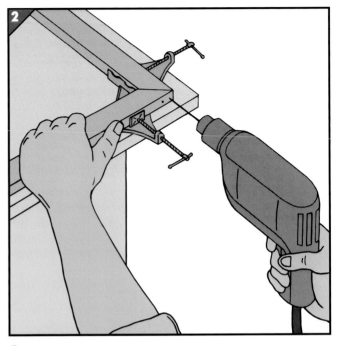

1. Mitering the frame corners.
Using a backsaw and miter box, cut each end of four 1-by-2s at a 45° angle as shown above. Make the long edge of each piece $\frac{1}{4}$ inch shorter than the corresponding edge of the opening for the screen.

2. Joining the pieces.
◆ Secure two adjacent sides of the frame in a corner clamp, then remove one of the sides and apply glue to the end. Reposition it in the clamp.
◆ Drill two $\frac{1}{16}$-inch pilot holes into the corner *(above)* and drive a 2-inch finishing nail into each. Repeat this procedure to join the other three corners.
◆ Staple screening to the frame *(page 211)*.

3. Adding the molding.
Cover the staples with $1\frac{3}{8}$- by $\frac{1}{4}$-inch lattice strips, mitered to match the frame pieces. Align the outer edges of the lattice strips with the outer edges of the frame, and fasten them with $\frac{3}{4}$-inch brads driven near each edge at 6-inch intervals.

Extending the Life of Wood Structures

The major causes of damage to porches and decks are rot and insects. Spongy, discolored wood indicates rot; piles of wood fibers or detached wings signal insect activity. If insects are present, exterminate them before trying any repairs.

Widespread damage may require replacing the entire structure, but in most cases, the affected parts can simply be repaired or replaced. With the exception of porch flooring, which is usually protected by weather-resistant paint, make all repairs with pressure-treated lumber to pre-vent rot and galvanized nails and hardware to prevent rust.

Using a Jack: Before replacing a post or a column, support the structure above with a screw-operated, telescoping jack. Use a bell jack—a strong, bell-shaped screw jack about 1 foot tall—under a low deck or porch. Before using either type, grease the threads so the jack will operate smoothly.

Periodic Checks: After the repair has been completed, a little routine maintenance can prevent further trouble. If the porch or deck is painted, scrape clean and repaint any blisters or cracked areas as soon as they appear. If the structure is not painted, treat it once a year with a wood preservative. And regular inspections for rot and insect damage will catch any problems before they become severe.

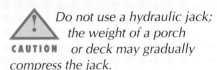

> ⚠ **CAUTION** *Do not use a hydraulic jack; the weight of a porch or deck may gradually compress the jack.*

 **SAFETY TIPS**

Protect your eyes when hammering nails and when using a circular saw. Wearing earplugs reduces the noise of this tool to a safe level. Wearing a dust mask is advisable when sawing pressure-treated lumber, which contains arsenic compounds as preservatives. And be sure to wash your hands thoroughly after handling pressure-treated wood. Finally, wear a hard hat when handling heavy objects overhead.

PATCHING A TONGUE-AND-GROOVE FLOOR

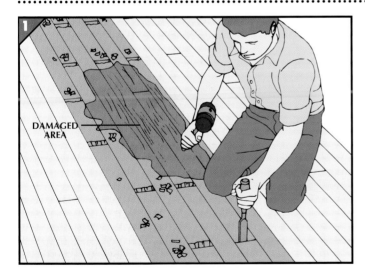

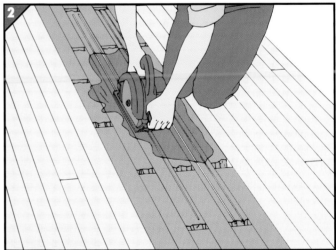

1. Chiseling floorboards.
With a 1-inch wood chisel, chip deep grooves across each damaged floorboard on both sides of the damage.
◆ Center the chisel on a joist, with the tool's beveled edge facing the damage. Drive the chisel straight down to cut deep across the board.
◆ Reverse the chisel, move it about $\frac{1}{2}$ inch closer to the damaged area, then drive it toward the first cut, chipping out a groove.
◆ Repeat for each damaged board, staggering the grooves so that adjacent boards are not cut over the same joist.

2. Removing the boards.
◆ With a circular saw set to the thickness of the floorboards, make two parallel cuts down the middle of every damaged board that is longer than damaged boards next to it. Start and stop the saw just short of the chiseled ends, and complete the cuts with a wood chisel.
◆ Use a pry bar to remove first the middle strip, then the tongued side, and finally the grooved side of each board. The remaining boards can be pried out without sawing.

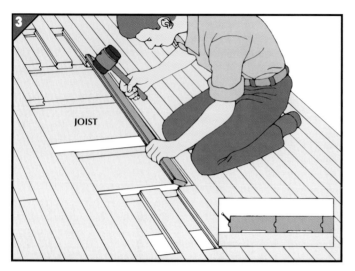

3. Inserting new boards.

◆ Where no floorboard blocks the way, tap a replacement into position with a rubber mallet, fitting the grooved edge over the tongue of the undamaged board next to it.

◆ Drive a $2\frac{1}{2}$-inch finishing nail through the corner of its tongue into the joists below *(inset)*.

◆ Fit as many boards as possible this way. For any pieces that cannot be wedged into place, use the alternative method described in Step 4.

4. Installing the final boards.

◆ Where a neighboring floorboard hinders fitting a replacement, chisel off the lower lip of the new board's grooved edge. Place its tongue in the groove of the adjacent board, and drop its trimmed edge into place *(inset)*, tapping it gently with a rubber mallet to seat it.

◆ Nail the board at each joist with two $2\frac{1}{2}$-inch finishing nails, set at an angle to minimize shifting of the board. Countersink the nails and fill the holes with wood putty.

STRENGTHENING JOISTS

Reinforcing a joist.

To strengthen a weak joist, fit a new joist alongside the existing one, as shown above.

◆ Cut a joist having the same dimensions as the original, then bevel one of its edges to ease installation *(inset)*.

◆ With a helper, rotate the new joist into position atop the beam supporting the deck and fasten it to the ledger board and ribbon board with 7-inch galvanized angle plates held by $1\frac{1}{2}$-inch nails.

◆ Nail the two joists together with $3\frac{1}{2}$-inch nails, staggered top and bottom at 12-inch intervals.

◆ Finally, nail the floorboards to the top edge of the new joist.

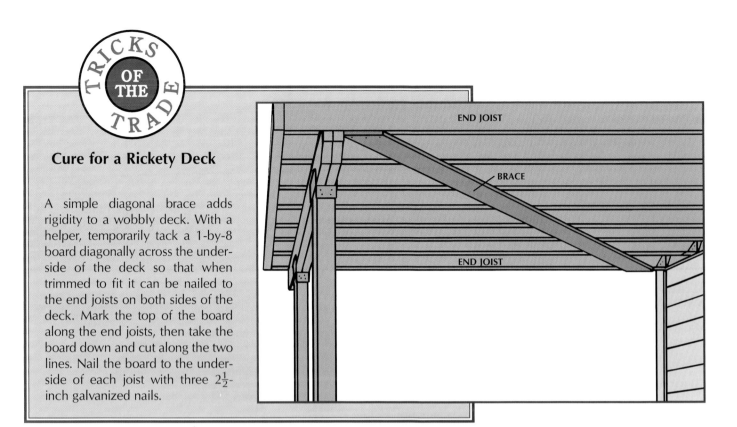
REMOVING PORCH POSTS AND COLUMNS

1. Jacking a porch roof.

◆ Set the jack on a 2-by-12 board and line it up between the roof header and the floor joist nearest the damaged column.

◆ Extend the jack's telescoping tubes so that the top is about 2 inches from the roof header. Lock the tube in place with the steel pins provided.

◆ While a helper holds the jack plumb and steadies a second board atop the jack, extend the jack by turning the screw handle. When the jack is snug against the boards, give the handle a quarter turn—enough for the jack to support the roof without lifting it.

2. Disassembling the support.

◆ To remove a porch post or solid column *(above)*, use a handsaw to cut through the post in two places about 1 foot apart. Knock out the middle section with a mallet, and work the top and bottom sections loose. Install a new post using the hardware from the old post.

◆ To remove a hollow column *(above, right)*, make two vertical cuts, opposite each other, down the length of the shaft with a circular saw. Then make a horizontal cut around the middle. Pull the two upper sections apart and remove them, staying clear of the capital in case it falls—it may not be nailed to the header.

◆ If the capital is attached to the header, detach it with a pry bar; to free the capital from the post, cut it in two. Remove the two lower shaft sections and the base.

◆ Check the post inside to see if it is damaged, and replace it if necessary. Cover the post with a new shaft, capital, and base.

SALVAGING A DECK SUPPORT

Reusing a ground-level footing.

◆ First, support the deck with a jack set near the damaged post, then cut off the post flush with the top of the footing. Chisel the bottom of the post from the footing.

◆ Fill the resulting cavity with new concrete. Then use a plumb bob to establish the postion of a J bolt directly under the beam. Push the J bolt into the concrete *(inset)*.

◆ When the concrete has cured for 24 to 48 hours, attach a post anchor to the bolt.

◆ Cut a new post to fit between the beam and the post anchor. Nail it to the post anchor and to the beam, using the original hardware if possible.

Building up a buried footing.

♦ To prepare the new footing, support the frame with a jack, dig down to expose the top of the old footing, and cut off the post as close as possible to the footing. Fill the hole with concrete, covering the remnants of the old post by at least 8 inches.

♦ Measure and cut a new post long enough to sink about 1 inch into the new footing, and set it into the concrete.

♦ Hold the post plumb while a helper fastens it at the top. Brace the bottom of the post with scrap lumber to hold it plumb *(inset)*. Allow the concrete to set at least 24 hours before removing the jack.

NEW CONCRETE
OLD CONCRETE

Splicing a weak post.

When only the upper or lower part of a porch or deck post is rotten, you can splice in a new section instead of replacing the whole post.

♦ Support the deck on a jack and saw through the post just outside the damaged area. Measure and cut a replacement section long enough to sink into a new footing if one is needed *(above)*.

♦ Cut an L-shaped notch, half the thickness of the post and 6 inches long, in the end of the undamaged section, and a matching notch in one end of the replacement section. Clamp the notched sections together and drill three $\frac{3}{8}$-inch holes through the joint, staggering their positions. Counterbore the holes for nuts and washers, then secure the joint with $\frac{3}{8}$-inch carriage bolts.

♦ Attach the other end of the replacement section to the deck or footing.

Holes, pockmarks, and cracks in concrete can usually be filled with patching mortar. The procedure to use depends on the size of the flaw. Cracks and holes less than 1 inch deep can be brushed clean and filled with tough latex or epoxy patching mortar. Epoxy compounds are slightly stronger and more water-resistant than latex ones.

Major Repairs: Larger flaws must be dressed with a cold chisel before

patching. Epoxy and latex mortars may be too expensive for filling big cracks and holes. Moreover, they are unsuitable for mending concrete steps *(opposite bottom)*. Instead, use bonding adhesive and prepackaged patching mortar—a dry mix of sand and cement to which you add water.

A Test for Failed Concrete: Such repairs may not suffice if the concrete around a flaw crumbles when chiseled, a possible sign of widespread

deterioration. To test for overall soundness, drop a tire iron in several places. A sharp ringing noise indicates firm concrete; a dull thud signals crumbling beneath the surface. Concrete that fails this test is best broken up and rebuilt.

SAFETY TIP
As shown here, wear goggles and gloves when chiseling concrete.

PATCHING A LARGE HOLE OR CRACK

1. Preparing the damaged area.
Chip out the concrete in the damaged area with a cold chisel and a maul to a depth of about $1\frac{1}{2}$ inches. Undercut the edge slightly so that the bottom of the cavity is wider than the top *(inset)*. Clear away the debris, then wet the area with a hose. Blot up excess water with a sponge.

2. Adding the adhesive and mortar.
◆ Brush bonding adhesive evenly around the cavity, and wipe up any spills around the edge of the hole with a rag.
◆ Wait for the adhesive to become tacky—usually from

30 minutes to two hours, depending on the brand—then prepare the sand-and-cement patching mortar according to the manufacturer's instructions. Trowel the mixture into the hole before the bonding adhesive can harden.

3. Smoothing the patch.

Level the surface of the mortar by drawing a wood float back and forth across it several times. Remove excess mortar around the edges of the patch with a trowel; then, before the patch hardens, wipe the edge joint smooth with burlap or a rag. Cover the patch with a towel or a piece of burlap. Keep the cloth moist for a week to be sure that the patch cures completely.

REBUILDING A CRUMBLING STEP CORNER

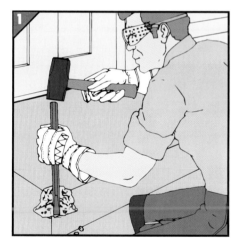

1. Preparing the corner.
◆ Chisel away the damaged corner until you reach solid concrete on all sides, then flatten the bottom of the cavity and undercut the sides slightly. Clear the cavity of debris.
◆ Cut form boards to enclose the corner and contain the mortar. Brace the boards in position, even with the top of the step, and nail their ends together at the corner *(right)*.
◆ Coat the inside of the form boards with motor oil, and paint the cavity with bonding adhesive.

2. Filling in the corner.
◆ After the adhesive has had a chance to become tacky, trowel in sand-and-cement patching mortar and tamp it down to fill the entire hole. As the patch begins to harden, level the surface with a wood float and remove any excess mortar with a trowel.
◆ Cover with burlap and keep the burlap damp for a week.

Index

A

Air-entraining agent: 190
Angled-corner decks: curved decking, 55-56; example, 9; framing, 40-42
Angle irons: 63
Architectural review boards: 6
Attached decks *versus* freestanding decks: anatomy, 18, 19; example, 11; joists, installing, 34-39

B

Batter boards: 110-111
Beams: band, 109, 116; bracing, 33; attached to notched post, 100; built-up, 28, 29; cantilevered, 18; fastening to 6-by-6 posts, 31; flush, 19; installing over patio, 31; installing band beam for porch, 116; for low deck, 31; materials and tools for, 28; size and spacing, 20; splicing, 30; split, 32; standard installation, 28-30
Benches for decks, building with back: 136; leg and back assemblies, 140-141; integrated with angled railing, 144-145; materials and tools, 136; seat and back slats, 142-143; structure, 140
Benches for decks, building backless: 136; and railing, 69; leg assemblies, 137; attaching to deck, 138; frame, 137; materials and tools, 136; seat slats, 138; seat supports, 137; storage area, 138-139; structure, 136
Benches, curved, for patios: 195
Bird's mouth: 122; cutting, 127
Blocking: 34, 38, 39
Brick: laying for piers, 113; mounting ledger boards to, 110
Brick, rubbing: 196
Brick pavers: 174, 176; cutting, 177; laying in mortar, 196-197; patterns with, 175. *See also* Patios, brick-in-sand; Patios, brick-in-mortar
Brickset: 177
Building codes: 92; and railings, 69; and stairs, 60
Bull-floating: 191

C

Carriages: 104, building, 120-121
Columns, classical: for porch, 133; removing for maintenance, 216
Concrete: curing, 190; finishing surface, 190, 192-194; for footings and slabs, 14, 190; forms for, 182, 187, 188; handling, 15; materials and tools, 15; mixing by hand, 15, 190; pouring footings and piers together, 26; pouring slab for patio, 191; pouring slab for stairs, 61; ready-mix, 190; setting posts in, 25; testing,

218. *See also* Patios, brick-in-mortar; Patios, concrete; Patios, flagstone
Concrete, repairing: 218; materials, 218; patching large hole or crack, 218-219; with patching mortar, 218; patching step corner, 219
Concrete pavers: 174
Crown: 38

D

Deck coverings: 160; vines for, 165
Deck coverings, building: 160; angling louvers, 162; erecting posts and beams, 161; installing eggcrate pattern, 164; installing louvers, 162-163; installing rafters, 162; installing reeds, 163; installing slats, 165; installing snow fencing, 164; lumber dimensions, 160; materials and tools, 160; using vines, 165
Deck wrench: 49
Decking: 14; radius edge, 14; maintenance, 208; protective finishes for, 208-209
Decking, installing: basic pattern, 48; capping edges, 73; at corners of wraparound deck, 52; curved, 55-56; diagonal pattern, 53-54; fascia, 50; fastening, 48; finishing edges, 48; materials and tools, 48; notching for railing posts, 71; around obstacle, 57; spacers, 49; splicing boards, 49; trap door, 48, 58-59; using invisible clips, 50-51
Decking, repairing: 213
Decks: designs, 8-12, 13; with hot tub, 12; lumber sizes and spacing, 20; maintenance, 208; materials for, 14, 20; openings in, 11, 43; planning, 4-15; over patio, 31; platform on, 9; site selection, 6-7; structural design, 18-19
Decks, building: bracing, 28, 33; attaching to flat siding, 22-23; cutting overlapping siding, 24, 95-96; fascia, 50, 56; fastening ledger, 22-24; footings, 21, 25; foundation, 21; framing openings, 40, 43-45; in-stalling beams, 28-30; installing beams for low deck, 31; installing joists on attached deck, 34-38; installing joists on freestanding deck, 34, 38; layout, 21-22; lumber sizes and spacing, 20; making angled corners, 40-42; making rounded corners, 55-56; materials and tools, 21, 28; octagonal, 42; over patio, 31; setting posts, 25; trap door, 58-59; using metal bases for, 26-27; using pier blocks, 21, 27. *See also* Benches for decks, build-ing; Decking, installing; Railings, building for deck; Railings, building for stairs; Ramps, building; Skirting for deck, building; Stairs, building
Decks, freestanding: 11, 19, beams, 28, decking pattern, 53; joists, 38

Decks, low-level: 10, 11, 12, 56; attaching beams, 28; ramp for, 67-68
Decks, multilevel: 9, 10, 11
Decks, multilevel, building: 84; front to back, 86; lower level, 84; materials and tools, 84 platform, 84-85; side by side, 86-87; steps, 84, 87, 88-89
Decks, repairing: 213; bracing, 215; joists, 214; posts, 215-217
Decks, second-story: 12, 92; structure, 93
Decks, second-story, building: 92; attaching ledger board, 98; cutting siding, 95-96; foot-ings, 94; framing openings, 106; installing beams, 100; installing angled railing, 103; installing slanted railing, 106-107; installing joists, 101; installing ribbon board, 101; land-ings, 102, 105; laying out, 93; making angled corners, 102-103; materials and tools, 92; setting posts, 94. *See also* Railings, building for deck; Railings, building for stairs; Stairs, building
Decks, wraparound: 10; multiply curved, 56

E

Eggcrate roof: for deck, 164-165
Electricity: wiring hot tubs, 91
Expansion joints: 182, 186, 196

F

Fascia, flexible: 56
Finishes for decks: 208; applying, 209
Flagstones: 196. *See also* Patios, flagstone
Flashing: installing at corners, 115; installing on side of house, 24, 97
Flooring: installing on porch, 119
Footings: 21; building up for post replacement, 217; pouring for posts, 25, 26, 94; pouring with piers, 27; reusing for replacement post, 216
Forms for concrete: 182; curved, 188; permanent, 187
Framing of house: identifying, 92; fastening to, 23
Framing anchor, multipurpose: 35
Framing square: 123
Freestanding decks: 11, 19, beams, 28, deck-ing pattern, 53; joists, 38

G

Gates, building for railings: colonial, 80; traditional, 81
Ground fault circuit interrupter (GFCI): 91
Grout: 196; latex-base for tile, 200
Grout bag: 197
Grout float: 205

H

Hardware: for decks, 14

High decks: 12, 92; structure, 93

High decks, building: 92; attaching ledger board, 98; cutting siding, 95-96; footings, 94; framing openings, 106; installing beams, 100; installing angled railing, 103; installing slanted railing, 106-107; installing joists, 101; installing ribbon board, 101; landings, 102, 105; laying out, 93; making angled corners, 102-103; materials and tools, 92; setting posts, 94. See also Railings, building for deck; Railings, building for stairs; Stairs, building

Hot tub: incorporating in deck, 12, 89, 90; wiring, 91

I

I-beams: fastening ledgers to, 23, 92

Insect resistance: pressure-treated lumber, 14, 208

Invisible decking fasteners: 50-51

J

Jack, bell: 213; used to replace post, 216-217

Jack stud: 167

J-bolt: 114

Joint filler: 197

Jointer, convex: 193

Joist hanger: 36

Joists, deck: 18, 19; blocking, 39; bracing, 215; cripple joist, 43, 44; installing on attached deck, 34-38; installing on freestanding deck, 34, 38; materials and tools, 34; reinforcing, 214; rim joist, 37-38; size and spacing, 20; splicing, 36; trimming, 37

Joists, porch: adjusting length, 117; corner, 118; installing, 116-117

K

King stud: 167

Kneerail: 168

L

Landings: for ramp, 67; for stairs, 66, 102, 105

Latch: installing on gate, 81

Lattice: cutting, 153; for deck privacy, 150; for porch crawlspace, 121

Ledger board: deck, 18, 21, 92; fastening over flat siding, 22-23; fastening to wall with overlapping siding, 24, 98; and framing of house, 23; porch roof, 124

Legal restrictions: and decks, 6. See also Building codes

Lookouts: 122; installing, 131

Low-level decks: 10, 11, 12, 56; attaching beams, 28; ramp for, 67-68

Lumber: for deck structure, 14, 28; for decking, stairs and railings, 14, 20; for porch, 108; substitutes for, 14

Lumber, pressure-treated: handling, 14

M

Masonry: attaching ledger boards to, 110

Mason's rule: 113

Microcutter: 203

Mortar: 196; latex-base for tile, 200

Mosaic tile: 200

Multilevel decks: 9, 10, 11

Multilevel decks, building: 84; front to back, 86; lower level, 84; materials and tools, 84 platform, 84-85; side by side, 86-87; steps, 84, 87, 88-89

Muriatic acid: cleaning grout from brick, 197; not used on flagstone, 199

N

Nails: 48

Nailer, power: 119

Nippers, tile: 204

Nosing: 60

O

Obstructions, building decks around: 40; decking, 57; framing, 43-45

Octagonal deck: 42

Ogee molding: 121

Overheads: construction, 160-165; examples, 11, 13, 165; posts, continuous, 21, 33

P

Patios: 174, maintenance, 174

Patios, brick-in-sand: 174, 176; circular pattern, 180; cutting bricks, 177; drainage, 176; edgings, 178-179; excavating, 177; gaps between bricks, 174, 176; herring bone, 179; laying brick, 179-181; laying out irregular site, 178; laying out sand bed, 176; laying out site, 177; materials and tools, 176; patterns, 175; scallop pattern, 181

Patios, brick-in-mortar: 196; edging, 196; expansion joints, 196; grouting, 197; laying brick, 197; materials and tools, 196; preparing slab, 196

Patios, concrete: 182; aggregate topcoat, 194; bull floating, 191; calculating slope, 182; calculating volume, 182; combined with redwood slabs, 193; concrete, 190; curing concrete, 190; edging, 192; excavating and grading, 183; excavating and grading curved-shapes, 188; expansion joints, 182, 186; finishing surface, 190, 192-193; flagstone effect, 193; forms, 182; installing curved forms, 189; installing forms, 184-185; installing permanent forms, 187; laying wire mesh, 186, 189; materials and tools, 182, 190; mixing concrete, 190; screeding concrete, 191; screeding gravel, 185; skid proof surface, 192

Patios, flagstone: 196; cutting, 198; expansion joints, 202, 205; grouting, 199, 205; laying out, 196; laying tile in mortar, 199, 204

Patios, tile: 200; cutting, 203-204; laying out, 202-203; materials and tools, 202; patterns, 201

Pavers: brick, 174; concrete, 174

Piers: brick, 113-114; pier blocks, 27; for porch, 108, 113; pouring, 26

Planters, building: 146; finishing top, 148-149; materials and tools, 146; sealing gaps, 149; sides, 147-148; structure, 147

Platform, adding to deck: 84-85. See also Transition levels, building

Plunge cut: with circular saw, 96

Plywood: bending, 188

Porch flooring, repairing: 213; patching tongue-and-groove floor, 213-214

Porch screening, building: 166; doorframe, 167; door latch, 171; doorstop, 171; framing, 167-168; hanging wood-frame door, 170-171; installing mesh with spline molding, 166, 170; installing stapled screening, 166, 169; materials and tools, 166; molding for framed screens, 168

Porches: 108; structure, 109

Porches, building wraparound: attaching ledger board, 110; brick piers, 113-114; columns, 133; installing band beam, 116, 117; installing double corner joists, 118; installing flashing, 114-115; installing jack joists, 118; installing joists, 116-117; lattice screen, 121; laying flooring, 119; laying out footings, 110-112; materials and tools, 108; planning, 108; pouring footings, 112; railings, 133; securing frame, 117. See also Roof, building for porch; Stairs, building for porch

Post bases: 27

Post caps: 29, 70

Posts: bracing, 33; continuous, 21, 25, 33; deck, 18, 19, 20; footings for, 18 21, 25, 94; locating, 21-22, 93; metal bases for, 26-27; mounting beams on, 28-33, 100; notching, 100; porch, 124; setting in concrete, 25, 94; size and load, 20, 21; using 6-by-6, 28, 31. See also Railings, building deck; Stairs, building

Posts, repairing: 213; replacing, 216-217; removing, 215-216; splicing, 217

Pressure sprayer: for deck finish, 209

Q

Quarry tiles: 200

R

Rafter length factor: 123
Rafter plate: 122, dimensions, 123
Rafters: 122; cutting, 126; dimensions, 123; installing, 127; ridge line, 126; tail line, 126
Rafters, hip: 122; installing, 127; making, 127
Rafters, jack: 122; installing 128; making, 128
Railings, building for deck: 69; angled, 103, 144-145; and benches, 69; blocking for, 39; colonial spindles, 74; colonial style, 74-76; installing posts, 70-72; integrated with benches, 144-145; materials and tools, 69; shaping posts, 70; slanted railings, 106-107; traditional spindles, 77, 78; traditional style, 77-78. *See also* Gates, building for railing
Railings, building for porch: 133
Railings, building for stair: 69; installing colonial, 77; installing posts, 73, 104-105; installing traditional, 79; materials and tools, 69
Railings, deck: designs, 69, 79; prefabricated, 76
Railings, stair: 69
Rake: on porch roof, 131
Ramps: structure, 67
Ramps, building: 60; beams, 67; landing, 67; modules, 68; piers, 67
Ribbon board: 93
Rise: total and unit for rafters, 123; total and unit for stairs, 60
Roof, building for wraparound porch: attaching ledger board, 124; attaching rafter plate, 124; cutting rafters, 126, 127, 128; design, 122; erecting posts, 124; installing ceiling with vents, 132; installing fascia, 131; installing gutters and downspouts, 131; installing headers, 125; installing lookouts, 131; installing rafters, 126-128; installing rake, 131; materials and tools, 122, 132; sheathing, 129; shingling, 129-130; squaring frame, 125; venting, 130
Roof, hip: structure, 122
Run: total and unit for rafters, 123; total and unit for stairs, 60

S

Safety: cutting bricks, 176; when digging near utilities, 21, 92; handling bricks, 176, 196; handling concrete, 15; handling joint filler, 182; working with mortar, 108; handling muriatic acid, 197; handling pavers, 174; handling pressure-treated wood, 14, 21;

handling stone, 197; handling tile, 200; handling wire mesh, 182; handling wood finish, 208; sawing and drilling, 92; using power tools, 21, 213; working with overhead objects, 213; working on roof, 129
Screed, making: 185
Screen, building around deck for privacy: 150; frame, 151; installing lattice, 152-153; installing vertical boards, 152; materials and tools, 150; structure, 150
Screen, porch: for crawlspace, 121. *See also* Porch screening, building
Screens, making wood frame for: 212
Screens, repairing: covering holes, 210; rescreening aluminum frame, 210; rescreening wood frame, 210, 211; solar, 210
Senior cutter: 203
Shade, controlling deck: 160; with eggcrate pattern of wood and slats, 164-165; with louvers, 162-163; with reeds or snow fencing, 163-164; with vines, 165
Shingles: for porch roof, 129-130; hip, 130
Siding: attaching ledger to flat, 22-23; cutting through overlapping, 24, 95-96
Site plan: for deck, 6, 7
Skirting for deck, building: adapting for traditional railing, 156; bracing, 157; installing boards, 155-157; installing door in, 158-159; materials and tools, 154; structure, 154
Slab, concrete: pouring for stairs, 61. *See also* Patios, concrete
Stairs: structure, 60
Stairs, building for decks: 60, 103-104; carriages, 104; concrete slab for, 61; between deck levels, 86; determining dimensions, 60, 61, 103; installing railing posts, 73, 104; installing risers, 64; installing treads, 64, 65-66; landing, 66, 102, 105; making stringers, 62-63; materials and tools, 60; open risers, 66; top step below deck height, 63. *See also* Railings, build for stairs; Transition levels, building
Stairs, building for porch: base, 120; carriages, 120-121; installing risers and treads, 121; materials and tools, 120; planning, 120
Storage area under bench, building; 138-139
Stringers: 60; making, 62-63

T

Tiles: types, 200, 201; cutting, 200, 203-204. *See also* Patios, tile
Transition levels, building; 86; between deck levels, 87; to ground level, 88-89; wrapping around deck, 89
Trap doors: 58-59

Treads: 60; cutting 2-by-2s for, 65; making, 64; picture-frame, 65-66
Trees, building around: 40, 43-45, 57
Trowel, notched-blade: 204
Trusses: fastening to, 23, 97
Turn buttons: 168

U

Unit rise: 60, 123
Unit run: 60, 123
UV protection for wood: 208

V

Vents: porch ceiling, 132; porch roof, 129
Vines: 165
Volatile organic compounds (VOCs): and wood finishes, 208

W

Water level: 22, 95
Water repellents: 208-209
Weeds: control in patio, 174, 176
Wheelchair ramps. *See* Ramps; Ramps, building
Window well: framing deck opening around, 45
Wire clamp: 211
Wiring hot tub: 91
Wood, protective finishes for: cedar, 208; pressure-treated wood, 208; redwood, 208
Wraparound decks: 10; multiply curved, 56
Wrench, deck: 49

TIME®
LIFE
BOOKS

Time-Life Books is a division of Time Life Inc.

TIME LIFE INC.
PRESIDENT and CEO: George Artandi

TIME-LIFE CUSTOM PUBLISHING
Vice President and Publisher: Terry Newell
Vice President of Sales and Marketing:
  Neil Levin
Director of New Product Development:
  Teresa Graham
Director of New Business Development:
  Liz Ziehl
Production Manager: Carolyn M. Clark
Quality Assurance Manager: James King

**EDITORIAL STAFF FOR
THE BIG BOOK OF DECKS**
Project Manager: Jennifer L. Ward
Director of Creative Services: Laura
  Ciccone McNeill
Cover Design: Fuszion Art + Design, Susan
  Newman Design, Inc.
Special Contributors: Mel Ingber (indexer);
  Robin Bray / REDRUTH

Editor: Lee Hassig
Art Directors: Kate McConnell, Kathleen
  D. Mallow
Text Editors: Karen Sweet, Lee Hassig,
  Esther Ferington
Associate Editors / Research-Writing: Mark
  Galan, Mark G. Lazen

Administrative Editor: Barbara Levitt
Picture Editor: Catherine Chase Tyson
Assistant Art Director: Sue Pratt
Senior Copyeditors: Barbara Fairchild
  Quarmby, Juli Duncan
Director of Photography and Research:
  John Conrad Weiser
Picture Coordinator: Paige Henke
Editorial Assistants: Renée Wolfe, Amy S.
  Crutchfield, Patricia D. Whiteford
Director of Operations: Betsi McGrath
Directors of Book Production: Marjann
  Caldwell, Patricia Pascale
Special Contributors: John Drummond (il-
  lustration); William Graves, Craig Hower,
  Eileen Wentlant (digital illustration); Peter
  Pocock, Glen B. Ruh, Tony Wassell, Eric
  Weissman (text)

Sections of this book created by St. Remy
  Multimedia Inc.

PICTURE CREDITS
Front Cover: Ron Chapple / FPG Interna-
  tional LLC.
Back Cover: Pamela J. Harper / Harper
  Horticultural Slide Library.

Illustrators: James Anderson, Jack Arthur,
Terry Atkinson, La Bande Créative, Gilles
Beauchemin, George Bell, Frederic F. Bi-
gio from B-C Graphics, Laszlo Bodrogi,
Roger Essley, Charles Forsythe, Gerry
Gallagher, Dale Gustafson, William J.
Hennessy, Elsie J. Hennig, Walter
Hilmers Jr., Fred Holz, John Jones, Ken
Kay, Al Kettler, Dick Lee, Lennart John-
son Designs, John Martinez, John
Massey, Peter McGinn, Joan McGurren,
Kurt Ortell, Eduino J. Pereira, Jacques
Perrault, Ray Skibinski, Snowden Associ-
ates, Inc.

Photographers: 5: Ron Chapple / FPG International LLC. **10, 13, 43, 56, 79, 89:** California Redwood Association. **14:** Thermal
  Industries Inc. **17:** E. Alan McGee /
  FPG International LLC. **27, 37, 51, 59,
  70:** Robert Chartier. **47, 135:** © Com-
  stock, Inc. **49:** Cepco Tool Co. **66:**
  Western Red Cedar Lumber Association.
  76: CCD Design/Construction Inc. **83:**
  VCG / FPG International LLC. **123, 174,
  188, 200-201:** Renée Comet. **146:**
  Robert Mowat Associates. **165:** Pamela
  Harper. **173:** © Laura Ciccone McNeill
  1999. **185, 190:** Rick McCleary. **207:** Pe-
  ter Gridley / FPG International LLC. **209:**
  Osmose Wood Preserving Company.

Library of Congress
Cataloging-in-Publication Data
The big book of decks : a complete guide
  to decks, porches, and patios / by the
  editors of Time-Life Books.
p. cm.
Includes index.
ISBN 0-7370-0304-9 (alk. paper)
ISBN 0-7370-0306-5 (hardcover)
1. Decks (Architecture, Domestic)—Design
  and construction—Amateurs' manuals.
I. Time-Life Books.
TH4970 .B53 1999   98-49075
690'.893—dc21   CIP

ACKNOWLEDGMENTS
Les and Barbara Allison, Washington, D.C.;
Almost Heaven Ltd., Renick, WV; Ar-
chadeck, Richmond, VA; Josh Baker, Bowa
Builders, Arlington, Va.; Better Built Corpo-
ration, Wilmington, MA; California Red-
wood Association, Novato, CA; Harvey
Carmel, CCD Design/ Construction Inc.,
Columbia, MD; Cepco Tool Co., Spencer,
NY; Club Piscine-Le Supermarché,
Brossard, Que.; Ron Conner, Conner's Pool
and Spa, San Antonio, TX; Geoff and Meg
Dawson, Washington, D.C.; Jon Eakes,
Montreal, Que.; Joan L. Gregory, Vienna,
Va.; Reed Harper, Summitville Fairfax Inc.,
Alexandria, Va.; Hickson Corporation,
Smyrna, GA; Ben Hoenich, Glen-Gery
Brick, Wyomissing, Pa.; Mary Levine, Tile
Promotion Board, Jupiter, Fla.; Maxx Inc.,
Sainte-Marie, Que.; Robert Mowat Associ-
ates, San Francisco, CA; Osmose Wood
Preserving Inc., Griffin, GA; Pacific Group
International, Walnut Creek, CA; Simpson
Strong-Tie Company Inc., Pleasanton, CA;
Scott and Dibby Smith, Arlington, Va.;
Southern Forest Products Association,
Kenner, LA; Joe Teets, Centerville, VA;
Thermal Industries Inc., Pittsburgh, PA;
Trex Company, Winchester, VA; Western
Red Cedar Lumber Association, Vancouver,
BC; Joseph Wood, Wood's Shop Creative
Builders, Spring Valley, CA; World Floor
Covering Association, Anaheim, CA.

**Books produced by Time-Life Custom Publishing are available at a special bulk discount for promotional and premium use.
Custom adaptations can also be created to meet your specific marketing goals. Call 1-800-323-5255.**